Life Among
the Married People

Bret Carter

Copyright © 2016 by Bret Carter

Cover image designed by Alan Herberger
Interior text design by Brent Wilcox, *BackStory Design*

All rights reserved. Printed in the United States of America. No part of this book may be reproduced in any manner whatsoever without written permission except in the case of brief quotations embodied in critical articles and reviews.

10 9 8 7 6 5 4 3 2 1

this is for
Mom

*the first Married Person I ever met
who also happens to be one of the best*

Contents

PART 1
Manifesto AND **Disclaimers** — 1

   A Bachelor's Manifesto, 2
   Disclaimer: A Question of Sources, 4
   Disclaimer: Apology to the Reader, 4

PART 2
Orientation AND **Disorientation** — 7

   Arrival and Accommodations, 8
   Shovel to the Head, 9
   One and One is One, 10
   The Cootie Phase, 14
   The Fence, 15
   Introduction to Infatuation, 18
   The Importance of Plumage, 20
   The List, 23
   Anatomy of a Broken Heart, 27
   Es-Ee-Ex, 30
   Birds Sing, Bees Sting, 32

PART 3
Picking Flowers IN THE **Minefield**   35

    Slow Werewolves, 36
    Infatuation 101, 37
    Killing Two Birds, 39
    Standard Procedure, 41
    Going Unsteady, 45
    Predating Dating, 47
    The Invention of Dating, 50
    The Other List, 53
    Finding Someone, 56
    The Truth About Valentine's Day, 58
    Chocolate, Roses, Diamonds, 60
    Breakers and Breakees, 62
    Date, Then Hate, 65
    The Girl in the Alto Section, 67
    Music the Tyrant, 69
    Pre-Marital Dancing, 72
    Popcorn and Lies, 74
    The Laughing Machine, 77
    The Profound Insight of Youth, 80
    Husky Rogue, 82
    Sex, Then Love, 84
    Horse Power and Big Money, 86
    Dark and Dangerous, 88
    Elegant and Easy, 90
    Fabricated, 92
    Snobs and Slobs, 95
    Ring in a Pig's Nose, 97
    The Gigantic Arrow, 101

Red-Blooded, 104
Samson the Wimp, 106
The Third Wheel, 110
That Soft Clicking Sound Under Your Feet, 112

PART 4
Live FROM THE **Ruins** — 115

The Dark Truth About Cake Toppers, 116
WorldSpeak 1—It's My Life, 118
Love is God, 121
Someone to Solve Us, 123
WorldSpeak 2—Follow Your Heart, 126
Advanced Infatuation (Falling in Love), 127
How the Mighty Became Fallen, 131
World Man, Real Man, 135
One Thousand Women, 138
That Which Destroys Kings, 142
World Woman, Real Woman, 144
Wearing the Pants, 146
Recipe for a Doomed Marriage, 150
The Black Box, 152
The Ballad of Fred and Vanessa, 155
Pre-Nuptial Sabotage, 157
The Law of Amusement Parks, 160
Adultery Ground Zero, 161
Love and Amputation, 165
WorldSpeak 3—You Deserve to Be Happy, 168
Fool in the Water, 172
Backward Planet, 174

PART 5
THE For-Reals — 179

Cautionary Tale, 180
General Characteristics, 181
Rules of Engagement, 183
The Wedding, 184
Weird History, 187
Confessions of a Groomsman, 190
The Honeymoon, 192
The Naked Truth, 194
What the World Thinks the Christian Thinks of Sex, 197
Arranged Marriages, 199
The Dowry, 203
The Mystery, 205
True Love and Truer Love, 207
Living for Someone, 209
A Collaboration of Superpowers, 211
Contagious Faces, 213
Buddy System, 217
Burning the List, 219
The Excellent Husband, 221
The Excellent Wife, 224
Buying Canaan, 226

PART 6
High-Impact **Solitaire** — 231

The Cards You're Dealt, 232
Men are Stupid, Women are Insane, 233
The Circling Flame, 235
Old Maids and Spinsters, 238

CONTENTS

How to Win at Musical Chairs, 241
Boaz and Ruth, 243
Solitary Confinement, 245
Expiration Date, 248
Shipwreck Etiquette, 251
Girl and Friend, 254
A Tribute to Tricycles, 257
The Hug Drug, 259
The Significance of Sex, 262
Stigma of the Virgin, 265
Legitimate, 267
Rahab Rehab, 269
Foothold, 273
Guard Your Heart, 275
The Tree Inside Your Head, 277
Meet the Deceiver, 279
Captive Thoughts, 283
Appetite, 286
Her Hero, 290
The Joseph Tactic, 292
Flee and Pursue, 294
Playing Stupid, 296
The Masquerade, 298
The Last List, 300
The Curse of Good Looks, 303
Written in the Stars, 306
Someone Who Can Live Without You, 308
The Single Single, 309
Woe is You, 312
Yes, I Expect You to Be Alone, 316
Pricey, Wonderful You, 319
Opportunity Knocks, So Don't Knock Opportunity, 321

Five Seconds in Front of the Whole World, 323
The Art of Being Alone, 324

PART 7
The End OF THE **Comedy** 328

Acknowledgments *333*
Sources *335*

PART 1

Manifesto AND Disclaimers

A Bachelor's Manifesto

Since the following report deals with a part of the world relatively inaccessible to me, it seems suitable to make my own position clear from the start.

I am not married.

I have never been married.

The fact that I have never been married limits my personal insights about marriage.

A certain degree of my perspective on romance and marriage has been deeply influenced by movies, books, music, and television—none of which are necessarily reliable sources.

Various females have also been instrumental in shaping my views, but I will keep them incognito through false names—in the hope they will remember me fondly.

My family, most of who are married, has been a great source of insight in these matters and any useful advice found in these pages, I attribute to them and their wisdom as guided by the Bible.

I have lived among Married People my whole life and as such have had the opportunity to observe them in their natural habitat and learn a great deal about their behavior.

My position as an outsider (restricted as it is) might also be conducive to a certain amount of objectivity and should be considered valid to at least some extent.

Given that my circumstances are blatantly non-nuptial—that I do not have to remember an anniversary or that I freely wash colors with whites—it could be argued that my objectivity might actually have some value.

I am a Christian.

1 - *Manifesto* AND **Disclaimers**

I believe that other than the blatant evidence of Creation, the Bible is the only source of pure Truth accessible in this life.

The worth of any conclusions I reach in this book is ultimately measured by how much of it can be based on the Bible.

Due to the fact that I am male, some of my comments can be attributed to a naïve view of females, and if identified as such, can be summarily dismissed as the ranting of a bachelor.

Although my position as a single male *does* limit my input to a great extent, my gender does *not* automatically disqualify all of my observations about females.

Since it is not impossible that someone might read this who I once took to the movies or bought flowers for, I would like to use this opportunity to apologize for the dumb things I said and the dumb things I did, my only excuse being that I am male—which is no excuse.

Even though I intend to approach this whole endeavor with a smile, I have nothing but respect for the subject at hand.

It is my hope that writing this book will help me have a better grasp of the world of matrimony.

It is also my hope that this book ends up helping other people—single or married.

I sort of know how to cook.

I can sew a little.

I can do my own laundry, but as mentioned, I freely wash colors with whites.

Sincerely,
Bret Carter

January 2012

Disclaimer: Sources

There are good reasons to dismiss the following pages.

Parts of this book are based on personal experiences, essentially indulging a subjective point of view. These possibly deserve skepticism and even rejection. However, they are offered with the hope they might contain a small amount of truth. At the very least they might prove the author is capable of empathy.

This book has been influenced by several other books. Several of these are listed in the appendix. Please note that this author does not necessarily support everything presented in each book and is not necessarily recommending them.

Which brings us to the final source.

Parts of this book refer directly to Scripture. Since the Bible is the infallible Word of God, the reader is encouraged to take special consideration before dismissing anything responsibly built on this Truth, regardless of whether or not it conflicts with any previously held ideas. Like any of us, our agendas are subtle and powerful. Question your own judgment, but never the Bible. The reader is also urged to not be too quick to dodge conclusions with the standard loophole, "That's just your interpretation." A close look at Scripture will not reveal suggested guidelines, but reliable instructions.

Whether you are a Married Person or a Single Person, the Bible alone is strongly recommended as your primary field guide.

Disclaimer: A Warning to the Reader

This book is for Christians. This does not mean that a non-Christian is not welcome to read it. In fact, a non-Christian might even find it helpful. But many of the arguments made will be potentially offensive to those who do not hold to the Bible as the standard of Truth.

1 – *Manifesto* AND **Disclaimers**

A non-Christian is whole-heartedly welcome to turn these pages. But this is fair warning. Much of what this contains will be abrasive to world-ideas.

This book might be of use to Married People. It examines the system that leads to marriage. It also explores some of the general characteristics and pitfalls of marriage.

However, this book was primarily written with Single People in mind. I hope that you in particular will find encouragement in here and that it might help you not only understand Married People, but to also find your own place among them.

PART 2

Orientation AND **Disorientation**

Arrival and Accommodations

The trip was uneventful. On the average, it takes about nine months. There isn't much legroom, but amenities in a womb are first-class. There are "in-flight" meals and it's easy to get plenty of sleep. I was the only passenger.

For most, it's a rough landing. On approach, you are upside-down. Like most travelers, you don't really take note of the exit until it is absolutely necessary. And when you disembark, the change in climate is overwhelming. Much less humid.

I had no baggage to claim. In fact, in a very real way, *I* was the baggage.

There are photographs to document this. There's a man and a woman holding a newborn. That's me. The man and woman are my father and mother. I would eventually call them Daddy and Mommy (later shortened to Dad and Mom). I had just met my first Married People.

I was a stranger in a very strange land. I did not speak the language and knew nothing of the culture. However, Dad and Mom went to great lengths to make me feel at home.

These Married People took great care of me. They gave me food and clothes. My only real contribution during this stretch of time was to make sure neither of them overslept. Even though several photographs show them smiling, I suspect that sometimes those smiles grew tired.

They accepted me as one of their own.

One thing noteworthy in the photographs—my eyes are wide open. My parents often commented on how I seemed to be incredibly aware of everything around me. A very observant baby. Based on the snapshots, it would seem I never closed my eyes—that I never even blinked. If there was ever a person who knew how this world works, surely it would be the chubby one with the big eyes.

So you think I would have seen it coming.

2 - Orientation AND Disorientation

Shovel to the Head

The first stretch of my life is mostly lost to me. I do not have a ready recollection. Most people don't remember much about this part of their lives. Maybe God pulls a veil over that prologue to blur our existence down to a faint sensation of warmth and safety.

But there came a point in my life when something more distinct was etched in my brain. Appropriately enough, it was when I began to fully appreciate the fact there was another kind of human being on this planet.

I had always been aware of my mother, of course. Later, I was introduced to my sister. She arrived during the blurry prologue and my Married People cared for her as well. My sister was the one in the bassinet. She would later become my nemesis / partner-in-crime and eventually one of my best friends. But even with the foreshadowing of my mother and sister, nothing prepared me for the others.

I knew I was a boy and that I would someday join the ranks of men. But it was soon apparent we were not alone. There was another creature who occupied the other half of the world. There were those who were not like us.

The girl.

One of my first encounters with this species also happens to be one of my first memories. I remember the situation. I remember the outcome. But I don't remember her name.

We were playing in the sandbox. We were both probably around three years old. Two kids playing in the sand. For a while, everything was great. We were happy together.

I'm not exactly sure how the disagreement started. But it all came down to this: there was one little pail and one little shovel and both of us wanted the shovel. I had plans for the shovel and she also had plans for the shovel. Things escalated quickly. Communication broke down. She felt like I was suffocating her. She needed space. We both wanted different things. We were young.

I tried to take the shovel. She refused. I pressured her to reconsider, but she was adamant. I made it clear that I really wanted her to give me the shovel. Finally, she did—sort of. She gave it to me right in the head.

I could tell something was wrong. We were growing apart. There were tears—mainly mine. There was blood—all of it mine.

It was a difficult breakup. She went her way and I went mine. It was over.

This might have been the point when a basic truth was filed away in my head. Right next to the shovel-shaped dent above my right eye. There are two kinds of people and there exists between them a kind of intriguing tension. Even as the differences between them become more prevalent, each side becomes more determined to draw closer to the other. Sometimes this works out well. Sometimes it ends in tears. Fortunately, shovels are rare.

Today, somewhere in the world, there is a woman about my age, who might have a faint recollection of once hitting a little boy in the head with a shovel.

I forgive you.

After the sandbox incident, it was pretty obvious I would need to be more prepared. Especially whenever I ventured toward the female side of the world.

Whenever XY encounters XX, conflicts ensue. Boy is boy and girl is girl and never the twain shall meet—without complications.

One and One is One

It all started in a zoo. For twenty-four hours, the fish and the birds had it all to themselves. They swam through the water, they swam through the clouds—ocean and sky teeming with elegance. The dry land was barren. All the mountains and plains were a blank canvas. Night fell on flocks and schools.

2 – Orientation AND **Disorientation**

The next day changed everything. This sixth sunrise saw the arrival of the rest of the animal kingdom. God collected dirt and used it to make an incredible variety of living things. The land stirred with paws and hooves. The air was filled with roars and howls. A wild array of creatures leapt, crawled, slithered, galloped, and darted across the surface of the world. It was one big zoo.

But before this day ended, there was one more thing on the agenda. God took some more dirt and with this one-item recipe, He fashioned bones, flesh, and blood. He sculpted two lungs, two eyes, a brain. Then, like someone firing up a pilot light, God brought the being to life. The lungs began to breathe. The heart began to beat. The eyes began to see.

But this organism was drastically different from every other living thing. This one didn't really belong to the zoo. This one wasn't an animal. This one had a soul.

Adam stood in the midst of this menagerie. He stood on the ground that had only recently been just ingredients. And even though he was surrounded by myriads of organisms, in essence he stood alone.

During the fanfare of Creation, this was a noticeably awkward moment. God had given every other living creature the ability to duplicate. Except one. There Adam stood, the one and only rendition.

All the other living things could make more living things. It would have been incredibly anticlimactic if God had designed each creature to just live, fade, and then die, leaving only a zero where there had once been a unique, thriving masterpiece. The final result would have simply been a planet of bones.

Instead, God gave each living thing the means to make more versions of itself. Each living thing could reproduce. The method of reproduction varied. A large percentage could make offspring simply by dividing. Others could detach part of themselves, which would then grow into a new edition.

However, despite these numerous solitary solutions, in many cases, one would not be enough. Reproduction would require one male and one female.

This would also be the arrangement for human beings. One would not be enough. It would take two. God took a look at Adam and said, "It is not good for man to be alone; I will make him a helper suitable for him" (Genesis 2:18). I don't know if Adam spent enough time solo to actually be lonely or if he was still just getting used to existence. Regardless of his own feelings on the matter, God made the decision. When it came to human beings, one man alone wasn't the preferred standard of the Designer. So God made another human being.

As Creator, He had all kinds of options. If the primary concern was merely companionship, He could have just made more Adams. There was plenty of dirt.

But once again, God did something new. Instead of using the ground like He did with the animals and with Adam, this time He used a different ingredient. Despite popular belief, God did not use sugar and spice and everything nice.

Whereas the making of Adam was akin to sculpting, this was more like surgery. God anesthetized Adam and removed part of his side (Genesis 2:21). The original Hebrew language of the text implies it wasn't a tidy, dry rib. It was bone and flesh and some blood.

Quasi-philosophers wonder if Adam and Eve had belly buttons. Personally, I wonder if Adam had a scar. God "closed up the flesh" but did He seamlessly repair Adam or did He intentionally leave a trace of the process to remind this first husband and wife of their connection? *With this scar, I thee wed.*

So there stood Adam and there stood Eve. Then, of all things, apparently Adam decided to undo what had just been done. "The man said, 'This is now bone of my bones, and flesh of my flesh; she shall be called Woman, because she was taken out of Man.' For this reason a man shall leave his father

2 - Orientation AND **Disorientation**

and his mother, and be joined to his wife; and they shall become one flesh" (Genesis 2:23-24).

Hold on.

God had just made the one into two. Now Adam was saying the two would be one? Seems kind of like one step forward, one step back.

However, it's quickly obvious this was fine with God. In fact, it turns out this was God's intention all along. He endorsed this "one flesh" idea with great enthusiasm.

But why make two and then arrange for them to be one?

There's more to the story. Turns out, this man and woman would continue to be two separate people, but they would be connected through a bond called "marriage." This means that when God made man and woman, He made two. But when God made marriage, He made one. First, there was Adam and Eve. Then there was Adam *with* Eve. The first Mr. and Mrs. The first Married People.

Together, these two, who were now one, would be authorized to make more human beings. God would later emphasize that marriage was the only arrangement in which this process was authorized.

Adam and Eve reproduced and another individual stood on the earth.

They made more human beings and then more. Over time, they and their descendants accomplished one of God's primary assignments. "Be fruitful and multiply, and fill the earth" (Genesis 1:28). This continued for some time. Descendants had descendants. Eventually, the world was filled with human beings. Many of these human beings also became Married People.

However, today the process of becoming one of the Married People appear to be more complicated than it was for Adam and Eve.

One of Adam and Eve's descendants puts it rather well. "The course of true love never did run smooth." A little bit of investigation proves Shakespeare was right.

The Cootie Plague

Complications typically surface in elementary school. Here, boys and girls learn about sharks, planets, multiplication, and most of all, cooties.

Even though everyone is concerned about cooties, no one seems to know exactly what they might be. The only certain thing is that boys think girls have them and girls think boys have them. It is thought to be some kind of disease. Just like chicken pox or the measles, you can "catch" them. As soon as the outbreak is confirmed, everyone quickly agrees on a strict quarantine. Males and females separate into two groups, each warily eyeing the other.

Boys are generally more distressed about possible contamination. Girls also express aversion, but always with a smirk of insight that confuses the boys.

Years ago, the term "cootie" was actually used as a slang term for lice. During times of languishing hygiene, you could accuse someone of "having cooties" and be vindicated by tangible, crawling proof. A girl might very well distance herself from a boy if the inhabitants of his hair showed signs of migration.

The pandemic of the modern cootie, however, is exceptionally intriguing because of a behavioral paradox found in its victims. Both genders profess concerns about contamination, but both genders are also deeply fascinated by the carriers and they often manipulate circumstances to necessitate close proximity.

The cootie paradox is most easily measured in a ritual called "recess." The boy-girl tension which has accumulated in the classrooms, moves out onto the swings and the slide and the monkey bars.

At first glance, it might appear there are multiple games taking place. But in truth, all the games are merely components of one much larger *game*. It is the only game of significance to anyone on the playground.

It's most blatant form is tag. This allows interaction with

2 – Orientation AND **Disorientation**

cootie-carriers, even while sustaining a pretense of mutual loathing. It's a kind of predator / prey system. The females usually take on the role of predators. The boys are generally relegated to the role of prey. This analogy is somewhat faulty in that true prey usually do not laugh while being hunted down.

However, as the elementary years progress, there is a distinct shift. Everyone begins to realize that future interactions will require some finesse, and so both males and females fall back and regroup.

They become less focused on "tag" and more focused on activities that amplify their particular gender's characteristics. Females train themselves to be socially proficient by transforming even the most mundane moments into epic dramatic experiences. Males begin to pursue a variety of radical activities that will demonstrate their strength—or at least a basic coolness.

In a sense, the game of "tag" is still being played, only now with much more discretion and an incredibly complex set of rules.

After they regroup into two distinct herds, the males abandon their sworn repugnance toward the females. Whereas before, it was the girls who pushed for desegregation in the interest of romance, now it becomes the all-consuming agenda of the boys.

Solidarity among the boys dissolves quickly. Traitors appear. In defiance of strict cootie policy, boys step forward one by one, admitting attraction to the enemy. The girls arrive at this juncture much earlier.

Both sides express outspoken interest. Even so, a barrier remains. Now they face a border that is covered in conundrums. Trying to map out a passage is notoriously treacherous.

The Fence

Mom and Dad somehow figured it out. They got along just fine. Sure, like all Married People, they had disagreements, but they obviously loved each other. As far as I can remember, they never even once accused each other of having cooties.

Mom and Dad were the stability of my life. They held the world together. Whenever the day ended and darkness fell, my sister and I found ourselves with these Married People—safe and sound. Together, they took care of us. But each one had their own way of doing so.

Dad was the deep voice, the firm hand, and the driver of the car. He led the prayer at the table, he fixed things, he snored, and he laughed. He lectured and disciplined. He worked every day and lay awake at night, so that we could have food and clothing. He was Adam.

Mom was the soft voice, the whisper, and the cool hand on our foreheads. She carried a small Bible in her purse, she cooked dinner, she sighed, and she smiled. She raised her eyebrow and she shook her head. She worked every day and got up early to make sure we had breakfast and something to wear. She was Eve.

Since they were the first Married People I encountered, they set the precedent. From my perspective, they had always been Married People. They had always been together. Later, I learned they had once not even known each other. My dad was born in Colorado. My mom was born in South Carolina. Yet, the distance had been solved. Their paths had crossed.

I have seen pictures of the wedding. They are young, smiling, and married. A few moments before those photos were taken, they were not married. Then they were married.

They met at a church building in Denver. My mom thought my dad was married. My dad thought my mom was foreign. But despite this initial confusion, they became acquainted and eventually became Married People.

They had once been two separate individuals with no knowledge of each other. They had spent a huge part of their lives completely unaware the other even existed. Like everyone else on the planet, they had started out just like me. They were solitary and single. But the two of them became one. Even though

2 – *Orientation* AND **Disorientation**

I spent years living with them, the actual process of how my parents went from being strangers to spouses remained a mystery. It took me some time to start piecing it together.

After I had mastered walking and began to interact with other children, I picked up some basic skills. *Don't push. Share. Don't hit people with shovels.*

For several years, I applied these principles to both boys and girls equally. Whenever I happened to interact with the other gender, I had no agenda. There was no social intrigue. We just played. In my mind, the only difference about girls was they had longer hair.

Carol lived next door. She was a girl. I suppose I subconsciously knew she would not be interested in pretending to shoot each other or breaking stuff with a rock. She must have sensed I wouldn't be interested in acting out dramatic scenarios with dolls or making things pretty with a crayon. We had to find neutral territory.

There was a ball. Home movies provide some details. The ball was blue. Carol had dark hair and wore a yellow dress. I wore jeans, a plaid red shirt, and a crew-cut that implied preschool ROTC. I was enjoying the part of life where you are blissfully ignorant about personal appearance. Whether or not Carol thought I was attractive didn't even cross my mind. We were just playing a game.

Carol stood in her backyard and I stood in my backyard. We threw the ball back and forth over the fence. It was not a battle. It wasn't even a competition. *Here you go—here's the ball. Thanks. Here you go—here's the ball.* I suppose our parents came up with this arrangement. We could play together and still stay in our own yards.

It was sort of a Romeo and Juliet situation. We were separated by circumstances and our relationship was doomed before it even really began. Unlike the Montagues and the Capulets, our families got along just fine. In fact, to this day, my parents exchange Christmas cards with her parents. But as far as I can recall, Carol remained separated from me by that fence. It allowed us to interact, but it maintained a barrier that was beyond us to overcome. It probably didn't occur to either of us to try and climb it or go around it.

I don't know who eventually stopped throwing the ball. I don't know which of us stopped the game. Her parents or my parents might have called one of us in. Either way, it ended and we went into our separate houses. One day we moved and I never saw Carol again.

There was no pain. I did not gaze longingly out the back window of the car as we drove away. We had no reason for goodbyes because there had never been any real hellos. The fence had kept everything quite simple.

At that point in my life, I had no real interest in getting past the fence. But soon enough, trying to navigate the barrier between me and the females of the world would be my primary objective.

Introduction to Infatuation

Even though cootie plague protocol promotes a calculated disdain for the other gender, deep down, both males and females are inevitably attracted to each other. For a young mind, the desire can be baffling. But once he or she begins to openly admit that romantic possibilities are no longer anathema, there is a brief but rough stretch of life called "Puppy Love."

General fascination of the opposite gender begins to zero in on individuals. This new state of mind becomes so prevalent in the brain of the subject, they spend their time daydreaming about hypothetical conversations and wildly happy futures involving their current objective.

Those who experience Puppy Love settle into a permanent state of distraction. At the birthday party, they might be aware of the cake and ice cream. But mostly they are focused on the location of one particular person of interest. At school, the victim might be enthralled with squids or story problems.

2 – Orientation AND Disorientation

But their attention will keep veering to the back of the head of that one certain student who has caught their eye.

For our purposes, I would like to suggest that Puppy Love reveals a significant truth. There are levels of love. There is a spectrum of emotion measured in units of smiles, tears, and sleep deprivation. Here, on the low end, there is a love labeled with the disposition of a young dog. One might think of it as love in the form of an action figure. A realistic rendition, but not the real thing. It falls somewhere between cooties and "Like-Liking" someone.

The experience of Puppy Love is intense. Countless words have been spent trying to describe the feeling. Here are a few more.

A new and unfamiliar sensation appears just behind and a little above your breastbone. It feels like a brand new heart has been installed designed to radiate waves of painful happiness throughout your body, depending on the proximity of the one you "puppy-love."

It's like a gradual heart attack that never quite attacks.

It feels like sickness, but you don't necessarily want to get well.

An antiquated word that can be of use here is the term "smitten" (disastrously stricken or afflicted). For you do indeed feel you have been struck down.

It is an unresolved chord. A glow, a fire, a shard of hot winter jammed into your soul. Lub-a-dub, pitter-patter, etc.

"Puppy Love" captures the basic idea. It might indeed be puppy-ish. It frolics and grins and has no clue that the world has sharp edges. It is naïve and vulnerable. One minute it is intensely focused and the next minute its attention drifts. It typically has all the staying power of a puppy who spots a piece of bacon.

Adults often dismiss Puppy Love as laughable. They assure the "puppies" that even though it feels real, it is a very temporary and shallow thing. Ironically, many of these patronizing grown-ups indulge in similarly temporary and shallow pursuits that could be best described as merely adult "puppy-love."

It's called infatuation. It is the precursor of love. It can lead to love, but it can also destroy love. Mostly, it is an imposter. Infatuation makes crossing the fence more complicated.

The Importance of Plumage

Once you are afflicted with an undeniable attraction to the opposite gender, you become preoccupied with making yourself more attractive. From this point on, you become very concerned about how you are perceived by the opposite gender. Since you are now very interested in getting past that fence, you are ready to resort to strategies not unlike those used by many other living creatures. Great attention is given to plumage.

Clothing

Colors or patterns can flatter your appearance or make you stand out in the crowd. Modesty is a key factor (more on that later), but attempts to solve the distance between males and females is often based on the power of the closet.

Although Joseph's famous coat was not intended to lure the ladies, it was considered a sign of prestige (Genesis 37:3). In Esther's time, it was an honor for a man to wear a robe that had been worn by the king (Esther 6:8).

Specific brand names displayed with logos can alter the game in a big way. Any fashion-conscious person will admit an unofficial hierarchy of stores. Shopping on the higher end of this hierarchy can help ensure beneficial attention. Shopping on the lower end might hinder your progress.

Hair

Your parents no longer have to remind you to pick up a brush or comb. In your younger years, your bathroom mirror routine was mainly just a toothbrush, toothpaste, and occasionally soap.

Now, hair products appear. The female is more attentive in this area, presumably because she has more hair. She is much more likely to spend a great deal of time brushing and arranging her hair, specifically to capture the attention of males.

Although the male will probably not spend as much time with his hair, he is much more aware of whether or not his hair sticks out in ways that make him look stupid. Hair has been a prominent feature for centuries. In Song of Solomon, the girl is complimented about her hair (Song of Solomon 4:1). So is the guy, for that matter (Song of Solomon 5:11).

Body

Although clothing covers the majority of your body (in most cases), the general shape, weight, and height of your body are considered crucial. Females are more concerned with their weight. Males are more concerned with their height. Weight can be adjusted to a certain extent, but as far as height, not much can be done, other than regular applications of hope. Song of Solomon also focuses on this general physical attribute. "Your form is lovely" (Song of Solomon 2:14).

Face

The most noticeable aspect of you is your face. Even though the components of mouth, nose, eyes, etc. are standard issue, God provides an astounding variety. Each face carries its own unique arrangement of features.

Since your face seems so significant in regard to the fence, you end up spending a considerable amount of time in front of a mirror, examining all the contours with the intensity of a watchmaker. The female will often use make-up. The male will often resort to various expressions ranging from a scowl to a grimace, as an attempt to look mysterious or edgy.

King David had a handsome face (I Samuel 17:42) and Rachel was "beautiful of form and face" (Genesis 29:17).

Jezebel may or may have not been attractive, but she did use make-up, noticeably just before she was thrown out a window (II Kings 9:30).

Eyes

The two eyes in your face get more attention than the other features, such as your nose or mouth. Someone may very well find your nose to be cute, but the eyes can carry a certain aesthetic that far outshines the rest. After all, no one has ever referred to the nose as "the window of the soul."

Eyes are expressive and are unusually helpful when it comes to the fence. They can be used for secret glances, winks, or longing looks. They are of particular benefit to the female. Once again, Song of Solomon offers a good example. "Your eyes are like doves" (Song of Solomon 1:15) Rachel's sister Leah unfortunately did not have appealing eyes. She is described as having "weak" (or soft) eyes (Genesis 29:17).

Odor

Attraction is not completely determined by appearance. How you register in someone's nostrils can make all the difference. Many guys learn the hard way that their athletic prowess doesn't translate well to a girl's nose.

Once you become aware of this factor, baths and showers become more than just about making your family happy. In addition to soap and water, both females and males have been known to apply chemicals to their body to make themselves more aromatically appealing. The Bible also addresses this aspect of attraction (Song of Solomon 5:13).

Skills

Another way for someone to become more attractive is to develop their talents.

Sports can add a great amount of appeal, especially for the male, odor complications notwithstanding. The ability to throw or kick a ball can make a male extremely attractive to many females, even if he lacks appeal in his general appearance. Musical ability can also be a key factor, depending on the instrument chosen or the style of music. An electric guitar producing pop ballads can be beneficial. A clarinet serenading with polka classics—not so much.

There is something built into just about every boy that tells us we can make girls like us by doing dangerous things. You might end up with a Band-Aid or even a cast, but if a girl looks at you with admiration, then it was all worth it.

Maybe there's something built into just about every girl that makes them want to *see* boys do dangerous things.

Wow. He almost died. Now I love him.

Skills mainly benefit the male as far as attracting females. Due to the shallower criteria of the male, the female can have an amazing range of talents and yet remain unnoticed by those on the other side of the fence. This is only one example of a skewed system which we will address in more detail later.

These are the primary means of plumage. The affects you have on the eyes or nose or ears of those on the other side of the fence can make all the difference. Whether or not the other side responds in a positive way is completely unpredictable.

The List

There are some pretty tough things in life. One of the worst is the realization that just because you Like-Like someone, this doesn't necessarily guarantee they will Like-Like you back. In fact, in most cases, attraction is brutally lop-sided. Chances are, the majority of songs written ever since Eden address this sad truth.

As we grow up, we all began to understand there are levels of attraction. Some girls seem prettier than others. Some boys are more handsome than others. Learning where you fall on the scale can be fairly discouraging. It can become a haunting preoccupation.

It's strange. Much of our self-worth, if not all of it, is determined by the aesthetic appeal of our physical body—essentially just our container. It's disposable and biodegradable and built to break down. Yet, it typically determines a great deal in the world of Married People.

In sixth grade, all the boys in my class liked Mary. So did I. She was pretty and she knew it. Even the other girls knew it and many of them supported her as the Alpha Female. She did not seek out this position of honor. It fell into her hands naturally.

School was all about Mary. Every subject was Mary. If Mary paid even the slightest bit of attention to any of the boys, it was a huge deal. But no one seemed to know for sure if she in turn found any of us guys appealing.

One of the boys must have pieced together enough courage to try and find out. His cautious investigation took a strange turn. Mary was approached and asked—maybe by a curious female at this point—to list all the boys in the class in the order she liked them.

All of us boys welcomed this demeaning degradation. Any math quiz or spelling test on deck was of no concern. The all-consuming question for every male in that classroom was, "Where do I fall on Mary's List?"

Mary dutifully took a piece of paper and wrote down all our names.

Although at the time, the number next to my name on her list must have been far more important to me than any grade I might have received that year, I don't remember where I fell on the list. I know I wasn't at the top. But I also think (or maybe I just hope) that I wasn't at the bottom. I mainly remember being very enthusiastic about even being on the list at all.

Mary wrote down my name. She probably misspelled it and she might have even grimaced while she wrote it, but it was solid proof that she knew I existed. I wasn't high on the list, but at least I was in the system. I eventually learned there is no universal standard. There is no Master List. Even if I rated low on Mary's list, I could possibly rate higher on another's girl's list. There was nothing standardized.

All of the commotion around Mary culminated in an extended field trip to a place called High Trails. Sixth graders from several different schools spent a week at a campground in the mountains. All the school subjects were applied to the great outdoors. It was a chance to see the world in a whole new way. It was also a chance to pursue girls. The week was fun and interesting, but for all the guys, it was primarily an opportunity to flirt with Mary.

My friend Stewart, also among the Mary-smitten, decided to make the most of the situation. I don't know why he did what he did. He must have decided to see if he could get a higher rating. All I can say for sure is—he had guts.

Stewart enlisted the help of a kid named Archie, who was from another school. We had only met Archie at the beginning of that week. Archie had proven himself to be weird, but also wildly confident. He didn't seem to care very much about where he fell on anyone's list. He was the very definition of a loose cannon.

With the cunning of a military genius, Stewart approached Archie with detailed instructions for a reconnaissance mission. Stewart went to great lengths to make sure Archie understood all the nuances of the plan.

Just outside Mary's cabin were a few small pine trees. Stewart would hide behind one of these. Archie would then approach the cabin door and ask for Mary. When she came to the door, Archie, with great discretion, would ask Mary what she thought of Stewart. From behind the tree, Stewart would be within earshot, able to eavesdrop. He would hear for himself the glorious or the devastating answer from Mary herself.

If she expressed animosity toward the whole Stewart scenario, he could slink away somewhat unscathed. He could later even feign disinterest or repugnance. *Mary? Yuck.*

At first, it all went as planned. Stewart found his hiding spot behind the tree. It wasn't much of a hiding spot, because it wasn't much of a tree. It was along the lines of Charlie Brown's Christmas tree. It provided more camouflage than concealment. But it was dusk and if you didn't know Stewart was there, you wouldn't notice him.

I should emphasize—Archie was virtually fearless. He was the kind of kid who would eat a rotten banana on a dare or jab a mountain lion with a stick just to see what happened. That was one of the reasons Stewart chose him for this delicate mission. Archie had a tough sense of humor and seemed to thrive above all the silly social games. He was what he was. The other guys admired that kind of swashbuckling flair.

Stewart crouched there in his pitiful hiding place. Archie, fearless and suave, approached the cabin door, as planned. Archie knocked on the door and a girl who was not Mary answered. Archie did not tremble, he did not flinch. "Is Mary here?"

The girl disappeared for a moment and Mary appeared—looking somewhat irritated. The fact that Archie had come calling was obviously not any kind of dream come true. She stood there in preemptive disgust.

Archie didn't waste any time. With great tact and finesse, he turned and pointed at Stewart, barely concealed behind the pitiful tree. "He likes you."

Mary looked past Archie and through the tree at Stewart. My poor friend froze like a rabbit.

Awkward pause.

Mary rolled her eyes and closed the door.

The rest of us guys found out what happened. We gathered up pieces of Stewart and heard the horrible tale from his own mouth. It made us all shudder far more than any campfire ghost story. Stewart was so embarrassed, his grandchildren probably spontaneously blush.

When it comes to love, we often hide. Sometimes behind walls of iron three feet thick. Sometimes behind wretched trees. We send out signals or we send out Archies and hope that maybe there will be a positive response. Some, on the other hand, are brave enough to just walk right up and risk it all. *I like you, do you like me?*

But even so, we all get our turn being the blushing spectacle as we try to venture out and hide at the same time. The thrill of it all is often just the set-up for devastation. In the effort to eventually become one of the Married People, there is a lot of misery. Your racing heart, resonating with hope, is all the more fragile for it.

Anatomy of a Broken Heart

There is an organ inside the chest of every human being. It pumps blood through the body, pushing the color red up and down and all around. It faithfully clenches and relaxes 100,000 times every day whether or not you're awake or asleep. It does this if you focus on it. It does this if you ignore it. Unlike a tree falling in a forest, it continues to make a sound whether or not anyone is there to listen. It is one of the key components of life.

Hello, heart.

A cardiologist can tell you all about this amazing organ. He can tell you all about the elegant design and the potential diseases and flaws. But one thing that lies outside the knowledge of the cardiologist is the more figurative aspect of the heart—emotion.

Sometimes the heart is called the "seat of emotion." This implies emotion needs a place to sit down and the furniture of choice is the heart. Everyone knows this is all very symbolic, but it remains a steadfast image in our minds. Emotions come from your heart.

You can feel happiness in your heart. You can take something to heart. You can offer a heart-felt apology. Anger, joy, fear, and all the things that make a mood ring change color, all originate in the heart.

There are cultural variations. In the past, emotions were

said to originate from other parts of the body. The spleen was once thought to be the source of our anger. This misunderstanding still survives in the word "splenetic," which means "bad-tempered." People once thought the kidneys produced fear. They also thought the lungs contained sadness and the stomach produced anxiety. The Greek word used for the seat of emotion in the New Testament can be translated as "innards" (Colossians 3:12)—essentially your digestive system. However, the most durable "seat" is the heart.

As a side-note, this is a good thing, since the spleen, the kidneys, or the lungs would have drastically taken pop music in some bizarre directions.

The concept of emotions coming from the heart works well. When you have strong feelings, it does indeed feel like it's originating in your cardio area. However, of all the emotions that seem to thrive under the breastbone, love gets top billing.

This is why people give each other heart-shaped things on Valentine's Day. As an additional side-note, Hallmark would have also gone in some bizarre directions selling spleen-shaped jewelry or stomach-shaped candy. For that matter, an anatomically correct heart would have also not gone over very well.

The heart has won the honor of holding our love. It is generally considered the opponent of the brain—or at least a precarious ally. God did warn us that the heart is kind of a liar. "The heart is deceitful above all things and beyond cure. Who can understand it?" (Jeremiah 17:9). This is certainly an issue for Married People and those who aspire to be Married People. It is very possible for your heart to mislead you and that alone is worth much discussion. But for now, let's just consider the plain and simple fact that your heart can be broken.

When you begin to feel a strong interest in someone—whether it be Puppy Love or Like-Like or something stronger—the heart begins to feel fragile. It's a giddy despair, dependent on whether or not the person you are smitten with returns the same amount of interest in you.

In most cases, things do not go well. Rejection causes your chest area to experience something that could be described as gently excruciating. This is your heart breaking. The blood continues to move through the body. The heart itself actually does continue to pump. An MRI would reveal nothing amiss. But it does really feel as if your heart is suffering from multiple fractures.

The Bible has an account of a man with a broken heart. During a period of political upheaval caused by Saul, King David's wife Michal ended up with a new husband named Paltiel. Once the political upheaval stopped upheaving, David sent a man named Ish-bosheth to fetch Michal and return her to her rightful marriage. "Ish-bosheth sent and took her from her husband, from Paltiel the son of Laish. But her husband went with her, weeping as he went, and followed her as far as Bahurim. Then Abner said to him, 'Go, return.' So he returned" (II Samuel 3:15-16). We don't know much about this man. We do know that he felt something many of us have also experienced. A shattered, pulverized, demolished heart.

Essentially breaking someone's heart is like destroying the future. For some time, they have imagined the future a certain way. When rejection collides with the heart, the impact annihilates all those daydreams. The future is undone. You and the other person will not be together, after all.

It's not like we die when we're rejected. But it sure feels like it. The ache of not being loved by someone in a romantic way is its own special kind of pain. Saying your heart is "broken" works. No other word really captures the feeling. A broken brain or a broken gut just doesn't get it done. It's your heart that's broken. And it really does feel like there is a serious injury somewhere underneath your breastbone. It feels like damage. You want to be alone, but at the same time that's what you fear the most—being alone.

Sometimes, when Cupid hit me with an arrow, I wanted to hunt down that arrogant archer with a double-barreled shotgun.

One thing we do know. God created us with hearts that can be broken (and often are). But He empathizes far more than you might think. "The Lord is near to the brokenhearted and saves those who are crushed in spirit" (Psalm 34:18). The Creator is well aware of the pain and is eager to draw near and help you through it. He knows very well the condition of your heart.

With such pain waiting for anyone who attempts to cross the fence, one realistic option is to stay put. Don't risk anything. After suffering deeply from unrequited love, some withdraw completely. They seal off feelings of love, but they also wall up happiness along with it. Unless they get a happily-ever-after, they feel they can't be happy at all.

The problem with this solution is that you rob yourself of the blessings that come with having a heart to begin with. The bottom line is, if you care about anything or anyone at all, it will require you to stay vulnerable. That's the price of feeling anything.

With Mary's help and a few other girls, I quickly learned that having a heart was pretty painful. As a result, life would have some rough stretches. But I kept going. There was a lot more to learn.

Es-Ee-Ex

No way.

As I recall, one of my cousins enlightened me. Later, my dad confirmed my worst fears. It's all true. To a young mind it all seems pretty gross, yet—possibly intriguing.

These days it's difficult to get very far in life without stumbling on at least some of the general details. You can piece it all together to a certain extent through overheard indiscretions or pop music innuendos. Movies and television contribute to your data with all the subtlety of marching bands. Hopefully, the Married People known as your parents help you through this brain-rattling epiphany.

However, nothing can prepare you for full confirmation of

2 – Orientation AND **Disorientation**

what happens between a man and woman in order to produce babies. Shock and awe. It all seems so vulnerable and embarrassing. At first you even find it a little difficult to even say es-ee-ex. You find yourself wishing the stork explanation was the truth. A large bird leaving a bundle of joy on the doorstep is so much tidier.

I remember feeling relieved that I wouldn't have to deal with it any time soon. In fact, it seemed pretty improbable that it would ever happen at all. That was Married People stuff and I didn't need to worry about it.

But time goes by and gradually the idea becomes strangely more interesting for all of us. First, the idea of holding hands and even the kissing part doesn't seem as horrible as it once did. These things might be worth a try. Eventually.

But still—who in their right mind would interlace fingers with *you*? Who would want to smash their lips against your lips? It all becomes the subject of murmured comments and giggles. Sitting at a wedding, it suddenly dawns on you what the wedding night is all about. You've heard of honeymoons, but now you finally realize what will soon happen. Once you realize it, you can't un-realize it.

Your interest increases. What was once offensive to your smaller mind actually becomes a permanent presence in your grown-up brain. Along the way, you learn there are restrictions. You also find out there is much debate about what those limits are.

Some say sex is fine between "two consenting adults." Some say it should happen between two people only if they're really in love. Some say only Married People are cleared for it. The Bible says "sexual immorality" is wrong (I Thessalonians 4:3). So clearly there are lines to be drawn somewhere.

As you grow older, your thoughts on the matter are shaped by various sources. The general consensus seems to be that sex is a simple act with no complications outside of the concerns of birth control and prevention of disease. It is two people who connect briefly and then disconnect to return to unchanged individuality. But despite the trend to play down its importance, you do suspect an aura of significance. Lives seem either fulfilled or destroyed by it. Tears and smiles and deep resounding sighs of sadness or happiness can be traced back to it. Regardless of the world's insistence that it is a simple act, you sense there is something undeniably profound.

It is clearly precarious territory. Just for the sake of your very breakable heart, it would be wise to approach with some caution.

Birds Sing, Bees Sting

There were fables along the way. Before you arrived at the unedited truth, there were metaphorical euphemisms to hold off the questions for a while. Explanations varied.

The Foggy Island

Somewhere in a distant, unexplored part of the world, there is an island perpetually shrouded in mystery and humidity. Infants somehow accumulate in this misty place. They are eventually collected and presumably delivered by boat to eager parents.

The Cabbage Patch

Turn a cabbage leaf and there it is—a baby. This is a lot like discovering a snail in your garden. Except in this case, you take it home and raise it as part of your family. Cabbage seems like an odd choice to me. As far as I'm concerned, a strawberry or watermelon patch would carry a little more appeal.

The Stork

This explanation is less about the source and more about the delivery system. The storks might even get the babies from a cabbage patch on Foggy Island. This avian delivery system of infants is appropriately exotic. It is accomplished via a relatively unfamiliar creature, not a common dog or horse. It is a wild stork—a large one in fact, since it must be big enough to carry a six or seven-pound child. Oddly enough, the stork transports the baby in a bundle that resembles the bundle kids make and tie to the end of a stick when they're running away. The stork deposits the baby and leaves before being seen. Like UPS.

These explanations buy time. But there is yet another metaphor that shows up before the full disclosure. It is closer to the truth and even though a transitional explanation, actually contains some unintentional insight into the whole matter.

The Birds and the Bees

Here we have two drastically different creatures being used to provide a partial explanation through extended innuendo.

Birds produce eggs. Inside each egg is a baby bird. Then it hatches. It's born. This gently suggests to a young mind that maybe human beings are also born. They don't come from a mysterious island. They aren't delivered by a stork. They are born.

The bees are even closer to the delicate truth. A flower must interact with other flowers in order to make more flowers. Bees carry pollen from one bloom to another. This process not only results in more flowers, it also indirectly results in the production of more bees. This side of the double zoological symbolism approaches one of the more delicate aspects of the issue. The male and female must combine. Like flowers, they each contribute something to the project.

It makes you wonder why this mixed metaphor hasn't caused children to think birds come from pollen.

But eventually, all the pieces finally fall into place. Your eyes open a little bit wider. Then one fateful night, you lay awake with the abrupt realization that Mommy and Daddy have probably been up to things that baffle the imagination.

Before we move on, I would suggest there is yet another facet of this whole bird / bee concept. Reproduction notwithstanding, we can use this double zoological symbolism as a warning.

Along the path toward Married People, there are some good things and there are some bad things. There is a great deal of happiness, but there is also a great deal of sadness. It is a world of pleasure and it is a world of pain. Birds sing and bees sting. Both fly, but there are ominous concerns in the vicinity of honey.

As you grow up, for a while, you can believe that it's all good. You see couples walking hand in hand. You see Married People smile at each other. In general, the world of romance and love seems to work pretty well. But it doesn't take long to find out another truth.

There's a lot of bad stuff.

There are murmurs about indiscretions in the shadows. There are scandalous rumors. People shake their heads about other people. Pop culture and friends fill in the blanks. The final diagnosis is not encouraging. When the lights go down, there's a lot of dark in the darkness.

Even though the mistakes tend to happen mostly at night, broad daylight reveals the consequences. Once the sun comes up, there are obvious indications something is off. Tears and anger and betrayal and broken hearts. You find out about unmarried girls who get pregnant. You hear bravado from guys who think that sleeping around makes them a man.

Sometimes you notice problems even among Married People. Some of them have more anger than love toward each other. A wife suddenly abandons her family. A husband lets his career or hobby turn his family into a footnote. You learn the ominous word "divorce."

The comforting stories about foggy islands and storks fade fast. Just as you begin to be relieved that cooties are a myth, you discover there are darker threats that are all too real.

It isn't that the males and females find each other disagreeable. In fact, they are deeply drawn to each other. But in the collision of hearts, there is great potential for disaster. Even as love makes the world go round, the pursuit of love rips the world off its axis.

PART 3

Picking Flowers IN THE **Minefield**

Slow Werewolves

It's impossible to be completely prepared. The public school system, friends, and even a heart-to-heart with your parents can never fully brace you for the arrival of puberty. If you didn't get any warning at all, you might think you were suddenly afflicted with a terminal disease. You discover you have a brand new brain. A completely new state of mind. A completely new state of body. The transformation begins.

It is a metamorphosis, but less elegant than the caterpillar and its butterfly makeover. The caterpillar gets to hide away in a cocoon until it's over. That would be nice. You could go into your room, lock it, sleep for a few months and then emerge a new person.

Puberty isn't discrete. It's more like slowly turning into a werewolf. The key difference between puberty and lycanthropy is that when you go through puberty, you can never change back. At least a werewolf gets a break once in a while.

Regardless, eventually the adolescents emerge, blinking in the sunlight. The girls become obsessed with mirror-time and the daily challenge of camouflaging blemishes. The males now have Adam's apples that jut out like misplaced elbows. There is a lot of sweating and a lot of eating. When you're going through it, it's not hard to imagine yourself curled up on some foggy moor, as your writhe under a full moon.

What's even worse is that the females go through all this before the males do. It's not easy for a guy to maintain any shred of confidence, while girls tower over him physically and socially. It can bring a guy to new depths of humiliation to stand among blossoming girls, and feel like nothing more than a weed.

The aesthetic imbalance of gangly arms and legs eventually levels out, and for the most part the males find themselves resembling men rather than boys. The females look more and more like women rather than just little girls.

3 - Picking Flowers IN THE **Minefield** | 37 |

Once it's all done, on the far side of puberty, life is different. All the mysterious goings-on of Married People now seem feasible. It takes time to fully adjust, but there is one thing that is now definitely on track. The other gender has stopped being merely a curiosity. Now they are of great interest. At times, they even feel like an obsession. The flesh and bone machinery of your body feels like it runs on a more potent fuel. There are occasions when you feel like you're not driving it anymore. It's driving you. It can get to the point where you miss the days of cooties.

Infatuation 101

The almost violent transition of puberty doesn't just result in external changes. You could argue that the more significant changes occur on the inside. A hurricane of chemicals floods your circulatory system, drenching your heart, your brain, your everything. As these fiery potions shoot through your veins, everything in your world is measured by how it will affect your interactions with the opposite sex.

Every time you enter a room filled with people, you are keenly aware of your appearance, especially if there is anyone your age and even more especially if they are of the opposite gender. Your days are spent wondering whether or not you might be considered attractive. You dread being the center of attention, but at the same time, you also kind of want it. This constant distraction is like background static behind your every thought.

No one your age hides the truth anymore. You are attracted to the enemy. You are extremely interested in peace talks and would be more than willing to consider a treaty of some sort. But the shadow of rejection is always in the wings. All of this sets the stage for a higher level of infatuation.

You want what you can't have.

This particular form of infatuation is often referred to as a "crush." During the earlier stage called Puppy Love, you are "smitten" (struck). This new level is much more severe that just being smitten. It's a lot like actually getting crushed. It's like being put in that giant compactor at the junkyard and being reduced to a small cube.

Just as Puppy Love has been mistaken for love, so has this level of infatuation. To "have a crush on someone" might feel like love, but it is more correctly identified as a more intense case of infatuation.

Infatuation is not love. It is not as strong as love. Infatuation is a kind of counterfeit of love. It might very well lead to love, but it isn't really even an early form of love. Infatuation and love are no more the same thing than a housecat and a leopard. They have some common characteristics, but they're actually two completely different animals.

Infatuation is less like a form of love than a form of insanity. You and the real world go your separate ways. Your rational thoughts are drowned out by your giddy daydreams. Your mind settles down into a loop—the same thoughts over and over. *What are they doing? Where are they? How can I get them to like me?*

You lose sleep. You are like a musical instrument designed to only play one tune. Your heartbeat, your breathing—all your vitals—are all shaped by your "crush." The briefest conversation can make you float home. The slightest glance can knock you down. They are your prefix and your suffix, giving new meaning to every word. They are the subject of every romantic song. Every movie with a romantic angle is about the two of you.

It's agony. And you relish every moment of it.

It feels like your only hope for happiness depends on whether or not your crush gets crushed too. So you become determined to make it happen. You begin to develop better plumage. The male typically sets out to acquire a buff body, a fast car, or a chubby wallet. The girl typically sets out to acquire clothes. Yet, even as you adjust to this new game, everything gets complicated.

Killing Two Birds

For me, seventh grade was an exercise in stealth. I spent a lot of time just trying to keep a low profile. Bullies stalked the edge of the herd. Friends were scarce.

But in science class, I ended up with Rhonda as my lab partner. She had not been of particular interest to me before. I'm not sure I even noticed her until the teacher paired us off. I had no romantic agenda, but suddenly I was in the company of a girl my age on a regular basis. It was very new.

We weren't boyfriend and girlfriend. We were friends. She was a *girl* and she was a *friend*, but the two words had some space between them. Everything was fine.

We would talk about school. I would make her laugh. We dissected an earthworm together. Life was good. But then one day, everything changed.

It happened in English class. All of us were scattered throughout the library, while the teacher strolled around, overseeing our scribbles. I was deeply involved in a short story about aliens or something when several pairs of shoes appeared in front of me. I looked up.

Girls. They looked like they were here to talk to me. I didn't know any of them. But when one of them spoke, it started to make a little sense. They were emissaries. "Rhonda told us to tell you that David asked her to go steady with him and unless you ask Rhonda to go steady with you, she'll say yes to David and go steady with him."

I recall this being spoken in one breath and it seemed to come from the whole group—the collective. It had all the romantic tone of the Miranda Rights.

They stood and waited for my response, but they didn't seem necessarily interested in what my response would be. If anything, they seemed a little perturbed. Either it was because I was so clearly ignorant of protocol or simply because I did not rate very high on the Mary List. Or whatever the standard was at this school.

To make things even more confusing, I had no idea who David was. All I knew was that Rhonda expected a response.

I was only distantly familiar with the phrase "going steady," mostly from movies about the 1950s, where couples drank milkshakes and listened to jukeboxes. As far as I understood, "going steady" was kind of a distant cousin of marriage. An IOU for a promise ring, for an engagement ring, for a wedding ring which turned you into Married People.

The delegation left.

I felt pressured. But I also felt like my friendship with Rhonda was on the line. I didn't know exactly how this was all supposed to play out, but clearly I had to do something. As far as I was concerned, things were fine. But apparently there was something missing. Rhonda and I were supposed to not just be friends anymore. We were supposed to go to the next level. We were supposed to "go steady."

I didn't want to lose our friendship, so I put down my pencil and set out to look for Rhonda. I found her with the delegation. None of them thought privacy was in order. They simply watched me like I was an earthworm about to be dissected.

Rhonda wasn't smiling. She wasn't frowning. She just waited.

"Rhonda?"

"Yes?"

"Do you want to go steady?"

"Okay."

I fidgeted. There wasn't much else to add. "Okay."

I went back to my desk and picked up my pencil.

Nothing was ever the same again. From that point on, our friendship faded. It had become legislated. It was as if we were trying to follow a manual that contained all the proper procedures and protocols of love. But it had been misplaced or possibly reserved for only an elite few. All I knew was, I didn't have a copy.

From the moment we started going steady, we became unsteady. Rhonda and I continued to be lab partners, but our

conversations became stilted. Our hellos in the hall were stifled. For Valentine's Day, I bought a heart-shaped box of chocolates the size of a baseball mitt. My Dad drove me to an unfamiliar neighborhood. We found the house. I placed the box on Rhonda's porch with a short note:
Happy Valentine's Day.

By the time seventh grade was over, so was our friendship. I assumed that also meant we weren't going steady any more either.

On our own, Rhonda and I may have very well found our way toward something more, but relegated expectations killed our friendship. The unwritten rules of romance ruined everything.

They say you can kill two birds with one stone. I guess you'd have to be a pretty good shot. But it would help if the birds were close together.

And if they didn't see the stone coming.

Standard Procedure

"Going steady" is just one small step in a much bigger system. Here in the Western World, when trying to make any progress toward the realm of Married People, there are expectations.

During this effort to map out the proceedings, although these also involve men and women, we will refer to the male as "the boy" and the female as "the girl." For most of us, it went something like this:

Target Acquired

While in the midst of a group of people, you notice one person in particular. This particular person is either physically attractive or has some kind of charisma. Circumstances might prevent any further progress and the final result will only be stealing glances while pretending to look at something else.

Visual Confirmation

While stealing glances, there is the possibility the target will happen to look your way. You can increase the likelihood of this if you maintain your gaze without looking away or blinking. However, this approach has less chance of leading to an introduction than to a restraining order.

Initial Contact

If you are extremely confident, you can just walk right up and introduce yourself, relying on your good looks, your sophisticated demeanor, or your clever banter to make your target mutually interested in you. You can also manipulate an "accidental" meeting: *Excuse me, was that your toe?* A more discrete approach is to send a friend to run reconnaissance. Just make sure your friend's name isn't Archie.

Communication

Once you have established some kind of dialogue, conversation can be maintained in many different ways. Face-to-face is the best. In the old days, the only other options were phone calls and letters. Currently, however, this phase can be sustained through texting, and numerous other communication systems. (I met some Married People who found each other through Twitter).

Arrangements

If communication reaches an acceptable comfort level, the boy (typically) will suggest he and the girl take part in some event together. This is a point-of-no-return because now it will be difficult to hold onto any platonic pretense. Both are now very aware that at least one of them is romantically interested. This pending rendezvous is commonly known as the "date."

Preparation

Before the actual date, certain tasks must be completed. The boy washes the outside of his car and removes all fast food wrappers crammed under the seats. Both the boy and girl will spend a great deal of time making sure they are clean. Even if they have taken a shower earlier in the day, they will do another round of shampoo and soap. This is followed by applying chemicals to make them appear and smell attractive. A great deal of attention is given to the hair. Since girls usually have more hair, her prep-time is much longer than the boy's. This is also due to clothing selection. The typical girl spends more time on this as well. The typical boy aspires to merely find something that has recently been in the washer.

Security Measures

The boy arrives in his car or the family minivan. He walks confidently up to the door, but he knows he will now confront security. Although he would prefer the door to be answered by the girl, most likely it will be one of the parents. The most daunting possibility is the father. Typically, the father welcomes the boy with a handshake. The father uses the firm grip to express I-will-kill-anyone-who-is-a-threat-to-my-daughter. The boy is expressing I-like-your-daughter-and-please-don't-kill-me.

The Delay

Even though the boy and the girl have set a specific time, the girl is not yet ready. There has been some kind of complication with her outfit or her hair. Or she has discovered some last-second blemish she must now cover in skin-colored makeup. Or she simply wants to promote anticipation for the boy, who currently sits in the living room sweating high-caliber bullets, as he tries to make small talk with strangers. The boy might also be required to demonstrate finesse by having to interact with siblings or pets.

Rendezvous Point

Eventually, the girl comes into the room. The boy must then express cautious admiration for her appearance. Too little and he offends the girl. Too much and he offends the parents. Whether or not the boy and girl are having second thoughts, the date has been activated. At the front door, the father gives instructions about when the girl must be returned to her home. This is known as the "curfew." The boy quickly agrees to whatever time is named by the father.

Departure

The boy and the girl are now in the process of going "out." They walk to the car together, where he opens the passenger door for her. She knows how to open a car door, but he does this anyway as an expression of her value to him. Once they are in the car, they fall into stressful, small talk. If conversation falters, there is no one else present to save them. It's like when the safety bar on a roller coaster clicks into place. There's no turning back now.

Digestion

In many cases, the boy and girl will go to a restaurant to eat dinner together. This gives the boy the opportunity to spend money, which further supports the idea that he considers the girl to be of value. Menu selection is key here. Some foods should be avoided. Spaghetti and fried chicken are difficult to eat in an attractive way. Depending on the couple, as they sit across from each other, this is when small talk can eventually smooth out into "big talk."

Amusement

Although dates have included bowling or miniature golf, the standard choice is a movie. At dinner, the boy and girl face each other. In the theater they sit side-by-side, like in the car. However, instead of talking, they watch the movie. The darkness and proximity of the seats promote a fairly romantic atmosphere. Many discredit movies as a good choice for a date, but when the lights go down, the pressure to maintain witty banter is temporarily lifted. Afterwards, the movie gives them a common experience which they can then use to supply the conversation on the way back to the girl's home

The Return

During the drive back, the conversation might dwindle back down to small talk. If their time together has triggered greater interest, they will most likely plan another date. Either way, both of them sense this date is almost over. But there is still one last phase.

The Door

Once they arrive at the girl's home, the boy opens the car door for her and walks her to the door of her home. Because both of them have watched a thousand movies which involve a kiss at the door, there is now an awkward tension that is both exciting and horrible. With some effort, it's possible for them to maintain their composure by saying something like, "I had a great time." The girl goes inside and the boy drives away.

Going Unsteady

Adam and Eve didn't date. They didn't "go out." They didn't even get engaged. I suspect there wasn't even an official ceremony. They just got married. This sound overly simple to us here in the modern world, but you have to admit, things have gotten a lot more complicated since. More complicated than they need to be.

Granted, the first man and first woman did not have a wide selection. It wasn't like they could "shop around" or "play the field." There was no competition. But somewhere between Eden and Sweden, we've come up with so many stages of relationship, it's difficult to know exactly where things go wrong, or even where things go right.

When you first become interested, you can "like" or even "like-like" someone. As you get older, there are all kinds of other ideas that clutter the landscape. Over the years there has been "going steady," "hanging out," "sowing your wild oats," being "an item" or being "together," "hooking up," and "seeing someone." Just to mention a few.

From a distance, all of these might sound like efficient calibrations of an effective system. But if you take a closer look, you see the wreckage scattered everywhere. The truth is, this system is primarily efficient at destroying relationships and breaking hearts. Whatever we're doing, we're doing it very wrong.

Although some claim they are dating "just for fun," the underlying intent is the possibility of a closer relationship. But in order for there to be any progress, there has to be at least some form of loyalty. This often takes the form of being "exclusive."

This kind of arrangement was once sealed with the boy giving the girl his class ring or letter jacket. Since these items are borderline obsolete, the most recent equivalent might be posting on Facebook that you are "in a relationship."

In our efforts to establish this limited exclusivity, we have created several levels that have elements of marriage, without actually being marriage. They have the feel of durable love, but nothing in their composition contains any real commitment. The relationship might appear to be moving toward something real, but both people understand—there is an unspoken stipulation that either party can opt out at any moment.

The concept of "becoming one," first established with Adam and Eve, has been fragmented into attempts of *almost* becoming one. Anyone considering a lifelong commitment would be wise to approach with some caution. But the current situation is certainly not the best way to go about things. We are at the mercy of ideas about love that were never part of the original design. We have not improved things. We have merely invented a hundred ways to sabotage love. We have developed a system that is not unlike trying to cross a minefield. If you want to reach the other side, you're going to have stay on your toes.

It might help to consider what things were like before we came up with all this other stuff. It might help to look at how things worked before we invented dating.

Predating Dating

Although marriage can be traced back to Creation, dating is actually a relatively recent invention. From Eden up until about the 20th Century, there was no such thing. Between Day Six and Year 1900, a guy and a girl did not necessarily go out to dinner and a movie. For one thing, during the great majority of this time, there were no restaurants or theaters.

The Biblical record is filled with countless births. This is strong evidence that a dateless world did not hinder Single People from becoming Married People. The only conclusion possible is that there were other just as efficient or even better methods that might simply be unfamiliar to the 21st Century mind.

Although Adam and Eve were married, nothing is recorded about the details leading to their union. When Cain went east to find a wife, we have no information about how they ended up together. As far as I know, the first time any kind of process is mentioned is when Isaac and Rebekah got together. Keep in mind this marriage was like Adam and Eve, in that it was specifically arranged by God (Genesis 24:5; 24:27). Isaac's dad sent out a servant to find Isaac someone to marry. The servant found Rebekah drawing water at a well. He made arrangements with her family for her to return with him to meet Isaac (Genesis 24:15, 61). When she arrived, she saw Isaac walking across a field. As he approached, she put her veil on (Genesis 24:65). Then they got married.

That's pretty much it. As far as any pre-marriage interaction, there's nothing to suggest that Isaac took Rebekah out to eat. They didn't go for long walks or sit and watch the sunset while they shared their hopes and dreams. The account implies they simply got married. But it worked. There were certainly dysfunctional facets of their relationship as later revealed through in-house politics (Genesis 27:6-13), but these two people got married and stayed married.

Isaac's son Jacob had a similar experience. His wife was also discovered while she drew water from a well (Genesis 29:10). Moses also met his wife through the well-water program (Exodus 2:17). Saul too met some single girls that way (I Samuel 9:11). Saul didn't end up marrying any of them—but still. Back in those days, single guys looking to get married probably would have been wise to hang out at the nearest water source.

One key difference with Jacob and Rachel, however is that when they first met, he kissed her (Genesis 29:11). Don't raise your eyebrows. It was probably just a culturally acceptable, friendly greeting. After all, shortly after this, Rachel's father kissed Jacob (Genesis 29:13).

Another significant difference with Jacob and Rachel is that they did not get married right away. There is a stark contrast between how Jacob went about getting married compared to his parents. Whereas his mom and dad married shortly after meeting, it was seven years before Jacob and Rachel reached matrimony (Genesis 29:20). But even with this prolonged delay, there is also no record of them going on a date. The only thing that definitely happened was Jacob worked lot. In fact, he worked 2,555 days. Call it a long engagement, but it was no date.

As far as Isaac and Rebekah, there was zero time for dating. When she arrived at Isaac's place and met him, they did not even go out for coffee. They just got married.

With all this said, we can learn some things about dating from these two couples. First, there was no such thing as dating. At least not in the sense of what usually occurs today.

When it came to searching for a spouse, the search was fairly restrictive. It wasn't a matter of just casting a glance across the whole, wide world. There was the strict consideration that an "outsider" could result in complications. The primary concern was spiritual compromise (Genesis 24:3; 28:1). Marrying anyone who did not belong to God was considered a big mistake.

Maybe because of this restriction, there weren't a lot of options. When Rebekah showed up, Isaac just went with it. He didn't ask if she had any sisters. He didn't suggest the servant go back and get more so he could have a selection to choose from. To a great extent, the same was true of Jacob. He focused on Rachel right away. Although his future father-in-law complicated things when he tossed Leah into the situation, as far as Jacob was concerned, he met Rachel and then he wanted to marry Rachel—so much so that he was willing to work seven years to get her.

To us in the 21st Century Western Civilization, all this seems extremely weird and unromantic. Seven years would be enough to get to know someone. But the seven-minute arrangement between Isaac and Rebekah seems like a bad approach. They certainly didn't know each other. At best, Isaac and Rebekah were able to conclude they found each other attractive. There was no time for them to see if they really Like-Liked each other.

Even in the 17th Century, there was a glaring absence of dating. Yet men who were busy settling the New World wanted wives. Once in a while, the French government would commission a ship full of women to the New World. The single men would go down to the docks to pick a wife. There was a brief meet-and-greet, a practical pairing off, followed by an immediate engagement or even the wedding itself.

It might come as a shock to you, but the great majority of humanity throughout the great majority of history did not date. Yet, history is filled with Married People.

One would assume that if this new advent of dating is truly beneficial, then Married People should be better off today. But that is not the case. Everyone knows that the realm of Married People is messed up in profound ways. Whether dating is the culprit is debatable. But something is wrong somewhere. You can't argue that.

Whatever the case may be, we have convinced ourselves that dating is the way to go. Dating is certainly an improvement over some antiquated ideas that are downright scary. But it is definitely worth exploring how dating came about. Its origin might shed some light on our current situation.

The Invention of Dating

We look back on medieval times as the essence of romance. But actually, what we imagine about that stretch of history is mostly Hollywood fluff. When there were knights in shining armor and princesses in towers, marriages were mostly a matter of politics. A king of one kingdom would give his daughter to the son of the king of another kingdom. That way both kings would be related and less likely to try and kill each other. Marriage became less about nurturing love and more about preventing war.

Even the common people played the same game. Marriages were arranged along the lines of business deals. The parents closed the deal without much regard for the preferences of the couple. The boy and the girl might get some say-so, but the primary concern was how much both families might financially benefit from the merger.

In the recent past, families urged the daughter to "marry well." This meant marrying a boy who was wealthy enough to stave off poverty. Marriage wasn't love. It was dealing with the anxiety of starving to death.

Traces of this kind of thinking are still around today. Take note of the mother encouraging her daughter to marry a doctor or the girl who is swept away by a knight in a shining sports car.

In the midst of this cold approach to marriage, dating somehow came to life. Around the 19th Century, courtship became more formal and romantic. There was lots of swooning

3 – Picking Flowers in the Minefield

and poetic protocol. A guy couldn't just walk up and talk to a girl. There were elaborate rules. In the Victorian Era, some women communicated in code, using their fans. If she fanned herself slowly, that meant she was already taken. If she let the fan rest on her left cheek, that meant "get lost." If she fanned herself quickly, that meant she was available. If she let the fan rest on her right cheek, that meant she was interested.

Romantic etiquette also involved calling cards. When a guy and a girl were introduced, if the man was interested, he would give her one of his cards. When there was some sort of party, throughout the evening, multiple men might offer their own cards to the same girl. At the end of the evening, she would choose one of these potential suitors by giving him her own card. This meant he would be allowed to walk her home—chaperoned by her family.

If things progressed, during the early part of the relationship, they would spend time with her family. They would eventually be allowed, on occasion, to sit alone together outside on the front porch.

We've all smiled in condescension at these movies. The boy and girl sit on the porch swing while her parents keep a watchful eye through the front window. The couple struggles through stilted conversations, but somehow they are able to grow the relationship. Then one day, the boy shows up and goes into the sitting room with the father to ask for the girl's hand in marriage.

We shake our heads. Surely we've come a long way from all that stuff. Surely, we are much more sophisticated when it comes to love. Even though we might flinch away from Jane Austin's world, there is clearly something missing in our way of doing things.

Let's fast forward out of the 19th Century. We reach the 20th Century and this is when we see everything change in a big way. Standing outside of a girl's house, you'll notice some differences right away. The boy does not come over and spend time at the house. He does not eat dinner with the family. He does not sit on the porch swing. Instead of adding himself to the home environment, he removes the girl. He takes the girl on a "date." Chaperones, the family, and any other third wheels are left behind like a flat tire.

In the 20th Century, there were restaurants to go to. Movies to see. Couples were no longer tied down to the girl's home life. Couples were out and about in public. This was where their relationship would be measured. Before, it was the family who set the standard. Now it was the world who would redefine romance and even love.

The invention of the automobile escalated the shift. Before cars, a boy was most likely to be found at his own home with his family. Even if there was somewhere to go, there wasn't any easy way of getting there. But with cars, a boy could bolt his dinner, jump in a car, and head on down the road. This made him much more likely to capture a girl's fancy. Together, they would zip off in his "portable living room" (as some have called it), in which privacy could lead to all kinds of unrestricted activity.

World War II changed everything everywhere forever. Many, many young men went off to fight and never returned. Just like that, all the girls had a drastic shortage of suitors. Girls far outnumbered boys. The ratio was out of whack.

Some say this is when society started measuring the worth of a girl by the number of her suitors. Victorian times had its share of girls stringing guys along, but post WWII seemed to trigger an even greater propensity for girls wanting to be pursued by multiple guys.

Probably all of us have at least once or twice liked the idea of numerous prospects being interested in us. It's one thing to actually have one member of the opposite sex interested in you. It's a whole different boost to your confidence to have a crowd vying for your heart. Even though the war ended, this idea has remained.

Dating is a kind of mash-up of multiple ideas and standards (or lack of standards) that have accumulated during twisted times in history. But it is so much a part of our culture, it seems impossible to imagine approaching marriage without it.

The Other List

If you think about it, the whole concept of being Married People is a little strange. Two people who begin as complete strangers gradually become the exact opposite of complete strangers. By all appearances, they cross an entire spectrum of relationships—from unknown to known, from total disregard to total adoration. When you consider Point B in regard to Point A, it's kind of mind-boggling.

Although convoluted, to a certain extent the current path can be mapped out by factors of attraction. Mary made a list. But eventually so did I—and so did you.

Whether you did so intentionally or subconsciously, you gradually compiled a list of what you find appealing about the other gender. For most, the list is figurative, secreted away in their minds. Some have actually sat down and written it all out. This list is significant in understanding how Married People find each other.

There is no Master List. Each person has their own. It is custom-made, one-of-a-kind. However, for the sake of this field study, we will now examine a general, hypothetical version. What follows is by no means definitive—some of the following might not even appear on your list. But these might help us understand a little more about the process.

Physical Appearance

Each person comes in a variety of biodegradable containers called a "body." The face in particular has been known to trigger a reaction resulting in Married People.

The rest of the body has its own qualities, some of them depending on the gender as to which specific parts are the most noteworthy (cf. your own list).

Physical appearance is typically at the top of the list. There are certain body shapes and types of faces that tend to appeal to certain cultures, but this category is more subjective than you might think. There is no true universal standard.

For many people, however, physical appearance is not only at the top of the list, it is virtually the only thing on their list.

Personality

The personality is what's inside the container. This is the person's attitude and outlook—whether they are nice or angry or optimistic or whiny or shallow.

This attribute is often considered to be the opposite of physical attraction. This concept is enforced by the unspoken (and sometimes spoken) belief that a good personality and good looks are mutually exclusive. However, these two factors can be completely unrelated and uninfluenced by each other.

Even so, a bad personality can be a deal-breaker, regardless of how good-looking the container is. A great personality can be a deal-maker, somehow improving the person's appearance. One of the best makeovers a person can have is putting on some humor or honesty.

Interests

The level of attraction between two people can sometimes be boosted by common interests. If both the boy and girl have a passion for cooking or for skydiving, these can actually help instigate romantic possibilities. Spending time making chicken fettuccini together or leaping out of a plane and falling 10,000 feet together can make all the difference.

On the other hand, a lack of common interest can interfere. If you find platypus figurines incredibly fascinating and you meet someone who openly thinks that platypus figurines are stupid, this clash of interest might very well doom the relationship. The other person might be good-looking, they might be a pleasant person, but if they have ridiculed your passion, things might not work out.

Behavior

Even if someone scores high on all of the above, certain habits can take a contender out of the running. A person with stunning looks can quickly be demoted if they light up a cigarette or if their hobby turns out to be kicking puppies. On the other hand, a person can become more attractive if they coach little league or negotiate treaties with hostile countries.

Opinions of Others

When it comes to considering a candidate for romantic possibilities, some people will take and even seek the advice of their loved ones. The observations and input of parents, siblings, and friends lend an objective viewpoint. Although, the great majority let other things on the list trump this factor, the input of others has proven to be a very valuable guide.

Your Rating on Their List

It is a brutal truth that not everyone you find interesting will feel the same way about you. In fact, in most cases, potentially romantic interactions will result in one person being disappointed. If the other person's list disqualifies you, chances are their own rating on your list will fall accordingly. However, that same unavailability has also been notorious for increasing their rating, making them even more appealing for the very reason that they are unavailable.

Spirituality

This factor is listed last, not because it is the least important, but because on most people's list—it *is* listed last.

In most cases, the spiritual condition of the other person is an afterthought. All the other factors are given precedence. Once those scores have been tallied, only then is the spiritual factor brought into consideration for a final appraisal—if that.

For the great majority, this factor does not even appear on the list at all. However, for the record, there are those who are convinced this particular factor is the primary consideration.

Finding Someone

One of the most fascinating aspects of Married People is how they actually find each other.

Discounting arranged marriages, it's not always easy to locate someone you might want to marry. It would be different if an angel was involved, like with Isaac and Rebekah. That kind of match-making service would change everything. You would reach a certain age, then an angel would lead you or someone representing you to find your future spouse. That would be nice.

Today, we don't go to wells and wait for someone to draw water. There are other places.

Next Door

During your childhood, you might befriend someone your age who lives next door. As you grow up, you play games and watch TV together. Then lo and behold, one day you both realize you make each other's hearts race. This particular scenario is more likely to happen in the movies than in real life. Plus, in the movies, you stand on the porch and sing.

School

There are actually a lot of real-life stories about high school sweethearts. You meet someone in class or at an event. You start dating and you walk down the halls hand in hand. In some cases, you can become an annoying landmark in the hall, clinging to each other like parasites.

College

Higher education can provide you with a degree, but also a spouse. This situation is similar to high school except there is less parental supervision and worse food choices. Here, you also meet during class or an event. After you graduate, you get married, and you end up sharing memories and tuition debts.

The Blind Date

This is when your friends arrange for you to go on a date with a complete stranger. Sometimes your friends are motivated by good intentions. Sometimes they are just trying to even out the numbers. The ones who set up the blind date are eager for it to work out because then they can forever take credit. Occasionally, this works out well. However, it does not have a great track record. In many cases, an awkward dinner is followed by an awkward movie, finishing with an even more awkward goodbye at the door.

The Church Building

Congregations of Christians have proven to be a good source of potential spouses. You might fall for someone you've known for years. Or you might meet someone new. You notice a visitor, then partly under the guise of making them feel welcome, you introduce yourself. If there's a potluck, you get bonus time to try and make a good impression, while dining on casserole and coleslaw.

Singles Groups

This usually happens when a congregation begins to notice they have a surplus of Single People. Various devotionals and parties are scheduled along the lines of low-impact mixers. Strong friendships and marriages have been known to result from these groups. These can definitely be spiritually beneficial. They can also be a great source of Dr. Pepper and Doritos.

The Workplace

A conversation at work during a lunch break or collaboration on a project can lead to romantic interest. Suddenly, work doesn't seem as bad as it did before. On the plus side, if things go well, you can end up seeing that person almost every day. On the negative side, if things do not go well, you can end up seeing that person almost every day.

Online Dating and Social Networking

Not that long ago, even though it worked out for many people, meeting someone through the classifieds was not considered very stylish. Of course now, the online dating sites are quite stylish. You can construct a profile of yourself and post a flattering photograph, along with an assortment of details that markets you in a positive way.

Miscellaneous

There are all kinds of places for possible encounters which can eventually result in Married People. A grocery store, a coffee shop, a park—just about any place has been known to lead to romance. The one place that does actually seem obsolete and unlikely, at least in our culture, is to meet someone while drawing water at the well.

The Truth about Valentine's Day

Before we go any farther, it might be best to examine that one day of the year that might seem to capture the essence of Married People. Valentine's Day is every February 14th and woe unto the boyfriend or husband who forgets that.

You might be surprised about its back story. It's actually kind of a crazy conglomeration of different legends, customs, and assorted distortions about love.

It started with wolves. The people of Rome were concerned about their sheep and shepherds, so they prayed to Lupercas, an imaginary deity. He served as a talisman against the howling canines outside the walls. A day was set aside every year to honor Lupercas. The wolves eventually left, but the holiday remained. Someone later decided to take the day away from Lupercas and give it to Juno, the goddess who specialized in marriage. That's when love got involved.

In honor of this Juno Day, people did all sorts of weird things. Girls would write their names on a piece of paper and put it in a clay jar. The boys then drew a name and they were paired off with that girl for the day, or even for the year. Sometimes they even ended up getting married.

Another weird tradition involved girls lingering at their window early in the morning. The first guy they saw coming down the street was their guy.

Another tradition urged girls to go to the cemetery at night. When the clock struck midnight, she was supposed to throw seeds on the ground and say, "Hempseed I sow, hempseed I mow. He that my true love will be, rake the hempseed after me." Then she would run home, looking back to see if anyone was following her. This means that one of the prototypes of modern romance was the hope of being stalked on the way home from the cemetery in the middle of the night.

February 14th was ultimately chosen because it was believed birds chose their mates for life on this day. Somewhere along the line, two or three different guys named Valentine were associated with the whole thing. All of them were killed. This doesn't even count the Saint Valentine's Day Massacre, when seven gangsters were gunned down in a garage. It's probably unfair to include this last historical snippet, but anyone who has ever been shot down by their crush will allow this tangent.

This is where the trail of roses and candy leads. False gods, avian superstition, a bunch of dead guys, and the fear of wolves. A cynic might find this appropriate. Valentine's Day is the culmination of a bunch of weird ideas about love.

But anyone else might find Valentine's Day endearing. It's about flowers and chocolate. It's dinner at a nice restaurant or a poem. There are some great things. There are some not-so-great things. Valentine's Day can be a wonderful chance to express genuine love—a reminder of how much someone means to you. It is a chance for your love to shine a little brighter.

It can also be a brutal reminder to many people of how alone they are.

A balanced perspective of Valentine's Day is captured by the symbol of the armed cherub who haunts the world for the better part of February—Cupid.

The offspring of Greek mythology, he flits around and shoots arrows at people. One part of the legend says he carries two kinds of arrows. The arrows with golden tips are sharp and they make you become totally infatuated. The other arrows have silver tips that are dull. A hit by one of these makes you lose interest and run away.

Like the golden arrows, love can make you feel great. But it can also make you feel like you've been mortally wounded. All of us, at one time or another, have probably doubted that Cupid uses arrows. It felt more like he carries a Glock with hollow-point bullets.

Today, love does indeed seem to be mostly managed by a cross between a baby and butterfly, doling out affection in the form of ammo. He does not anoint you with perfume spritzers or clouds of confetti. He shoots you. And when you're hit, it really hurts.

Chocolate, Roses, Diamonds

In our culture, love can be measured in gifts. Units of affection measure the distance to the object of your affection. This system is used by the males in particular to express their feelings toward the females. Whether or not the system springs from strategic advertising or is simply a natural side-effect of romance is debatable. But there is an undeniable progression. Love moves from shallow to profound and if you want to map out its progress, consider the gifts. There are various subsets of what I am about to present, but for the sake of simplicity, I will present the three distinct levels.

Stage One—Chocolate

The least daring but deeply appreciated expression of love is chocolate. If a boy wants to openly express a romantic interest in a girl, this will most likely be his first choice. Chocolate is a substance derived from *Theobroma cacao* seeds and is partly composed of a molecule called Theobromine ($C_7H_8N_4O_2$). Theobromine literally means "god-food" or "food of the gods." It has an effect on the central nervous system similar to caffeine, but not as strong. (As such, it's easy to imagine a gentleman caller today showing up at a girl's door with an espresso.) However, when it comes to stimulating the heart, chocolate wins over caffeine. This is probably why people suggest that chocolate creates a buzz comparable to being in love. Heart-shaped chocolates are common, but squares and rectangles are also acceptable, especially if presented inside a heart-shaped box. Chocolate can certainly be used for more serious relationships, but here in the early stages, it is the safest choice.

Stage Two—Flowers

Once the relationship has been sustained for at least a brief time, various kinds of flowers can be used to further express interest. Flowers can also be given for non-romantic reasons, but they have proven to be especially effective in the arena of love. Just about any flower can be used—even dandelions, depending on the personal significance intended by the giver. However, the universal donor is a rose. Although other colors can represent other relationships, the color of love in this case is red. Again, red roses are probably best later in the relationship. Any sooner, might be considered too bold. This is not to say that some guys might be able to make it work early in the game, but the safest progression would be chocolate, then flowers.

Stage Three—Jewelry

This is considered to be the highest stage of gift-giving among Married People and those aspiring to be Married People. As with flowers, there are variations of this gift, but the pinnacle of this stage is notoriously the diamond. They are a girl's best friend. The corollary for the male is a dog. Whereas a diamond is forever, a dog is about thirteen years. I'm not sure what to say about that.

Due to its drastically unusual durability, diamonds are usually reserved to honor a long-term commitment. Again, to drive the point home, you can imagine how well most first dates would go if the guy showed up at the door, not with chocolate or red roses, but a diamond necklace. The endurance of each gift fits the level of love. Chocolate is quickly consumed. Flowers last longer, but eventually die. But jewels endure.

We all accept the basic idea of there being increments. When it comes to love, there is no simple ON and OFF. You might say the spectrum ranges from Puppy Love to Always-and-Forever. Since such a vast landscape can be so overwhelming, the oversimplification of the Chocolate—Roses—Diamonds scale can be useful for now.

But the most telling choice is the second one. You would think our culture would have preferred to focus on tulips or gardenias—something without thorns. However, with some disillusioned hindsight, I guess we would all agree. The rose was a wise choice. Romance is indeed suitably captured by the flower with thorns.

In case you missed it—that was foreshadowing.

Breakers and Breakees

Most everyone believes that the pursuit of love is the best way to be happy. But the truth is, it's the best way to get really depressed. There is great pain when it seems like everyone but you has someone. If your person of interest has zero interest in you, that really hurts too. But the most painful moment in the pursuit of love comes when the boy and girl have been dating and then one of them decides it's time to stop dating.

3 – Picking Flowers in the **Minefield**

It's called breaking up.

It's pretty rare for both people to want the break-up. Usually only one of the two wants to end things. The other one typically wishes to remain unbroken-up. But the one who wants to break up gets veto power. Unless both are willing to continue dating, it all comes to an end.

The one wanting to break-up (hereafter known as the "breaker") can choose from a variety of methods in order to disconnect from the one who does not want to break up (hereafter known as the "breakee"). Few of these methods are admirable and none are painless. Here are some thorns.

The Fade

The breaker allows a sense of distance to surface, hoping the relationship will die on its own. This is accomplished by being generally unavailable. This method is easy on the breaker at first, but normally the breakee will demand some kind of clarity. Things will then become quickly awkward as the breaker is forced to choose one of the other methods.

Face-to-Face

Considered to be the most respected form of breaking-up, ending the relationship with a face-to-face conversation is extremely difficult for both parties. The breakee of course experiences the painful impact of the decision. But the breaker must witness first-hand the pain they are causing. This method requires the breaker to have the courage to deal with a straightforward confrontation, which can be extremely awkward and emotional. There can be anger and tears. The advantage for everyone involved is that it is like ripping a bandage off—painful, but quick. Although this is arguably the most honorable method, it is never easy.

The Phone Call

Another option is the phone call. This provides some distance to lessen the intensity of the awkwardness. This benefits the breaker mostly since it allows the breaker to not see the pain on the breakee's face. In most cases, this method is less respected than Face-to-Face. It can actually be an indication of disrespect to the breakee and it generally indicates the breaker is a big chicken.

It is not impossible that some breakees might prefer the phone call, since it allows them to not be directly exposed to the presence of the breaker. On the phone, you can make your voice sound like the voice of someone who is not that upset. You can make your voice calm and steady, like the voice of someone who was actually considering being the breaker anyway. You can hold your true feelings in check until you cordially hang up.

Writing a Message

Sometimes it is difficult to find the best words for a break-up. Writing a letter or an email gives the breaker time to collect some thoughts—to choose phrases—that might lessen the pain for everyone involved. Sometimes Face-to-Face or The Phone Call risks the strong possibility of saying the wrong thing, escalating the difficulty of a situation that is already difficult.

However, sending a message in the form of a letter or email is arguably even less respectful in that it is often designed to primarily protect the breaker rather than the breakee. Delivering words without actually being present is not the best choice. The Dear John Letter might be suitable during times of war, due to unavoidable distance, but in all other cases, it is usually considered one of the last resorts.

The Friend

We are now getting to the bottom of the barrel, addressing some of the least courageous methods. Breaking-up through a friend provides even more of a safe distance for the breaker. The idea is to choose an arbitrator or mediator, hopefully one with tact and a way with words. This friend is then sent to deliver the news to the breakee. However, no matter how elegant the delivery, it is not much unlike using a contract killer. The kill is clean and the conscience of the breaker might be soothed for not having to see the face or tears of the breakee, but it increases the chance of humiliation for the breakee because a third party is now involved to witness their broken heart first hand. This method is generally frowned upon as the choice of cowards.

The Text

This is not the bottom of the barrel. This is when you set the barrel aside and start digging beneath. The worst possible way to break up with someone is by text (or any equivalent short message such as a tweet or IM). This is the most meager form of communication and shows disrespect to the breakee. It is considered a very scummy thing to do. Possibly the only thing worse might be to post the break-up message on the breakee's Facebook wall or on a Jumbo-tron.

Although Face-to Face is probably the most painful and awkward, it is recommended that the breaker use this method. It speaks better of the breaker's character and shows at least some form of caring to the breakee. If you're going to give someone a rose, at least have the courage to also be accountable for the thorns.

Date, Then Hate

There is a curious side-effect of break-ups that reveals something significant about the nature of dating. Almost always, when a couple stops dating, they don't just shift down to friendship or even cordial acquaintances. One, if not both, descend into something that strongly resembles hatred.

This animosity usually comes from the breakee. It's also possible during the turmoil of ending the romantic relationship, for the breaker to experience grim emotions. Given time, bad feelings on both sides can fade, but the final result at best is usually a cold distance. They used to be in love. Now they aren't even friends anymore.

Dating often resembles one-step-forward-two-steps-back. These two people began with neutral feelings, which changed to "love," which ended in something far less. No matter how true blue their hearts may have been during the romance, all the admiration and adoration usually falls into a level of animosity reserved for archenemies.

Most likely, the breakee is suffering from the shock of watching their hopes vanish into thin air. They have imagined the days to come in great detail, picturing various scenarios of happiness in which there is laughter and comfort. To have all of that ripped away can be nothing less than agony. It makes sense that no one wants to spend any more time around the one who has so thoroughly destroyed the future.

We should point out that if the breaker is still a compassionate human being, they also might experience pain through empathy. This deserves some consideration. It would not be realistic or fair to suggest the pain of the breaker is comparable to the pain of the breakee. The breaker has had the benefit of some time to gradually become accustomed to a future that does not involve the other one. They may even have someone waiting in the wings. The breaker has had time to prepare to abandon ship.

The breakee, on the other hand, is suddenly shoved overboard. Most likely, they have invested their heart completely. There is no one in the wings. There is only the sudden empty seat next to them. These wildly different positions naturally result in different levels of feelings.

But again, it makes you wonder. Dating seems to not be very well suited for finding love. It seems much more likely to ruin it. Dating is not a gentle exploration of souls. It is like a bad surgeon who leaves love cold on the table.

I'm happy to say there are exceptions. They're rare, but they do exist. Even after breaking-up, there are some who do salvage friendship. It can take some time, but it is not impossible that whatever connection they once experienced resurfaces in a new form.

Dating is assumed to be the best way to find love. If that was the case, even it fails, that love should decline gently into at least a friendship. If dating is really about love, why does it so often end in hate?

The only reasonable conclusion is that what passes for love during dating is almost never actually love. It's something masquerading as love. This means that dating is not really conducive to finding love as much as promoting its counterfeit, infatuation.

Anything based on infatuation will have a tendency to collapse into hatred. And it will collapse. It's just a matter of time. Even if it moves forward, unless it actually reaches love in the truest sense, what makes their hearts beat faster will be a precarious thing, easily broken—and ultimately doomed.

The Girl in the Alto Section

It doesn't take long to sense the danger. When it comes to dating there are all kinds of metaphors that could work. Let's call it a minefield.

Speaking only for the male side of the world, when it came to dealing with this minefield, there were two kinds of boys. There were those who crossed the mine field and there were those—me included—who watched with interest to see who would be blown to smithereens.

Several of the ones who crossed that dangerous distance actually made it. They went on dates. They held hands with girls. They kissed girls. They began to resemble Married People.

Some guys blew up. They approached a girl and she would reject him. She would laugh at him. One of my friends asked out a girl and she said, "How cute." And walked away.

The broken bodies of these brothers were enough to keep a lot of us from even trying. We were the happy few, the cowardly spectators. It was much safer.

We didn't actually talk to girls we liked. We just imagined talking to them. It seemed like such a ridiculous thing to do. To go up to a girl and suggest romance. Those of us on the safe side of the field limited ourselves to only gazing from afar.

You know how it is. Once you've pinpointed someone, you're always keenly aware of where they are. If you're in the same room, they become your true north, by which you calculate all your bearings. All roads lead to them. Any kind of brief encounter, no matter how mundane, becomes the milestone of the day.

I was in love with a girl in my high school chorus. It wasn't really love, but at the time, it sure felt very much like love. I didn't even have any other classes with her. Just chorus. Once a day, a bunch of us would go to the music room and form up in our groups. Sopranos, altos, tenors, basses. I was a tenor. She was an alto. I was enthralled.

Whether or not I sang the right notes didn't matter to me. Whether or not the teacher was happy with our progress didn't mean anything at all. The only thing I cared about was making sure my line of sight was clear so that I could see her.

Once in a blue moon I caught a glimpse of her in the hallways. But I knew that when it came time for chorus, she would be there. I never spoke to her. I just gazed from afar across the minefield and wondered what she was like.

You know what's funny? I don't remember her name. Not even a little bit. Not even the first letter. This girl who mesmerized me in high school—the one who made my heart feel like it was soaring—is just a vague memory now.

I was deeply infatuated because she was pretty, but I also blame music. Not only did music bring us to the same room for forty-five minutes. Music gave the room some magic. She was singing and I was singing. Not to each other, but still. Music made my daydreams feel a little less impossible.

But now—looking back, I'm not sure that music in a minefield is such a good idea.

Music the Tyrant

One of the most significant culprits that causes all kinds of delusions and false expectations about love is music.

A song can express the essence of your feelings. A song can help strengthen the bond between you and the love of your life. A song can also give a magical passionate glow to some of the dumbest choices you'll ever make.

Music is wonderful and powerful. Music is one of the most potent catalysts in existence. But when it comes to its control over the heart, it can be flat-out tyrannical.

One of the first things music does is divide people into tribes. We naturally gravitate toward people with similar tastes, but songs seem to bind people together quicker and stronger than just about anything else. A Scottish politician in the 1600s named Andrew Fletcher said, "Let me make the songs of a nation, and I care not who makes its laws." Music has the power to unite people and to shape their thinking.

Music can alter your appearance. Young people in particular seem more susceptible to music in that it often dictates their choice of clothing, hairstyle, and general philosophy of life. In many cases, you merely have to see someone enter a room and you have a good chance of deducing the contents of their playlists.

Music can help you attract the opposite gender. One blatant example is the steady thump you often hear in traffic. There is something to be said for immersing yourself in music, but chances are—what you are hearing is the auditory equivalent of a bird parading its bright feathers. *Hey, I like that song too. I'm in the same tribe. Want to go out?*

More than anything, music toys with our longing to belong. It gently carves ideas in our heads that have no true connection with reality. It is the equivalent of trying to pass off cartoons as profound philosophy. Yet, we are endlessly shocked when real life defies all the things we have been singing for so long.

Listening to music is a key influence in matters of love. But music can have an even greater effect, if you know how to play it. It can even improve your rating on the Mary List.

For a guy, singing in the high school chorus or playing in the orchestra doesn't really help much. I can vouch for both of these. Classical music is classy, but carrying a violin case usually doesn't make any girls swoon.

Being in the school band is probably better. If you're in *the* band, there are possibilities. But when it comes to playing music, your best bet is to be in *a* band.

This is one of the bizarre anomalies of our culture. Just about any guy who can play three chords on a guitar has the chance to become interesting to girls. He doesn't have to be kind or smart or even that good of a guitarist. All he has to do is strum the latest romantic ballad, and girls will appear. I would even bet the great majority of male musicians learned to play music not because of any real passion for the art, but because they knew it might get them girls.

If you amplify that guitar and find some friends who can play drums and bass, your rating on the Mary List can really soar. Talent and charisma help, but neither are absolutely necessary. Everyone knows. You don't have to be good-looking if you're in a band. You can capture the hearts of a whole gaggle of girls, even if you look like a gnome.

We have all felt the power of this particular species of music. There are bands today who have an insane following. They can pack a concert venue with enough fans to people a small town. But one of the first bands was so popular that if you weren't a fan, you were executed.

As far as I know, the band didn't have a name. Since it was the only band in town, they probably didn't need one. The only thing we know for sure is the manager's name was Nebuchadnezzar.

The king of Babylon built a 90-foot high golden idol and decided to use music to make sure the people gave it proper attention (Daniel 3:1-3). When it was all arranged, Nebuchadnezzar had an announcement made. "Then the herald loudly proclaimed: 'To you the command is given, O peoples, nations and men of every language, that at the moment you hear the sound of the horn, flute, lyre, trigon, psaltery, bagpipe and all kinds of music, you are to fall down and worship the golden image that Nebuchadnezzar the king has set up'" (Daniel 3:4-5). There's no denying this pop movement was a force to be reckoned with.

Whenever this band kicked in, there were consequences if you didn't drop to the ground. You wouldn't be escorted out of the concert. You were killed. "But whoever does not fall down and worship shall immediately be cast into the midst of a furnace of blazing fire'" (Daniel 3:6). It's kind of shocking to realize the real reason Shadrach, Meshach, and Abednego were thrown into a furnace. Pop music.

There is no such band today. Nebuchadnezzar's Furnace Fury—or whatever they were called—has dropped off the charts. But this weird milestone in music history might be a useful analogy.

Music is power. It isn't necessarily good or bad. Whether or not it results in you being burned alive could sway your opinion. But there are other issues that should also be taken into consideration.

Music can lie to you and make the lies sound so good. Music can stir your heart, but it can also shut down your brain. Music can dress up infatuation so well that it looks just like love. Songs can help you wallow in self-pity.

Let me emphasize—music can capture a flicker of true love. All of us have been shaped by music in positive ways as well. But mostly, music enables horribly inaccurate ideas about love. This is why many times "love" has as much staying power as the next boy band.

When it comes down to it, music can get you to surrender to a lot of stupid choices. It can get you to bow down to ideas that will ruin your life. Nebuchadnezzar's band might be long gone. But the music plays on.

Pre-Marital Dancing

Music makes you want to dance. Ask any little kid with his kid music. No one has to teach you. Given the right song, you can't sit still. It's built in. All of us have discovered our foot tapping as if it had a mind of its own. That foot wants to dance.

I'm not going to attempt a history of dance, but it might help to take a quick glance at recent decades. Dancing is as old as the Pentateuch, but during the 20th Century, it was a prominent moral issue—at least in our culture. A generation or two ago, even though the world thrived on school dances, proms, ballrooms, and clubs, Christians did not go.

The questionable compromises at sock-hops, the freaky abandon of disco, and the gritty indulgence of techno led to a lot of bad choices. A thousand cautionary tales of writhing and seduction fed the anxieties of parents, and rightly so. But in addition to wise caution, unfortunately there also appeared a blanket indictment of all things danceable.

I grew up in a time and place where dancing was considered to be a very questionable pastime. But as I grew up, I could see that the blanket indictment was not the most rational approach. To say that all dancing was wrong was kind of silly.

Square dancing was all right. Its very name inadvertently suggested a kind of un-hipness. Dancing for squares. Even the most adamant anti-dancers were likely to give this the green light. It was mostly devoid of anything provocative, and how could something be wrong if it was being used for PE credit at school?

Some of my friends in college got into line dancing. They seemed to consider this a safe upgrade. Not as blah as square dancing, but not as racy as dancing-dancing. There was movement in the vicinity of the opposite gender, but there was a definite distance.

It gets complicated. Slow dancing, close dancing, forbidden dancing, dirty dancing, break dancing. There are hundreds of ways to move the human body in response to music. In Babylon, you would just make your body bow down. Today, things have gotten a lot more elaborate.

For a while, for some, the simple solution was to just say, "Dancing is wrong." I suspect this solution came from an assortment of extreme solutions in the 1950s, such as throwing away dice and cards to prevent gambling. But condemning all dancing sounded like less than a thoughtful reaction when you were confronted with someone in tap shoes.

Here in the 21st Century, the issue is not as fuzzy anymore. The most common form of dancing is nowhere close to tap, line, or square. At a dance today you will find just about anything going on except subtlety. Dancing is so provocative and blatantly suggestive, it's laughable to argue these moves are anything less than sexual. Let's be honest. It's a mating ritual. The participants are reduced to strutting insects. Colors and movement. Although the seduction may not reach any culmination, the theme is clear. There is no pretense. It's all for the sake of having sex. Anyone who tells you otherwise is either lying or stupid.

Lust is wrong (Matthew 5:28). Causing someone to lust is wrong (Romans 14:13). When music is used to promote lust, it's wrong. Tapping your foot isn't wrong. However, moving in such a way that should only be seen by someone you're going to have sex with (a.k.a your spouse) is clearly questionable.

This is not that hard to figure out. Just the fact that dancing is primarily the pairing off of males with females is a huge clue. Almost always it's using music to boost your sexual attraction toward each other.

Dances typically drown you in music. It's a kind of auditory inebriation that erases conversation and even thought. The volume is up and the inhibitions are down. For a

Christian, this is clearly an issue. "Be of sober spirit, be on the alert. Your adversary, the devil, prowls around like a roaring lion, seeking someone to devour" (I Peter 5:8). Sober doesn't just have to do with alcohol. There is more than one way get drunk. You can do it with lots of shadows and lights, along with music so loud it makes your bones hum.

All this caution and criticism will be drowned out by the next track. Dancers want to dance. Regardless, eventually all music has one thing in common. All songs come to an end. No matter how many verses or endless remixes, it all has to finally find the last measure. And that's when the truth surfaces. You'll find it in the inevitable bright silence that follows your mistakes. Life will have a little less life. But hey—as long as it's got a good beat.

Popcorn and Lies

Someone sits down and writes something called a script. Once it's finished, a company pays money for this story and then hires people who are really good at pretending. These are called actors. A crew of experts film the actors as they pretend to have emotions while acting out the story. Once the film is put together, music is added to express specific emotions.

When the film is totally finished, copies are made and then sent out all over the world to buildings that then present the made-up story to millions of people. These buildings are called movie theaters. Later, the film will be put on DVDs. At that point, the story will be watched by millions of people in their own homes.

A lot of these stories explain to us what love is and how love works. These stories teach us about relationships and how to be happy. These stories are also very good at getting everything absolutely wrong.

Don't forget. They were written by some guy, using his imagination. Don't be fooled. Even the ones "based on a true story" bear only the slightest resemblance to the truth. They come from the make-believing of people. The films are built out of personal views and ideas that come from the perspective of the writer. Good acting and a great soundtrack only make them *feel* like truth.

A lot of our beliefs about life and this existence come from a variety of sources. Some beliefs we inherit from our family. Some we pick up from close friends. Some from books or songs or inspirational posters. My hunch is that most of our philosophies about life—and love in particular—can be traced back to Hollywood. The city of pretenders.

Not only do we look to this part of the world for insight on romance, we even see the actors themselves as icons of love. Here they come, down the Red Carpet, their first names fused into cute hybrids to show the depth of their relationship. Yet when it comes to marriages inside this starry circus, they are notoriously horrible. The average Hollywood relationship is laughably brief. Quicker than you can say, "and the Oscar goes to," they split up and fall in love with someone new. Hollywood churns out one film after another, teaching us about love. Lots of brief, empty flickers of love.

Given their track record, you'd think we'd be wary of their advice. But we buy it and then we *buy* it. Although virtually everyone involved in the process of making the story is most likely on their second or third marriage—or living with someone outside of marriage—or clearly has a biased animosity toward marriage—these are the ones we go to for insight.

We walk out of the theater, full of popcorn and Coke, believing that life works just like the screen told us. Love is something that just happens. Love sometimes forces you to abandon your promises. Love is easy and always fun.

Then we drive home and try to live our lives like the made-up stories. Dazzled by the physical beauty and the elegant words, we become convinced that our own lives can play out just like the movies. We collect romantic catch phrases and bring them into a relationship. Then we're shocked when there's no happy ending.

Here's some truth that might help. Hollywood is not really telling love stories. It's telling infatuation stories. This is why the movie ends with them falling in love. Hollywood is pretty focused on telling you *how* to get with someone. But Hollywood stinks at telling you how to *stay* with someone.

Whenever a film does brave the realm of marriage, it is typically filled with justification for adultery and a constant endorsement of all kinds of dysfunction, as if families saturated in angst and anger are cute. If you pay attention, you will get the distinct sensation that a lot of script writers are mainly out to soothe their own consciences. Nothing numbs regret like justifying your mistakes. Movies are primarily made by people who indulge their desires while trying to make life without God seem shiny.

It is so easy to allow movies to twist our thinking. When life fails as a romantic comedy, we sigh even as we cling to the hope that everything might still somehow play out like it does on the big screen. We are hypnotized by beautiful people and we grimace at the mundane washed-out lives we must face when we leave the theater. That's what Hollywood does. It urges you to look away from what you have, in order to pursue what you don't. It bedazzles with discontent.

No doubt, through a filter of wisdom, you can derive some benefit from these make-believe stories. In fact, I would even argue that maintaining your childlike ability to imagine is of great use to anyone. Movies can inspire to aspire. But to try and derive solid truth from the fable factory is a grand delusion we perpetrate on ourselves.

Approach movies with caution. There are some great stories, but there are a lot of dangerous ones. The main thing is, when the movie ends, when the lights come up and you go back out into the real world, don't leave your coat or your cell phone. But don't leave your heart there either.

The Laughing Machine

Television spills out thousands of stories from hundreds of channels. Since most of these stories somehow involve ideas about love, we should take a little time to take a closer look.

Whereas movies have a beginning and an ending, TV never stops. It provides a continuous stream of words and ideas that support all the things we learn at the theater. *Adultery is unfortunate, but a reasonable expectation. The whole marriage concept is inherently flawed. Divorce is no big deal and the children are resilient enough to take the whole ripping-a-family-apart-at-the-seams thing in their innocent stride, chuckling all the way.*

There's something you should know about the business of television. The people who produce TV shows have one primary goal above all others.

Keep you watching.

It really is that simple. Television is designed to be an endless flow of amusement, driven by near-desperation to keep your attention. This is because if you lose interest, you will do what TV execs and the advertisers consider the unthinkable. You will find the off button.

This is why one show flows right into the next, sometimes almost seamlessly. In order to keep you floating down this stream, they must keep you constantly entertained. In TV world, they can do this by creating suspense or by making sure everyone in the story is beautiful. But one of the best strategies to keep you amused is to make sure you laugh.

Laughing is great. "A joyful heart is good medicine" (Proverbs 17:22). But mindless snickering and giggling is actually kind of disturbing. There is a creepier side of laughter that television people know all too well.

One way to make people laugh is to write something funny and then have the actors say these funny things in a funny way. However, it's difficult to write something that's actually funny week after week. This is why you see a lot of stuff on television that is only mildly amusing or even just plain dumb. Bad television will often decline into regurgitated clichés that have drained chuckles out of couch potatoes for decades.

When the audience has become jaded by these reheated jokes and pratfalls, there are at least two other tactics available.

1) The Laugh Track

On many comedy shows, you will often hear laughter in the background. This is often because the show is performed and recorded in front of a "live studio audience." What many of us potatoes don't know is that the laughter of this "live studio audience" is not always what you are actually hearing. In post-production, pre-recorded (artificial) laughter is added. These sounds are placed right after the jokes. This helps the audience at home realize when it's time to laugh. Laughter is contagious and there is a much better chance of coaxing out a giggle if we hear how much this unseen "audience" finds the show just hilarious. Many times, the humor of the writing can't stand alone. Unadorned, the jokes are very unfunny. So laugh tracks are added to help out.

To give you some perspective, think how weird it would be if you were watching a dramatic show, and you heard some unseen audience in the background. If something shocking happened, you would hear a collective gasp. If something sad happened, you would hear a crowd of people weeping. But we've gotten used to the laughter. We hardly even notice it anymore.

2) Shock Humor

When comedy writers are not able to think of something genuinely clever, there is another tactic available. The tactic is easiest to spot with stand-up comics. If they don't have witty quips or insight, they typically resort to crude jokes and foul language. The shock of profanity or even near-profanity is used to trigger automatic laughter. The audience giggles not because there is anything clever said. The laughter is triggered by discomfort or the childish mentality of giggling at words scrawled in a high school bathroom.

All of this is important to consider while living in the realm of the Married People. Those who are married or those who aspire to be married can become easy victims of one of the more dangerous traits of television.

Learning to laugh at sin.

This can do a lot of damage. It helps rewire our thinking in regards to love and all the things that corrupt love. Adultery, sex outside of marriage, lust, suggestive language, homosexuality, using God's name without reverence and just about anything you can think of is delivered to us with giggles. The joke is made and it is followed immediately by canned laughter. After a while, even a Christian will find himself smiling or even laughing right along. Laughing about sin.

It might seem like such a mild concern. But as one my teachers once put it—once they can get you to laugh at something, you're one step closer to accepting it. Any Christian is supposed to "hate evil" (Psalm 97:10). Anyone who truly belongs to God will "abhor what is evil; cling to what is good" (Romans 12:9). When we laugh at sin on television, this develops a disregard for God's commands. Shouldn't that bother us a little? Shouldn't something that is offensive to my Father also be offensive to me?

There is great concern about movies with highly immoral content—and rightly so. Television is currently blurring its own lines of immorality to compete. But don't be fooled by the rating system of censorship. Sin is not so easily mapped out.

Television is thought of as a lesser evil. But if you're paying attention, you might even argue it is a more dangerous evil because it is far subtler, because it is always in our homes, and because we sit in front of it and laugh.

Enough years of hearing a machine laugh at sin will ultimately undermine the seriousness of breaking God's commands. Things that are costing people their souls have become punchlines.

The Profound Insight of Youth

Television has not only taught us to smirk at the destruction of souls. It has also given us a front row seat to watch the methodical execution of the traditional family. Good luck finding any current show dealing with a father, a mother, and children, free of dysfunction. With disdain toward the older shows, prime time provides thirty-minute doses of families involving premarital sex, homosexuality, and a slapstick approach to adultery.

In the midst of all this light-hearted dysfunction, there is often bonus deception slipped into the mix. TV teaches us that when it comes to romance, the younger generation has it all figured out. In the olden days, there was a TV show called *Father Knows Best*. Those days are gone. Today, the underlying mantra of most shows is *Children Know Best*.

I'm sure the cliché is familiar to you. A young couple "falls in love" and start sleeping together. When the older people (Boo!) oppose this, the young lovers (Yay!) distance themselves from everyone, because the older people (Hiss!) "just don't understand."

The older people are presented as naïve or completely irrational. They are bitter over having not lived their lives to the fullest and don't want anyone else to be happy. The young lovers have somehow tapped into the wisdom of the universe and their love will sweep them far away from all these people who obviously hate love.

Television is particularly helpful in promoting this delusion by making parents seem stupid—especially the father. This show would be called *Father Knows Nothing*. Everyone knows there are fathers who are ignorant and foolish. But not all of them are.

3 - Picking Flowers IN THE **Minefield**

Television teaches us that the older generation is so out of it, that their advice is essentially obsolete. The only older people who can be trusted are the ones who act like the younger people. You know—the ones who also make fun of such outdated things such as purity.

It is a well-known basis of the television industry that all its marketing generally plays to the young. Marketing also plays to the older people, but mainly to older people who are trying to act like they are young. In our culture, one of the primary gods in our pantheon is youth. Anything that defies this deity is rejected as simply uncool.

The sad thing is—deep down, many of us do believe the younger generation has a better grasp of life. After all, they have so much energy and they're so tech savvy.

There was an older couple who were members at the congregation I attended in Colorado Springs. Once, when they were watching television together, a news report came on about children using computers. The old woman turned to the old man and said, "I don't know. Sometimes I wonder. Maybe children today are smarter than we were."

The old man nodded. "Yeah. Maybe." He turned to his wife. "But can they plow corn?"

When it comes to the dazzle of modern toys, young people might be ahead of the game. When it comes to setting trends and being edgy, they might be ahead in that game too. But when it comes to anything other than games, they are not the best source of insight. When it comes to basic survival (plowing corn) or matters of true significance such as love, it might be best to consult something other than the nearest whirlwind of hormones.

But that doesn't play well on television or in movies. In pixel world, love means cutting yourself off from the older generation and gazing into each other's enabling eyes. It is the means by which a whole generation can indulge infatuation, bolstered by a thousand TV shows that teach us those who have true wisdom are to be ignored.

This is when you're supposed to laugh.

Husky Rogue

My friends and I made up a game. Before I tell you about it, let me make a disclaimer.

I'm not suggesting you play it. Some of you might even find it insulting or offensive. I only bring it up though to poke a little bit of fun and to make an observation.

It's called "Husky Rogue" and here's how you play:

> Go to your local bookstore and find the Romance section.
> Do not play the game if anyone is browsing this particular area. This is a matter of courtesy. The game sort of makes fun of this particular genre and it wouldn't be nice to be giggling at something someone likes—right in front of them. Wait until the arena is clear.
> The object of the game is to look for certain words. Finding specific words in particular gives you points. Caution—some books in this genre are unfortunately crude. Tread carefully.
> There are three ways of searching for the words.
> 1) You can skim the titles.
> 2) You can thumb through a book and pick a random page.
> 3) You can read the last paragraph on the last page. (This is usually the most entertaining.) We all know that many (not all) books in this part of the bookstore are well known for being blatantly cheesy. Many times, the extra cheese can be found at the very end.
> While doing one of these three things, if you come across certain words, you get points. These points are awarded as follows:

- Every time you find the word "husky" as in "She heard his husky voice as he walked across the moon-swept leaves." That's worth one point.
- Every time you find the word "rogue" as in "He was a sly rogue who was often seen wandering the ruins of Stormwind Castle." That's also worth one point.
- If you find both "husky" and "rogue," you automatically win.

Most of the fun is just enjoying the extra cheese.

Another friend of mind suggested that the following words also be added to the list for points: "brooding," "chiseled," "smolder," and "sultry." Recent tournaments have also allowed "highlander" and "scoundrel."

It was only after we made up this game that I learned that experts actually do research to find out which words resonate the best in the romance book business. Some even suggest you can do a fair analysis of current romantic desires based merely on the titles of that section of the bookstore.

Of all the genres of books being published today—general fiction, thrillers, sci-fi, horror, mystery, etc., the number-one selling genre is romance. But as you can imagine, these countless volumes are not necessarily the best source of wisdom when it comes to love. Many a reader is swept away by ideas about romance that are only cobbled-together daydreams of the author. Many a sad true story in real life can probably be traced back to the many fictions lined up in this particular part of the bookstore.

When we try to find love the same way it is found in *Husky Highlander* or *The Brooding Rogue*, we only find a new kind of unhappiness. With our minds saturated with worldly expectations, it is no wonder so many people find reality less than appealing.

Any book is a potential corruptor. One might even argue that the written word is far more effective in rewiring our thinking than any screen ever was. Words are powerful and the written word infiltrates on a much deeper level. This is not to say the romance genre is wrong, but it would serve anyone well to keep a watchful eye on books that are designed to make you swoon.

Sex, Then Love

It's probably time to get something out of the way. It's going to rattle some cages. What I'm about to say next is considered nonsense by the great majority of the world. Sad to say, this will also be dismissed as nonsense by those who consider themselves to be Christians. In fact, to many people, what I'm about to say will sound like the laughable rants of some stuffy matron, sitting in a front pew, turning around to wag her self-righteous finger. But we might as well get it over with.

Let the record show—sex outside of marriage is a sin. It doesn't matter if the two people really love each other, or if they are swept up with overwhelming passion, or if the stars are aligned, or they are seeking comfort in a world that has grown cold. Sex between unmarried people is wrong.

For those who are interested, this is what God says about it. "Marriage is to be held in honor among all, and the marriage bed is to be undefiled; for fornicators and adulterers God will judge" (Hebrews 13:4). "For this is the will of God, your sanctification; that is, that you abstain from sexual immorality" (I Thessalonians 4:3).

There.

It's kind of impossible to make any progress in understanding Married People until that one simple truth is in place. Sex is designed to take place only between husbands and wives. If a person is approaching Scripture with rational thinking and no personal agenda, this is the one and only possible conclusion. You can call it "sleeping together," or "making love," or "friends with benefits," but if two unmarried people are having sex, God calls it sexual immorality and it can cost you your soul.

3 – Picking Flowers IN THE **Minefield**

Music, movies, TV shows, and books have so completely overshadowed this basic truth, most people won't get angry if you take a stand. You will simply be dismissed with laughter.

One of the most twisted concepts in this regard—brought to you by your friendly pop culture—will appear in the average TV show, especially the hilarious [sound of laughter] comedies.

A boy and a girl are attracted to each other. They really like each other and begin to be physically intimate. Then, if they feel like the time is right and both of them are responsible enough as far as birth control and disease prevention, they have sex.

Those who are relatively selective in their partners are more admirable. But even those who aren't very selective will be presented as "adventurous."

If you pay attention you will notice an interesting truth that shows up in some of the dialogue. After one time or multiple times of having sex, one or both of the two people begin to "have feelings" and eventually during a passionate moment or under comedic duress, they eventually summon up the courage to stammer, "I love you."

This reveals something profound. You see, as far as the world is concerned, sex is first. Then, if emotions grow, you eventually get around to saying those three magic words, "I love you." As far as our culture is concerned, sex is merely a kind of elaborate handshake. To say "I love you" is so much more. It means commitment.

Which leads us to the heart of the problem. The world thinks sex doesn't require commitment.

God designed all of this to be the other way around. "I love you" as expressed through the commitment of marriage is first. Then once that commitment is in place—sex.

The world's sequence of events suggests sex is not as significant as saying "I love you." There are all kinds of TV shows and films in which someone says "I love you" and the other person is stunned into silence. Those three magical words are so magical that there is some hesitation. By saying "I love you," the first person has presented the most intimate exchange there is. Sex was just fooling around. Marriage is a possible afterthought. All the glory and significance of a relationship is summed up in just speaking the words, "I love you."

A nice thought. And let's toss a few crumbs of kudos for at least thinking that love is important. But this is actually a very subtle yet powerful degradation of sex.

The hesitation before "I love you" indicates that the words are very important and not to be taken lightly. There is an impending commitment. Any hesitation before sex is a token formality. Sex receives no such honor as the hesitation before "I love you."

The explanation is simple. The reason sex is passed over lightly is because the desire to take part in the physical act is extremely strong. Reducing it to a casual level clears the way for people to do what they want to do. Which, when all is said and done, is the true agenda of a whole bunch of things.

Having sex and then hesitating before saying "I love you" is a world-trick, shifting the honor of love so that selfish desires can be indulged.

It's kind of cute and kind of sad that the truth can be found in the old rhyming game girls used to chant while skipping rope. "First comes love, then comes marriage, then comes the baby in the baby carriage."

Horse Power and Big Money

When it comes to pursuing romance, males and females have a knack for making bad choices. However, both have the potential to be foolish in their own special way.

Girls have been known to be won over with automobiles. A brand-new sports car will turn heads even if the driver is the scuzziest of losers. If he is driving the most stylish of combustible engines, he will suddenly become a candidate as a "good catch."

To be fair, there is a deeper significance. It's not just the car. A lot of girls are attracted to the status. Being in the right car can improve a girl's image. *Look at the guy I got. He drives this car and I'm in the passenger seat and you aren't. Doesn't it look good on me?* Ironically enough, given the fickle nature of the average guy, one of the very girls she snubs will most likely be her replacement.

A very expensive car implies money. In many cases, the vehicle is funded by the driver's mom and dad, but that doesn't seem to matter. Driving a car his parents bought doesn't have the same stigma as a guy living in his parent's basement.

Luxury attracts a lot of girls. To her, the flashy car is the golden coach that will whisk her away to the fancy dress ball.

Being drawn to men primarily for their wealth is the beginning of many a sad story. It's not only a bad way to find a man, it's a bad way to live life.

We have all heard the verse. "For the love of money is a root of all sorts of evil, and some by longing for it have wandered away from the faith and pierced themselves with many griefs" (I Timothy 6:10). Yes, yes, the misquoted verse. It doesn't say "money is the root of evil"—it's "the *love* of money." Even then we all quickly disqualify ourselves. I'm not in love with money. We're just good friends. But when a girl uses cash value to shape her consideration of a potential boyfriend, it sure looks like love to me.

The story is a tiresome cautionary tale. There are enough movies and reality shows to demonstrate the common unhappy ending. The girl gets a rich guy and then is surprised when her man ends up spending women as quickly as he does his cash.

Our culture is so infected with this money issue, we have come up with prenuptial agreements. This is a blatant indication that the relationship is precarious at best and will ultimately end in a lawyer bout to decide how much of the money leaves with the Woman-Formerly-Known-As-Wife.

God has put up red flags all over the place, trying to warn us how easily riches can mess with your souls. "You have lived luxuriously on the earth and led a life of wanton pleasure; you have fattened your hearts in a day of slaughter"

(James 5:5). He has warned "those who recline on beds of ivory and sprawl on their couches" (Amos 6:4). Don't rely on luxury, because everyone at "the sprawlers' banqueting will pass away" (Amos 6:7). A life (let alone a romantic relationship) built on dollars never has a happy ending.

Money is famously unreliable. Like one guy said, "Money talks, but all mine says is 'Goodbye.'" Luxury is temporary and is guaranteed to abandon you. "Make sure that your character is free from the love of money, being content with what you have; for He Himself has said, 'I will never desert you, nor will I ever forsake you,'" (Hebrews 13:5). Money has a tendency to go away. It will often leave you. It will always forsake you.

This is also true of the men who are made of money. He too, is not inevitably bad, but rich men who are defined by their riches tend to have a nature very similar to cash. They go away.

Dark and Dangerous

There are more than a few mysteries out there. Suspicious rumors about Roswell, New Mexico. Conspiracy theories surrounding the assassination of JFK. But one of the greatest mysteries of this universe is why nice girls are attracted to bad guys.

In the grand scheme of love, this is one of the most prevalent and significant flaws in the selection system. It has been a source of great frustration for virtually every male—to be passed over for a grittier and more troubled rogue, who seems to have no distinctive characteristic other than a greater potential for becoming a felon. In some cases, he's not even attractive. As long as he shows a propensity for behaving badly.

Apparently, for some girls, a male's disdain for rules and a sneering lack of respect make her heart go wild. There are plenty of variations for her to choose from. There's the standard leather jacket on a motorcycle. There's the skateboarding criminal with his beltline slung around his ankles. There's the sneering goth with so many piercings, that during a strong wind, he sounds like a piccolo. There's also the clean-cut fake who appears to be have morals, but is merely a façade for a corrupted soul.

Whatever the personal preference, many girls will pursue or allow themselves to pursued by the bad boy. Believe it or not, in countless cases, Boy doesn't get Girl. Bad Boy gets Girl.

One theory is that when a female sees a disheveled rebel, it triggers some distortion of the mothering instinct. In her mind, or at least in her subconscious, she is convinced she can repair this broken thug. She believes she can see something of value in him that no one else can see. He is a diamond in the rough. She will excavate him from his angst and shine him up real pretty. Then everyone will see what she has always seen, the moment she laid eyes on him.

To her, it doesn't matter if there are a hundred broken hearts bobbing in his wake. It doesn't matter if his words are grimy or cruel. It doesn't matter if his purity is a faint memory. The girl convinces herself she will be the magic charm. She will somehow transform this oily toad into a shiny prince. It's just that unlike most frogs, it might take more kisses.

Maybe it's not as complicated as all that. The explanation might be more simple.

There is something nestled in all of us that tends toward degradation. The book of Romans makes some interesting points about this default setting. "And just as they did not see fit to acknowledge God any longer, God gave them over to a depraved mind, to do those things which are not proper" (Romans 1:28). When we allow our minds to run away from God, our choices soon follow after, resulting ultimately in the degradation of our bodies.

The Bad Boy is just the ticket for this descent. It's very possible that when it comes to a girl's attraction to a spiritually corrupted boy, her motivation is far from admirable. She might just be wanting to dabble in the world. In her mind, she can always move onto something more safe when she's done "experiencing the world." Whatever "nice" there is about the nice girl could actually be superficial. She is more interested in what she wants rather than what God wants. So she strolls hand-in-hand with her dangerous fellow into the dark descent that waits for anyone who turns away from God. Even "nice" girls.

Whatever the case, there's one thing I've noticed for certain. While many girls want a dangerous boyfriend, virtually no wives want a dangerous husband. Any wife in her right mind wants a safe one.

No woman wants a husky rogue with a wandering eye. Ultimately, she will want a real man. A real man will need to deal with the real challenges of real life, from depositing checks in the savings account to changing dirty diapers. In the realm of the Married People, a swashbuckling scalawag with abs just doesn't work.

Elegant and Easy

Females have flaws in their selection system, but so do males. The main difference is that a guy's bad choices are almost always focused on physical attraction. A guy is not likely to be intrigued by a girl in a Porsche, unless she's good-looking. He is also less likely to pursue the female equivalent of the husky-rogue-fixer-upper if she isn't pretty.

As a borderline presumptuous, self-proclaimed representative of my gender, it is my responsibility to be honest. For most males, it all comes down to whether or not she's hot.

However, just as there is a tendency among many girls to be interested in the "bad boy," there is a similar tendency for males to show the same foolishness in pursuing the "bad girl." Sad to say, the male rarely has anything resembling a mothering instinct to protect the girl. His agenda is built on the hope of seeking physical compromises. Whether or not he is consciously aware of this true agenda, even the most principled male is often swayed by a flirtatious or scantily clad female. In turn, whether her own nature is a blatant promiscuousness or a more discrete depravity, many a "good guy" will go after a "bad girl."

So to be fair—any girl has the right to claim their own conundrum about guys. Another great mystery of the universe is why do "Good Guys" go after "Bad Girls"?

As with girls, a guy drawn to a "Bad Girl" can also simply be seeking a partner to indulge in degradation. The "depraved mind" of Romans 1 is a factor in this situation as well.

As unlikely as it might seem, it is possible a guy might pursue a spiritually dangerous girl out of some misguided attempt to rescue a floundering "damsel." I suppose this could be a faint parallel to the mothering instinct.

Regardless of motivation, the truth is ultimately seen among the Married People. Many males might be attracted to a female who dresses immodestly and who compromises her purity when their dating. But not so much when they're married.

A wife who dresses provocatively draws the attention of not just her husband. Other eyes linger on what belongs to him. That's not conducive to a happy marriage.

A guy may want a flirty girlfriend, but virtually no husbands want a flirty wife. Any husband in his right mind wants a modest one. No sane husband wants a wife that offers herself visually to wandering eyes. A real woman will need to deal with the real challenges of real life, from depositing checks in the savings account to changing dirty diapers. In the realm of the Married People, the strutting vixen in the short dress just doesn't work.

The conclusion of the matter here is not encouraging. There are profound flaws in our selection system—on both sides. There are contradictory standards. We want one thing when we're dating. We want something completely different when we're married.

This implies something pretty important. There is higher quality of expectation in marriage that is seriously lacking in the dating process. Not only that—whatever is admirable in marriage is not just absent in dating. During the dating process, all the good things of marriage are actually ridiculed and undermined. The basic nature of dating is antagonistic to marriage. Standard dating is not only a less than effective way of finding someone to marry, it is also a process that preemptively sabotages marriage.

It would seem wise to at least hesitate. There is something seriously wrong about the process we use in becoming Married People. Our culture is often quick to criticize the "institution of marriage." But that isn't where we find the problems. The truth is revealed in the games we play along the border of marriage. The seeds of almost every marital issue are found in the path getting there.

Fabricated

First, let's welcome Adam and Eve!

The original trend-setters—these garden-variety innovators are wearing outfits made from fig leaves. Although the style lacks functionality, it does carry a certain savoir faire. And nothing says shame and guilt like a thrown-together ensemble made with forest debris.

The very first fashion statement was not about aesthetics or prestige. The fig leaves were desperate measures to deal with embarrassment (Genesis 3:7). The style didn't last long. It was creative, but foliage fashion was truly pathetic and quickly faux pas. God provided a much more effective and meaningful solution—animal skins. (Genesis 3:21). The animal skins were efficient in that they probably did a much better job of covering Adam and Eve. The animal skins were also meaningful because of the price tag.

It's not likely God just created animal skins. In order to provide proper clothing, He killed two animals. This was a huge decision. In all of Creation, these two animals were the first things to die. On this brand new planet teeming with life, death arrived on the scene because of the sudden necessity for clothing.

Which should get our attention.

From Eden on, the issue of clothing would remain considerably significant. Since they were officially evicted from paradise, Adam and Eve would need clothing not just to avoid humiliation. They would also now need covering to deal with hostile environments. As their descendants increased and spread across the world, many of them would be facing harsh climates. This led to an additional purpose for fabric on human bodies. Clothing kept the world from killing you. You needed something to wear in order to be comfortable, but mainly to not die.

But eventually, something strange happened. We came up with a whole new reason for clothes. Somewhere along the way, we started using clothing for status.

Yes, it keeps me from being naked. Yes, it keeps me from getting frostbite. But notice how it makes me look better than you.

Certain kinds of fabric and certain colors began to indicate wealth or position. As crazy as it seems, even though it started out with shame, clothing has become transformed into something that expresses the exact opposite—pride.

One outfit in particular is famous in this regard. "Now Israel loved Joseph more than all his sons, because he was the son of his old age; and he made him a varicolored tunic" (Genesis 37:3). Favoritism caused a lot of problems in Abraham's lineage, but when Jacob (Israel) gave his son Joseph this famous coat of many colors, it sabotaged the family. It caused so much trouble, this many-colored coat was eventually given one more color. "So they took Joseph's tunic, and slaughtered a male goat, and dipped the tunic in blood" (Genesis 37:31). This status symbol ended up becoming a gruesome Exhibit A in an unsolved mystery. Whether or not Joseph wore this coat to just be comfortable or to honor his father's gift, the animosity directed toward him was because of its association with pride—at least in the eyes of the beholders.

Jesus later targeted snobby scribes about their pursuit of "places of honor." One particular characteristic of these braggarts was how much they loved to wear long robes (Mark 12:38-39). They didn't wear them for practical reasons. They did it to be admired. It was pride.

The new Christian Lydia made a living as a specialist in one particular color of clothing (Acts 16:14). For the upper class of that culture, purple was all the rage. It was the equivalent of today's brand name clothing. Anyone who was anyone could stand out like a grape in the desert.

Today, we are certainly motivated to put on clothes to avoid shame. We are also motivated to dress according to the weather forecast. But in this culture, our primary criteria for clothing is how good we look. If a color or fabric makes us more attractive, we choose that. If it makes us stand out from the rest of the crowd in a beneficial way, we choose that.

I'm not going to argue that we should avoid looking attractive or pleasing to the eye. If something complements our skin tone or general appearance, that's fine. But we've reached the point where clothing has become almost indistinguishable from the person wearing the clothing. People build their very identity and self-worth on what they wear. But we don't dress to express the truth of who we really are. Clothes are more about presenting an image and image trumps substance. The time and effort we could be using to actually improve ourselves is spent purchasing decorative materials. We are cakes made only of icing.

Ingenious marketing has turned us into walking billboards. To make sure people know we have name-brand clothing, we sport logos, anchoring our self-worth in the companies we endorse. We do for businesses what athletes do for millions of dollars. We don't even do it for free. Nope—we pay *them*.

All of this is of special concern along the path to Married People. When a person's self-worth is based on how they look, clothing ends up being used as one of the main strategies to attract someone. It is not unlikely that two Single People can find themselves manipulated into a lifelong commitment through the lure of just an attractive face and strategic fabric. Being entranced by the outer accessories of a person alone does not a happy ending make.

God, of course, is focused on the truth— the real person underneath the clothing, even underneath the skin. A real marriage is made of real people. But we get caught up in decorating the exterior—the very aspect of us that is wearing out. Our skin has a tendency to wrinkle as badly as cotton. We have been tricked into neglecting our eternal self and emphasizing the one aspect of us that is extremely temporary. We have come a long way since Eden.

Snobs and Slobs

Clothing has caused a lot of trouble. It has motivated people to look down on those who don't dress the same as they do.

When it comes to people being judgmental about clothing, the Bible is very judgmental. God condemns people who mistreat anyone not dressed as well as them. Anyone who adjusts their kindness towards people based on their clothing are called "judges with evil motives" (James 2:4). Those who we might think of as Dresser-Uppers can easily fall into the trap of looking down on Dresser-Downers. Holding to the cultural anthem of "clothes make the man," the wearers of ties and semi-formal dresses can get a little uppity. In so doing, they prove their case. Clothes do indeed make the man. They make him arrogant.

On the other hand, those who live in T-Shirts and ragged jeans can get a little disrespectful. Dresser-Downers have often used this passage in James as a license to justify their own preferences. Everyone knows the scenario of the guy who doesn't own a suit and how his "Sunday best" might be overalls and scuffed boots. But there's a big difference between that guy and the guy who shows up at weddings and funerals in his yardwork duds, trying to pass of his lack of respect for the event as some kind of Everyman chic.

No one is supposed to look down on anyone because of their clothes. But we are also told, "Show proper respect to everyone" (I Peter 2:17). A Christian should never intentionally wear clothes that present disrespect. Perpetually living in your own personal Casual Friday just because you like it doesn't speak well of your respect toward others.

What we wear can be a reflection of our level of respect for the event we are attending. Dressing down might not be an expression of contempt, but in many instances it is clearly an expression of disregard. Our respect toward God is obviously vital, but so is our respect for other people. If overalls is the best you got, then mission accomplished. Times change and styles change. But if someone wears something simply because he can't be troubled to take other people's feelings into account, this is disrespect and makes him just as wrong as the uppity snob.

Of course the assembling of Christians is often the proving ground. In some church buildings there is a slight tension between two camps—the Dresser-Uppers and the Dresser-Downers. It would be so wrong for someone to scowl or murmur about someone who showed up looking sloppy. But any Christian who has even the slightest awareness of the respect we should be expressing toward God and the honor we should show our brothers and sisters will at least do their best to dress in such a way that demonstrates an effort toward respect.

Paul, in his efforts as a Christian, described how he would "try to please everybody in every way. For I am not seeking my own good but the good of many, so that they may be saved" (I Corinthians 10:33). Your responsibility of respecting others trumps whether or not you resemble a pop icon. And just in case you didn't know it, using some kind of artistic angst to look intriguing or endearing is only another flavor of insecurity and immaturity.

It's a fine line. The guy in the suit and tie looks down his nose at anyone who is not arrayed like him—and he is wrong. The guy in the ratty shirt and jeans who dresses with defiance, daring to make conclusions about his character—he is also wrong.

How perfectly disastrous that our enemy effectively uses the means used to initially cover sin, to cause even more sin. Self-righteous judging and unkindness and disrespect and irreverence all tangled together because of the plain and simple necessity of fabric.

In a way, clothes do *not* make the man. But the man makes the clothes. In other words, it is the character of the person that determines what they will wear. Granted, a higher dress code affects the behavior of the person, but it is the character of the person that guides them to make choices in the right direction. This means not only taking their preferences into consideration, but also the effect it will have on those around them.

This issue is of significance to both genders. But it is the woman who typically and unfairly finds herself entangled in the snare of fashion. Concern about modesty is legitimate.

Ring in a Pig's Nose

Let's ask Adam and Eve about modesty—before they sampled the Tree of the Knowledge of Good and Evil.

Adam shrugs and Eve tilts her head in curiosity and the question fades into silence. Standing there in all their unclad innocence, they look at you in confusion. Modesty?

At that particular moment in history, clothing was irrelevant. Later, sin would drastically alter their perception. Abruptly, nudity would be associated with the shame of sin.

When they made the disastrous decision to disobey God, everything changed. Just like that, the issue of modesty was born. In a sense, every day when we get dressed, we pay tribute to the loss of Eden.

I'm sure you've noticed. The great majority of the world is not naked. Although Married People are cleared for being alone together unclothed, the general consensus is that we cover up our bodies.

A completely objective approach might consider this odd. After all, it's not like there's any mystery about what is being concealed. Each gender is pretty much standard issue. God came up with two human body designs and that's it. Yet, there is a profound significance in covering up. There is also much debate about how much to cover up.

You would think it would come down to a simple equation. It seems like it would just be a matter of deciding on how many square inches of skin should be visible. Less skin, less sin.

I'm not trying to trivialize the issue. The world does plenty of that. The world mocks anyone trying to hold to a high standard of modesty. Any caution is considered prude insecurity. However, God considers it to be a significant issue. In fact, as far as He's concerned, the clothing issue is crucial to the safety of souls. Any trivialization would be out of place.

There has been a lot of debate about how much clothing and what kind of clothing. Women in particular are the focus. This has always been the case, since it could be argued that the physical form of the woman is much more of a distraction to men then the physical form of men to women. Not that it doesn't trouble both sides—but we all know. Women are at the heart of this concern.

In our particular time and culture, the female shape is a prevalent image. There are daring attempts to push the limits of nudity, without actually being unclad. Whereas the original purpose of clothing was to protect the wearer from shame, today it has become something that toy with shame. The world progressively defies the repercussions of Eden and calls the rebellion "fashion."

But let's be fair. What seems like a simple black and white moral choice is complicated by the fact that the definition of modesty itself fluctuates. As much as we might seek to pinpoint a standard of square inches, different times and places alter the standards.

Let's admit there are certain styles and trends that flatter feminine beauty without compromises. There are ways of emphasizing the femininity of the woman without sacrificing classiness. But the business of fashion is mostly about pursuing a provocative appearance.

One of the reasons so many women fall for this is because the world has twisted the definition of "beauty." It peddles the idea that being attractive is the equivalent of looking sexually promiscuous. We are besieged with marketing that worships immodesty. Beauty is in the eye of the advertiser.

A girl is no longer the difficult-to-win princess. She is not the treasure of one "prince." The modern woman is dressed to seduce the whole world. Everyone is her suitor. She abandons her nature as a valuable treasure and offers up her beauty along the same lines as overstock in a discount bin.

Almost every woman now measures her worth by how many men desire her. Whereas this degradation was once limited to shady magazines, today women are fooled into thinking that edgy poses and Facebook flirting are merely "glamour shots."

This kind of thinking is part of why women and girls will wear something clearly designed to emphasize sexuality. Some know exactly what they're doing. Others are fooled into thinking of the outfit as simply being "cute."

Women are focused on whether or not they look good. Very little attention is given to the possibility they might cause trouble for the souls around them. This is of absolutely no concern to most females, but any Christian woman who shows up at the assembly wearing a distracting outfit is no friend to any man there. She is a thorn, opposing the very purpose she is supposed to be honoring.

History reveals some interesting truths about modesty. Time and culture show an obvious shift in definitions of propriety. What seems almost mundane in some times and places would be quite scandalous in other times and places. In the 19th Century, men were enthralled to the point of writing poetry, if they glimpsed a woman's ankle. It was a little racy. But an exposed ankle in the 18th Century wasn't just racy. It implied prostitution. If you lived in the 1st Century, a shaved head suggested prostitution.

Many fashion police have criticized a passing female and commented about how she "looks like a streetwalker." What that particular appearance might be has obviously changed over time. But regardless of these dodgy historical details, it should tell us something about our particular time and place. Fashion trends have manipulated the tastes of the people to the point that there is no longer a drastic distinction between a "respectable" woman and a prostitute.

What a girl wears to cover the outside is connected to what she is like on the inside. The woman in Proverbs is "dressed as a harlot" (Proverbs 7:10), but her character is also measured by the "cunning of her heart." Even if a girl is dressed modestly, a cunning demeanor can make her immodest.

Girls quickly realize their potential to be attractive. From then on, her choice of clothing can be an expression of her heart. Her decisions will reflect her true character. Skillfully designed clothing can complement her beauty, but it can also degrade it.

One thing to keep in mind is that there are qualities of a woman's beauty that belong only to her husband. If she isn't married, she is not cleared to use her physical attributes as lures to get one. To put herself on display for all males reduces her to an advertisement. Even as she strives for self-worth and admiration, her value declines.

Like all things, the enemy is eager to promote degradation. God warns a woman she can be the victim of such a plot. "As a ring of gold in a swine's snout so is a beautiful woman who lacks discretion" (Proverbs 11:22). The contrast is drastic almost to the point of being offensive. The fact that a girl can be beautiful leads to specific concerns. If she lacks discretion—the ability to make good choices—she will have a tendency to abuse her beauty to the point of degrading herself. She will make herself into something that is much like squandering a beautiful ring in the nostrils of a pig.

A woman caught up in the deception of pursuing her own sexual allure is in the process of making herself a discount item. In sales, an act of desperation is to start dropping the price. This makes it less exclusive and more accessible. The world presents immodest fashion as glamour, but it is nothing less than pushing women to sell out. To be less than the woman God designed her to be.

A Gigantic Arrow

Modesty is not always about the amount of fabric. Sometimes the issue is whether or not the clothing is associated with certain kinds of behavior. Good luck to anyone trying to prove he's not a racist, if he's dressed like the Grand Wizard of the KKK. And don't expect a warm welcome at PETA if you wear a mink stole.

Immodesty is difficult because it is an ever-shifting target. But it is not just about lust-inducing exposure. It's even more than just shady connections. Although these should be taken into consideration, these alone can lead to shaky arguments.

Let's go to where we can have solid footing. God's thoughts on the matter are plain and straightforward. "But immorality or any impurity or greed must not even be named among you, as is proper among saints" (Ephesians 5:3). The NIV translation is also helpful here. "But among you there must not be even a hint of sexual immorality, or of any kind of impurity, or of greed, because these are improper for God's holy people." For a Christian, there should be no question about his or her sexual integrity. Not even a hint. This would include the way they dress. Any clothing that implies compromises in physical intimacy would easily fall under the category of immodest.

But notice that clothing is not even mentioned in this passage. That's because the issue of modesty is much more than just clothing. There is more to modesty than meets the eye. Misusing physical attraction is not the only concern. "Your adornment must not be merely external—braiding the hair, and wearing gold jewelry, or putting on dresses; but let it be the hidden person of the heart, with the imperishable quality of a gentle and quiet spirit, which is precious in the sight of God" (I Peter 3:3-4). Just because someone is not trying to be provocative doesn't mean they are modest. It's also immodest to dress in such a way to brag about wealth.

Another passage also addresses how immodesty can actually have nothing to do with sexual allure. "Likewise, I want women to adorn themselves with proper clothing, modestly and discreetly, not with braided hair and gold or pearls or costly garments, but rather by means of good works, as is proper for women making a claim to godliness" (I Timothy 2:9). Although lust is a valid and prevalent concern, it is not the only concern. You can also be held accountable for using your clothes to display your economical standing.

The word "adorn" in this particular passage comes from the Greek word *komios*. It's how we came up with the words "cosmetologist" and "cosmos." It might seem there's nothing in common between the Hubble Telescope and Madge's Beauty Emporium, but both involve *komios* since they both have to do with "harmonious, appropriate, and orderly arrangement." The idea is that there is an acceptable sense of order.

Even though the word might taste outdated, "propriety" captures the idea. If clothing does not have propriety—if it is inappropriate, causing the disorder of lust, the disorder of a questionable image, or the disorder of promoting snobbery, then this is immodest.

3 - Picking Flowers IN THE **Minefield**

This meshes with so many other truths. The Bible explains that the outside can be an effective measure of what's inside. You can deduce someone's character based on his actions. "You will know them by their fruits" (Matthew 7:16). You can deduce his character based on his words. "For his mouth speaks from that which fills his heart" (Luke 6:45). You can also deduce the character of a person by their choice of clothing.

Notice, I did not say judge them. To be unkind to them or gossip about them because of their clothes would be just as wrong as dressing immodestly (James 2:4). But just as a person is responsible for their actions and words, they are also responsible for their choice of clothing.

All of this actually leads to a very simple concept. Trouble ensues when you become focused on drawing attention to yourself. It's lack of humility.

Since the physical appearance of women has more powerful impact on her beholders, concerns surrounding what she wears are more obvious. God condemns the woman who indulges her pride with her adornments. "Because the daughters of Zion are proud and walk with heads held high and seductive eyes, and go along with mincing steps and tinkle the bangles on their feet, therefore the Lord will afflict the scalp of the daughters of Zion with scabs, and the Lord will make their foreheads bare" (Isaiah 3:16-17). Arrogance in the form of fashion is a defiance of humility and will ultimately lead to humiliation.

God is not irritated by those who are proud. He does not just shake His head in disapproval. He opposes them (James 4:6) If someone has trouble pursuing humility, He will help them find it.

Clothing is a key factor in the realm of the Married People. A Christian's responsibility about their interaction with fabric goes far beyond dressing provocatively. The real problem can be traced back to selfishness. God zeroes in on that basic tendency in all of us to put the focus on ourselves. For women, it might come in the form of parading your Louis Vuitton handbag or dying your hair magenta. For men, it might be posing next to your Midnight Blue 1969 Shelby Mustang or dying your hair magenta. Not that magenta is evil. Except after Labor Day probably—I don't know.

Deep down, we all know the true agenda for a lot of our clothing—drawing attention to ourselves. There is a difference between someone who accessorizes themselves to be presentable as determined by the occasion and someone who is determined to make sure there is a giant arrow above their head, pointing down at them to the exclusion of all others.

Red-Blooded

As unfair as it might seem, the pitfalls of fashion are mostly a girl issue. But now it's time to pick on the men. We do our share of flaunting and preening, but for the most part we are not as good at inducing lust as we are at being defeated by it.

In order to get anyone to sin, the enemy must make the sin seem harmless. Even as the Bible emphasizes how sin is nothing less than a disaster, the enemy sets out to tone it down. If possible, he will help us make light of the sin.

This is what's happening with pornography.

Even before it became so readily available, there was a common idea promoted everywhere that young men are just expected to indulge their attraction to girls. "After all" (always said with a smirk) "he's just a red-blooded American boy."

It's difficult to say why drawing attention to the color of the boy's blood is relevant—or for that matter why the attention is placed on his national heritage.

The blood concept seems to imply that given the hormonal nature of his body—the fact that testosterone and assorted puberty cocktails flow through his circulatory system, it is unreasonable to expect him to restrain his desires. To place such restrictions is unrealistic and unfair.

Being that he has born in the US of A might suggest that he has rights. Or at least lives in a prosperous nation that allows him the opportunity to aspire to the moral mediocrity of all the other young male citizens around him.

Whatever the reasoning (as such), the idea is that you can't expect a male to rein in his passion. After all he has "needs."

With this stage set, the arrival of prominent, ubiquitous pornography is given the green light as yet another somewhat innocent pastime of the red-blooded American boy.

Not long ago, porn and general sleazy pics were the fare of shadowy excursions haunted by the potential for horrible embarrassment. There was skulking and slinking and a desperate anonymity. A male might indeed glance or leer or linger, but there was nothing admirable about it. It was assumed to be something you resisted. Something you tried to avoid.

Today the porn business has appropriated the sin and made it much more acceptable. Jokes are made about men searching for porn. The only requirement is strategic discretion. One should keep the indulgence private, but there are no other expectations. The fact that he is feeding his lust is treated as laughable and natural. After all, he is red-blooded and he is an American.

Pornography is one of the primary money-making ventures on the internet. Billions are being made growing the parasite of lust infecting far more many men than we might think. They are deceived into thinking it's to be expected. It's just how the male body works.

God differs on this. "But I say, walk by the Spirit, and you will not carry out the desire of the flesh" (Galatians 5:16). "Beloved, I urge you as aliens and strangers to abstain from fleshly lusts which wage war against the soul" (I Peter 2:11). God is warning us of danger. The side-effects of degrading your desires are numerous and devastating. Lusts leads to crippled libidos, dependence on fantasy, and the methodical dismantling of souls.

Most men don't fight lust. Most men just shrug and smile. But what is most disconcerting is that many women put up with it. They not only put up with it, they chuckle right along, as if their man's sexual degradation is some sort of boyish endearment.

Lust is incredibly powerful and dangerous. Downplaying it with trite jokes makes it even more so. It has been the downfall of many a strong man.

Samson the Wimp

There was a dead lion by the side of the road. Anyone passing by might have thought the animal had been attacked by another lion. Or something bigger. By the looks of it, something incredibly strong had ripped the beast apart. But a beast had not killed this beast. This particular animal made the fatal mistake of taking on a man named Samson (Judges 14:5-6).

In the city of Ashkelon there were several dead bodies. This city, situated on the coast of the Mediterranean, was abruptly disrupted when a man single-handedly fought and killed thirty men, casually removing the clothes off the corpses as if he was on some kind of savage shopping spree. Samson again (Judges 14:19).

Later, there was a "great slaughter" which left behind a whole lot of dead Philistines. It was a drastic case of revenge brought to you by Samson (Judges 14:8). When more Philistines set out to retaliate, Samson decided to hide out in the territory that belonged to Judah. But the Philistines came knocking, demanding that the men of Judah turn Samson over to face their revenge for Samson's revenge. It was re-revenge.

It didn't go well for them. Even though Samson was thoroughly tied up with ropes, he got loose and wreaked some more havoc. Improvising, he picked up a donkey bone and killed a thousand more Philistines (Judges 15:15). Makes you wonder what he could have done with a whole donkey.

Later in Gaza, the people got up in the morning to discover their city gate was gone. The whole thing—the doors, the posts, everything—had been ripped away. It was just gone. Later, they found it on top of a mountain. Turns out, Philistines had been planning an ambush in the middle of the night for Samson. But the ambush had been cancelled when at midnight, Samson walked to the city gate and wrenched it out of place and carried it on his shoulders up to the top of the mountain. The ambushers must have lost their nerve when they watched their intended victim rip the entrance of city out of the ground and stroll away with it on his back (Judges 15:2-3).

But a missing city gate was merely sneak previews for Gaza. Later, Gaza was devastated on an epic level. The news must have certainly traveled fast. If you had lived nearby, and if you were curious enough to go check it out, you would have seen a massive pile of rubble. Inside the rubble were three thousand bodies. Three thousand and one to be exact. Samson himself was also entombed in the wreckage (Judges 16:27-30). This was Samson's final display of strength. The grand finale of a man who muscled his way through the world in memorable ways. His feats of strength would be so well-remembered, his name alone would resound as a synonym for steely abs. But there was another side to Samson that had nothing to do with dead lions and broken buildings.

Samson was very strong, but he was also very weak. The moment his name is spoken, we see him gritting his teeth, pushing against the pillars, the final moments of his life perfectly capturing his character. But whereas Samson received incredible strength through the Spirit of God, he received incapacitating weakness through his eyes.

Everyone knows this strong man was brought down by a woman named Delilah, who defeated him with that famous haircut. But it's very important to know that she was not the first woman to tamper with this man.

When we first meet Samson in Scripture, right away we learn he is a man who is distracted by good-looking women. "Then Samson went down to Timnah and saw a woman in Timnah, one of the daughters of the Philistines. So he came back and told his father and mother, 'I saw a woman in Timnah, one of the daughters of the Philistines; now therefore, get her for me as a wife'" (Judges 14:1-2). This was all pre-Delilah. We don't know who this woman was, but the main thing to notice here is that Samson didn't know who this woman was either. All he knew was that he saw her. At the risk of offending those who still believe in love at first sight, it is safe to say that Samson's criteria for women was pretty shallow.

In fact, Samson's parents pointed out that when it came to looking for a girl, his standards needed some improvement. "Then his father and his mother said to him, 'Is there no woman among the daughters of your relatives, or among all our people, that you go to take a wife from the uncircumcised Philistines?'" (Judges 14:3). They were trying to guide him toward the standard that God expected from those who followed Him. Fraternizing romantically with anyone who didn't belong to God was a bad idea.

Samson's rebuttal reveals a significant truth about him. "But Samson said to his father, 'Get her for me, for she looks good to me'" (Judges 14:3). When it came to tearing up and smashing things, Samson's brutish strength made him unstoppable. But when it came to women, he was very stoppable. In essence, when it came to women, he was nothing more than a wimp. This would turn out to be the perfect strategy for Satan to use in order to turn this man of strength into a puppet manipulated by winks and smiles.

Don't be fooled by the next verse. "However, his father and mother did not know that it was of the Lord, for He was seeking an occasion against the Philistines. Now at that time the Philistines were ruling over Israel" (Judges 14:4). Samson being enticed by this girl's looks was "of the Lord," but that doesn't mean God was pleased with this kind of shallowness.

3 – Picking Flowers in the **Minefield**

God often uses poor decisions to bring about His will (Genesis 50:20). Just because Samson's life ultimately resulted in good things doesn't mean there was anything good about his tyrannical libido.

As the account progresses, we see a pattern not only of power, but a pattern of stumbling and faltering, due to Samson's tendency to be distracted by his attraction to women. Men are designed to be attracted to women, but Samson let this desire completely run his brain. He was great at ripping apart lions and general combat, but Samson was horrible when it came to dealing with women.

Samson was especially vulnerable to persistent nagging. Long before Delilah, Samson was married. His wife used tactics eventually used by Delilah. She whittled away Samson's determination, ultimately getting him to reveal information that would undermine his plans. "Samson's wife wept before him and said, 'You only hate me, and you do not love me; you have propounded a riddle to the sons of my people, and have not told it to me.' And he said to her, 'Behold, I have not told it to my father or mother; so should I tell you?' However she wept before him seven days while their feast lasted. And on the seventh day he told her because she pressed him so hard. She then told the riddle to the sons of her people" (Judges 14:16-17). Just like Delilah, it was a matter of persistence and playing off Samson's desires. Granted, his wife had been threatened in order to make her weasel the information out of her husband, but it shows us the recipe for defeating Samson. To make him falter, add one woman.

Delilah follows the same protocol of hounding him and casting doubt on his love for her. "Then she said to him, 'How can you say, "I love you," when your heart is not with me? You have deceived me these three times and have not told me where your great strength is.' It came about when she pressed him daily with her words and urged him, that his soul was annoyed to death. So he told her all that was in his heart and said to her, 'A razor has never come on my head, for I have been a Nazirite to God from my mother's womb. If I am shaved, then my strength will leave me and I will become weak and be like any other man'" (Judges 16:15-17).

Delilah was not some kind of super-seductress. Samson had been setting the stage for her his whole life. Every woman that shaped his decisions because "she looked good" weakened his mental stamina just a little bit more. By the time Delilah arrived, Samson was a man waiting to be undone.

In a way, his grand and gruesome finale was poetic. His eyes were destroyed. The very things that had caused him to linger and look at women. In the end, I'm happy to say, even though he lost his sight, he regained his insight and finished well.

But this manly man should be a cautionary tale to all men. We might have power, but if we're not careful, that power is quickly overpowered by our attraction to women. Once he became blind, Samson saw this all too well.

The Third Wheel

Let's take a moment to step into a 19 Century parlor.

"Oh my darling," he says.

"Oh my own true love," she says.

"Ahem."

Just like that, the moment is ruined. It's usually a scowling spinster doing needlepoint in the corner. Sometimes it's a parent strategically entering the room on the pretense of announcing dinner. Sometimes it's even the little brother who wanders in to retrieve a toy. But whatever form it takes, it is a most unwelcome presence.

Meet the chaperone, the killjoy, the third wheel. The hall monitor of love.

The poor, young couple is reduced to shy glances. True love is stifled, smothered, and possibly even snuffed out.

Almost all of us have suffered this extra person. Almost all of us have *been* this extra person. I remember one time in particular being stuck in a situation where it was very clear that things would be running a lot smoother if I wasn't present.

Tricycles notwithstanding, a three-wheel arrangement can be very awkward.

But the chaperone was invented for a very specific reason. They were placed in the situation in order to make sure the potential lovebirds behaved properly. The word "chaperone" comes from the concept of a "hood" or "cape." The idea was that this person would watch over the couple (maybe the girl in particular) to help prevent any bad decisions.

Today, we laugh. We think the whole idea of a chaperone is hilarious. That kind of thing belongs to our naïve ancestors or possible contemporary backward countries with out-of-date principles.

Today, the goal is to reduce the situation down to two. Two's company, three's a chaperone.

That third person changes it all. That extra person interferes. It would all be much better if there were only two.

If you crunch a few numbers, you will soon discover that one is definitely the loneliest number, but two can be as bad as one—or worse.

The fact of the matter is, we still need watching over. Quickly shrugging off the rest of the world in order to "get to know each other," is the opening line of a lot of sad stories. A happy ending is going to require a little more caution and a lot more wisdom.

The truth is, it's impossible for any couple to not have a chaperone. Now I'm reduced to sounding like the matron in the corner with the raised eyebrow.

God is watching you.

You see, if you truly believe God exists and that He is omnipresent and omniscient, then it will shape every decision you make. To quickly dismiss this is a form of atheism. An occasional twinge of guilt doesn't mean much. Stubbornly continuing on toward physical impurity is just another way of ignoring God

In the romantic shadows, it's easy to forget Him.

Don't fool yourself. We still need watching over. The dating world is flawed and if you blindly push through this broken system, it might make your heart beat faster, but it also tends to make it break faster.

This doesn't mean being alone together is automatic forfeit of the game. But don't be too quick to scoff at the wisdom of a third wheel. Being with other people is often a smart choice.

That Soft Clicking Sound Under Your Foot

This isn't working—at least not as is. Either the system has been sabotaged or it never really worked to begin with. Dating is cluttered with traditions and trends and twisted ideas about love.

I'm sure we've all got our personal metaphors, but let me suggest one more. Dating is nothing less than trying to pick flowers in a mine field.

At first, when you're very young, it looks like just a beautiful field of roses and daffodils. *So this is love. I never understood before. But now I get it.*

So you pursue love. Sometimes it feels like you found it. Sometimes you blow up.

It's no wonder some of us just stand paralyzed, afraid of taking even one more step. Some people make a very different choice. They just keep grabbing flowers and keep blowing up. After being reduced to smithereens several times, their mangled heart crawls into marriage. That isn't likely to turn out well.

But let me tell you something I learned about mine fields.

Thanks again, Hollywood, for getting it wrong. In a lot of movies I've seen, if someone steps on a mine, there is a click underfoot, but the explosion doesn't necessarily happen immediately. The mine will go off only after the weight of the person is removed. In other words, once the person who steps on the mine lifts his foot—smithereens.

This delay allows the victim to possibly figure out a way to place a substitute of similar weight on the mine and possibly save his life. It allows him the chance to be a hero and get everyone around him to reach a safe distance. This also gives him a chance to come up with profound last words. Maybe some advice like, "Don't try to cross minefields." Either way, the one standing on the mine has some time to ponder lots of things.

But in the real world, that's not how it works.

This is how it works.

Click-Boom

That's it. There's no delay. There's the guy stepping on the mine and then there's the mine unraveling him in a glorious explosion.

Continuing with our metaphor, don't be in such a rush to sprint out into the minefield. We all want those flowers, but without some guidance, you will inevitably step on a mine. And there is no delay before the explosion. Once you're involved, there isn't really time to think. Once you're already standing on the mine, thinking-time is over.

It's probably better to do your thinking ahead of time. Before you start skipping around out there collecting your daisies and daffodils. If you do some thinking first, you might even reconsider your path. This minefield might not be the best way to get where you're going. It's littered with the debris of countless broken hearts.

On the other side—that's called marriage. Many Single People were able to reach the other side to become Married People. Even from way over here, you can get a pretty good view. Some of them seem pretty happy. But some of them don't seem happy at all. In fact, I don't know about you, but I see a lot of wreckage over there too.

PART 4

Live FROM THE **Ruins**

The Dark Truth About Cake Toppers

As it turns out, all Married People aren't happy. For a long time, I thought they were. They seemed so—together. In fact, to me most of them seemed as if they had always been together. So much so that it was hard to imagine them ever having been Single People.

Gradually, television and movies provided my disillusionment. I saw a lot of shows where Married People stopped being married. These shows enlightened me about the grim side of marriage.

Real life confirmed my suspicions. Married People are not always happy. Many of them are sad or even miserable. Many of them get divorced and never see each other again.

I've got some bad news. Not only are there problems with the dating process, there are incredible problems even after the fact. As bad as the minefield of dating is, the landscape of marriage on the other side is even worse. Wedded bliss seems to last as long as the wedding cake. Those two little figures on top of the icing can serve as a dark omen.

Almost every wedding cake has them. Toy versions of the bride and groom, standing on a field of fondant, holding hands, gazing out at the future. But right after the wedding, the cake begins to disappear. Piece by piece, bite by bite, all the hope of that special day is consumed.

Despite all efforts to salvage some cake, even if a piece is carefully wrapped and secured in the freezer, eventually even that last piece will also be gone.

And the happy toy couple? They end up in a box, wrapped in tissue paper.

Don't let the cynicism of a long-time bachelor get you down. But as we set out to walk these ruins, it would serve our purposes to take note of a well-known statistic that has achieved the prestige of being a cliché.

More than half of marriages end in divorce.

This means, from a coldly objective view, it would not be

outrageous to close a wedding ceremony with the flip of a coin. Heads—we stick, tails—we ditch.

Marriages have a pitifully short lifespan. This brevity has become so common, that it is often considered to just be the nature of the beast.

You can hear it in the excuses that surface in the aftermath of a divorce. "We were married too young." "We fell out of love." "We both wanted different things." When it comes to tidy excuses for the demise of a marriage, it's easy to find the variety pack.

At least half of marriages come to a cold, cruel end.

Half.

If that was the standard rate of survival for air travel, we would never set foot on a plane again. Yet, two by two, we venture aboard marriage, either thinking we are the lucky exception or that ultimately it doesn't matter. We can always just opt out and try again with someone else.

Brace yourself—it gets worse.

Not only do most marriages end in divorce. It's probably safe to say that most of the ones who actually do stay together are not happily married. The 50% who continue to plod along toward the golden anniversary are not always that thrilled about the trip. Even your most devoted romantic has to admit—a whole bunch of Married People are settling into something that smells a lot like a consolation prize. There's no wedded bliss here. They end up just existing together. All the dazzle of the wedding has faded completely. It's as if life ate all the cake out from under them.

From where you're standing, it might look like there's something rotten in the state of matrimony. Trying to map a path through the minefield is bad enough. But then you realize there are even greater dangers after that. It's kind of scary.

Don't blame it on the 21st Century. Modern life hasn't killed marriage. The culprit is human nature. Things have always been bad. Just because the divorce rate has gone up doesn't mean things are getting worse. It might be a relief to know we were *never* any good at it. The only thing that has possibly changed is that today, ending a marriage is easier and considered to almost be fashionable. In past decades, people tended to stay together because divorce was too scandalous. They didn't stay together because they were in love. They stayed together because it was more convenient.

These are hard truths. You're not going to find any of this at Hallmark. But it's important to know the condition of this realm before we take a closer look.

We're going to take a brief stroll through the rubble and try to identify the causes. There are certain ideas that prey on marriage and we need to see these culprits for what they are. The only way to keep believing in happily-ever-after is to be fully aware of the things that destroy it.

WorldSpeak 1—It's My Life

The world teaches us things. It shapes our thinking and eventually provides ideas that surface in specific catch-phrases.

I think of these worldly mantras as WorldSpeak.

We pick them up along the way and we assume they're true. We hear them on TV or from fellow employees or even members of our family. They are repeated often and even though they are not necessarily based on any real wisdom, eventually we believe them.

The demise of many a marriage probably comes from listening to what the world has to say. The damage can be traced back to certain WorldSpeak phrases that we either say out loud or that we sustain in the back of our minds.

Locating WorldSpeak phrases is sometimes difficult. They're not always easy to spot or identify. But once you do see them for what they are, it's hard to unsee them. They are exposed as counterfeit truth.

This first one I want to point out is usually found in arguments.

"It's my life!"

This is useful for promoting your agenda despite not having any real argument to support your case. It sounds legitimate even as it defies logic. It essentially works as a get-out-of-responsibility card.

"It's my life" can also be translated as "Leave me alone and let me do what I want to do" or more to the point—"Don't interfere with my selfish plans by confronting me with annoying things such as accountability or morals."

Even before we address this from a Christian perspective, there are so many reasons why this particular WorldSpeak phrase is so very not true. It is about as far from the truth as you can possibly get.

It is *not* your life. "Your" life in a very real way belongs to numerous people. It belongs to the ones you love and the ones who love you. It belongs to your friends. It belongs to the people you work with every day. This is all because of a very simple reason. Your life has an effect. You are not a neutral entity easing through this world without actually touching it. The decisions you make affect other people. Unless you're living in a yurt in the Yukon Territory, don't resort to this particular bit of nonsense. Even if you are that Alaskan hermit, your continued absence alters the equation of humanity—and even that has an effect.

This particular WorldSpeak phrase is even less true for a Christian.

First of all, saying, "It's my life" can only be spoken by someone who is being selfish. God holds Christians accountable for selfishness. Self-sacrifice is not exclusive to exceptional Christians. It actually defines a Christian. "Do nothing out of selfish ambition or empty conceit, but with humility of mind regard one another as more important than yourselves; do not merely look out for your own personal interests, but also for the interests of others" (Philippians 2:3-4). It's hard to find even the smallest nook or cranny in this passage that might allow room for such an idea as "It's my life."

But when it comes to Christianity, we're just getting started. There is a much deeper level that opposes this World-Speak. "Or do you not know that your body is a temple of the Holy Spirit who is in you, whom you have from God, and that you are not your own? For you have been bought with a price: therefore glorify God in your body" (I Corinthians 6:19-20). It's very simple. You don't belong to you. You've been paid for. Christianity is nothing less than slavery and a slave is the last person who can say, "It's my life."

If you're married, there is even less room for this World-Speak. When you get married, you don't belong to you anymore—even more so. If you're married, you belong to your spouse. "Wives subject to your own husbands, as to the Lord" (Ephesians 5:22). "So husbands ought also to love their own wives as their own bodies. He who loves his own wife, loves himself" (Ephesians 5:28). If you're a Christian, you belong to God. If you're a Christian husband or wife, you belong to God and your spouse.

Every decision you make as a Married Person effects countless souls, but the biggest effect will be on the one who is joined to you. That means any sin you allow to remain in your life is not just endangering you. It is not just corrupting you. The spiritual struggle for Married People is much more profound. The fight involves more than just one person.

When Nehemiah was put in charge of repairing the ruins of Jerusalem, he made some extremely significant strategic decisions. One is very relevant to Married People. "When I saw their fear, I rose and spoke to the nobles, the officials and the rest of the people: 'Do not be afraid of them; remember the Lord who is great and awesome, and fight for your brothers, your sons, your daughters, your wives and your houses'" (Nehemiah 4:14). Nehemiah positioned people in families because he knew they would fight harder. He knew a husband would fight harder if he was fighting to protect his wife and children.

This is an essential truth that seems lost on many Married People. At the very least, you are fighting for two souls. It isn't your life. To make any decision with that WorldSpeak driving your brain is pure selfishisness. More than likely, you will find this thorn jabbed into the heart of many troubled marriages. One or both of the Married People have bought this lie.

See it for what it is. Please notice the wreckage around it. Let's move on.

Love is God

The greatest threat to love is love. Believe it or not, every day we destroy love with love.

We watch movies about love. We read books about love. Most of the songs we listen to are about love. At this very moment, a large percentage of the world is pondering the possibilities of falling in love. We are in love with love and we love to hope about love and how maybe loving love will cause love to love our love in return. We love to love love.

The truth is—we destroy love with its counterfeit. We only think we want love. What we really want is something much less. We take actual love and try to renovate it. We gut it. Determined to get what we want, we take love apart and then cry over the pieces.

Even then, when we end up with something that falls short of what we hoped for, we still rely on worldly ideas of romance. It strikes the chord in us again and again. *Oh, if only I could have true love. Where is love? What is love?*

It's not as complicated as we want it to be. Here's the short version. God is love (I John 4:16). There. That's it. Not such a mystical secret after all. The One who created us is the very definition of love. All other definitions which do not include Him are, by definition, not love.

You might have infatuation or an empty longing. You might have jealousy or obsession. You might have some pitter-patter or lub-a-dub, but any real love has to be connected to God. "Beloved, let us love one another, for love is from God; and everyone who loves is born of God and knows God" (I John 4:7). Love can be passionate. It can involve intense attraction, but without the Creator, it will flounder and die. He's the one who designed it. As much as this will make a lot of people mad, it's the undeniable truth. If it doesn't include God, then it ain't love.

All those songs. All the movies. They're not really about love. They're about passion and attraction—just small components of real love. Unless there is something more profound connecting these various fragments, you will end up with something that doesn't last. True love lasts. Pieces of love fade.

When it comes to romance, we don't really love love. We love the periphery of love. We love the edges of it. We like to skim the surface. But when it comes to actually being really in love in the truest sense of the word—when we discover there has to be commitment and self-sacrifice, we veer off.

You can see it in the stories we tell ourselves. The great majority of the tales we love to hear are the ones where people find each other and fall in love. But the story ends there. The world can get you as far as the border. After that, it's a mess.

The world loves the dance—the lead-up. But not so much the follow-through.

This is another big reason why marriages don't last. Many Married People don't have the real deal. They might have all the unconnected pieces of love, but if these pieces remain unconnected, they will inevitably flicker out. That's when a lot of Married People convince themselves it's time to move on. They abandon True Love #1 and move on to True Love #2, where the fade begins yet again.

Love becomes a destination where no one really arrives. Even the ones who stay together—those without God have only fashioned a comfort based on familiarity. The dream they had when they were younger has dissolved. They have refashioned "true love" in more practical terms. They started out as mesmerized romantics, but the end of the story for most is cozy disillusionment.

Let's call it as it is. It's idolatry. We worship our idea of love. We sacrifice to it. We obey it. We devote our lives to it. Love is our god. But unlike the true God, it will not only fail to give us happiness, it will rob us of it.

Someone to Solve Us

As much as we flinch away from the idea of arranged marriages, we're pretty okay with it if the arranging is done by mystical forces of the universe. The idea of allowing our family to be involved in our love life is preposterous. But as far as leaving it to fate or destiny or the stars—that's just fine.

One of the most damaging deceptions thriving in our culture is the idea that all of us have a "soul mate" who is our cosmic destiny—a person who will provide us with peace and fulfillment. If we can just find them.

For the record, the Bible is very clear that God is all-knowing. This means He has complete awareness of who ends up with whom. It's also not a reach to think He is instrumental in arranging the obvious blessing of two people finding each other, if they follow His will.

But as far as "it is written in the stars" or "we were meant to be," it's important to know that at the heart of this idea is a very dangerous lie.

Here's the lie. Someone other than God can give you peace and fulfillment.

The truth is, without God, there will be no peace or fulfillment. "There is no peace for the wicked" (Isaiah 48:22). "They have made their paths crooked; whoever treads on them does not know peace" (Isaiah 59:8). Unless God is included, life will remain crooked and unfulfilled. The only real peace is with God. "The steadfast of mind You will keep in perfect peace, Because he trusts in You" (Isaiah 26:3).

When Jesus looked out over humanity, He mourned how they rejected peace even as they longed for it. "If you had known in this day, even you, the things which make for peace. But now they have been hidden from your eyes" (Luke 19:42). Only God through Jesus has "the things which make for peace."

No one else can give you this. Even the best human being you can find, in and of themselves, does not have "the things which make for peace." This alone is the source of many problems for Married People. They go into the marriage believing there is at least a little destiny in the mix, expecting their "soul mate" to provide something that only God can give them. Many Married People are miserable because they are disappointed that marriage lacks this essential feeling of fulfillment.

The truth of it is, when people are looking for love, without even realizing it, people are actually looking for God. That empty feeling, that deep sensation that your life is starving for some kind of purpose—it's a lack of God. Even those who claim to be Christians and merely dabble in religion miss the point. As long as their efforts to connect with the Creator remain half-hearted, they will continue to feel the void.

Even the world senses this emptiness. There is a great deal of intellectual, literary fiction that explores the idea of sex taking people to a higher level of existence. Even ungodly people have described sex as a spiritual experience. Many a philosophical writer has delved into the idea that there is something meaningful just beyond the veil of lust. All the romanticism is meant to find something that resonates with our souls. They know it's more than a drug rush of hormones. It is a glimpse of something significant. It is a realization that there is a built-in loneliness in all of us. But the unrealized sad ending to all these aspirations is that as long as they ignore God, they will only find more emptiness.

Without God, the search spirals into degradation. People will follow this false love even through dark turns, seeking fulfillment in the most degraded ways. They mistake the buzz of sex for happiness. But this existential lust will leave them as mere junkies shuddering for the next hit. Even though the cascade of feelings seems so fulfilling, it only leads to deeper emptiness. They don't realize they are clinging to physical intimacy because they are attempting to fulfill their souls. They are trying to find God through a physical collision with someone else's body.

This parallel is legitimate. God compares the husband / wife relationship with the relationship between Jesus and the church (Ephesians 5:22-33). There is something about the interaction of a husband and wife in a marriage that is inherently spiritual. The world is detecting traces of this deeper purpose even as it dabbles in the shallow end. That's what any romantic tryst is fumbling to be. But anything they achieve on their own is only a faint echo of what God intended. They are sincere in their search, but the coordinates are way off. It is merely a shadow of the mystery.

As a result, many people move through life believing that any real purpose will be found in another person. It's all backwards. Instead of using a spiritual path to reach love. People use love to reach something spiritual. Bring all this into a marriage and failure is inevitable. The hopeful heart expects their one-and-only to give substance to their life—substance that only God can really provide. When they realize they have ended up with someone who can't make them feel like life has a purpose, the hopeful heart then decides there's only one possibility. The galactic dating service was wrong. They have accidentally been paired with the wrong person. They owe it to themselves—nay, to the universe—to break with the imperfect match and connect with a more promising one. So they set out to find the next "right person." It is a sad search always ending with two empty shells clinging to each other.

Searching for someone to solve us is a doomed undertaking. It is a quest that will always fail. Married People are confused because they have found the "right one," but they are still lacking "the things which make for peace." This trail is littered with abandoned spouses, neglected sons and daughters, and the general debris of life that collects behind the selfish.

We want someone to make our lives have meaning. We want someone who will fill us with a sense of purpose. And no human alone can do that. We cannot solve each other. As long as God is kept out of the equation, it will always add up to zero.

World Speak 2—Follow Your Heart

Disney movies are nice. Disney movies are inspiring and optimistic and for the most part, family-friendly. Disney movies fill your childhood with happy memories and they stir your imagination.

But Disney movies and many others of their kind are also the primary perpetrators of World Speak 2.

"Follow your heart."

This enchanting phrase sounds incredibly sweet and innocent, but it does just as much damage as "It's my life."

If by "follow your heart," you mean, "Aspire toward great achievements and develop your talents, trusting that you can do so much more than you're doing now," then great. Good idea.

But if by "follow your heart," you mean, "Now that you are faced with a significant moral decision, you should now rely on your emotions for guidance," that is a horrible idea.

Following your heart (a.k.a. following your gut, instincts, intuition) is about as wise as using a dousing rod or a Ouija Board. "The heart is more deceitful than all else And is desperately sick; Who can understand it? (Jeremiah 17:9). All by itself, your heart is only good at deceiving you.

God talks about those who rejected the truth. He said they "became futile in their speculations, and their foolish heart was darkened" (Romans 1:21). Without the Word, you are reduced to speculations (guessing). In other words, you're reduced to following your heart. When it comes to decisions that matter, your heart is not the best resource. It is fickle and blind.

To get a real sense of what following your heart can do for you, read the book of Judges. It is one of the darkest stretches in history. The cause of the darkness is made very clear in the last verse of the book. "In those days there was no king in Israel; everyone did what was right in his own eyes" (Judges 21:25). You won't see a Disney rendition of Judges any time soon. Doing what is right in your own eyes does not lead to happily married princesses. It is the fast-track to trashing your life.

With so many Married People following their hearts, it's no wonder we're seeing so much rubble. Venturing off together without God's Word only leads to guessing. Failure is inevitable.

The only way to have any true clarity about anything is to rely on God's guidance. Follow His Word, not your heart. And don't follow the hearts of other people. Unless they're living their lives based on the Word, their input is highly suspect. Follow the Word and those who follow the Word.

Following your heart might work if you're trying to escape a witch's tower or if you're trying to figure out which frog might turn into a decent suitor. But in real life, the heart alone is unreliable. There are countless people who trudge through sad days now because they followed their heart.

It's not that your heart is disposable. God wants your heart. He considers it highly valuable. It is an excellent follower. It's just a horrible leader.

Advanced Infatuation (Falling in Love)

This brings us to the most complicated level of infatuation. Before we continue, it's important to point out again that infatuation in and of itself isn't bad. The problem is when we mistake it for love.

Stage One is Puppy Love and when you grow up, you realize it is merely a shadow of the real thing. It is a powerful feeling, but it's just a sneak preview of things to come.

Then comes Stage Two: The Crush. Hormones mercilessly take your brain hostage and transform you into an obsessed puppet with all the clarity of a sleepwalker. At this stage, the feelings are strongest when the object of affection is unattainable. You want what you can't have. Just like Stage One: Puppy Love, it feels real, it is powerful, but it typically has the lifespan of a mayfly (approx. 2 days). Despite the intensity, the brevity reveals the truth.

It's not love.

You can imagine how antagonistic the response would be if you told someone in the midst of Stage Two Infatuation they weren't really experiencing love. So brace yourself. There's going to be even more animosity when I break the news about Stage Three: Falling in Love.

No such thing. You can't *fall* in love.

But everybody believes you do. We don't even question it. Falling in love is just part of life. Everyone knows it. When it comes to true love, one of the main factors is gravity. If it's the right person, then you just "fall in love."

Falling is normally considered a bad thing. Mostly because falling implies there will soon be some kind of impact, resulting in damage or even death. However, falling with a parachute is pretty cool (so I've heard) because there is the exhilaration of flying and you have the added plus of surviving.

Falling in love can be kind of like that. There is a kind of breathless thrill and sometimes it does feel like you might be in the process of almost dying, but in a good way. It is a wonderful agony.

As far as our ideas about love, there might be something ominous in the specific direction of the movement. An inevitable descent from higher to lower.

But the most significant characteristic of this idea of love is that it promotes the belief that love is not a choice.

This is where the parachute fails. Or rather the parachute analogy fails. The falling involved in "falling in love" is not a choice. Skydiving takes planning and rational thought and cautious preparation. Falling in love rarely includes any of these things.

It's an unplanned falling. The kind where you are walking along minding your own business and you trip, or you lose your balance at the top of a flight of stairs, or you step into an open elevator shaft.

The basic idea is that you don't have any control whatsoever. You might make the initial compromise in your equilibrium, but after that, gravity (or love) takes over. You are a victim of the laws of nature.

The essence of this is captured in a phrase that should at least get Honorable Mention in WorldSpeak's Greatest Hits— "You can't choose who you love."

At first, this sounds very sweet. Isn't it a nice thought that we all just go around accidentally plunging into love? *Whoops, I love you. And whoops, I love you too. And go figure, I can't seem to keep my balance, whoops again—pardon me—I love you as well.* If you're emotionally clumsy, you might very well end up just falling in love with all kinds of people.

But a darker aspect of all this is seen in another phrase, that defies the laws of physics.

Falling *out* of love.

You hear it all the time. Almost as much as the falling-*in*-love thing.

It's always used to explain why someone is abandoning someone else. *Sorry—I fell* out *of love.* They are referring to the same person who they fell *in* love with, but now the process has reversed (completely out of their control) and they have fallen upward out of their passionate devotion—the same passionate devotion they would have once bitterly defended as "true love."

There is a current widespread tendency to remove everyone's ability to choose. Whereas God made it a point to make sure we are free moral agents, the world urges you to relinquish that privilege and become a victim. A victim of your environment, your genetics, your love. Whatever the case may be, you are ultimately absolved of any real responsibility because you are just responding to stimuli.

"Falling in love" fits right in.

God designed us to be able to make choices. He intentionally made it a point to make us very different from the rest of existence. All other things follow a program or pattern. Planets orbit and animals follow instinct. We have the wild and powerful ability to make decisions about our behavior.

But there are a thousand excuses lined up for you to deny yourself this ability to choose. One of them is that you have no input about who you love.

Married People become married, deceived into thinking that Stage Three Infatuation: Falling in Love is what will make it all work. They expect the chemical buzz to hit them on a relatively regular basis and they will just keep "falling in love" regardless of any effort on their part. It is not unlike a virus. You just catch it and then you experience the side-effects naturally.

But true love is not so precarious. Real love is a choice. Which is a good thing. Because true love loves people when they're lovable, but also when they're *not* lovable. "And if you love those who love you, what credit is that to you? For even sinners love those who love them. And if you do good to those who do good to you, what credit is that to you? For even sinners do the same" (Luke 6:32). Loving the lovable is nothing. That's easy. True love is found in loving each other when you're unlovable. Like my dad used to say. True love is being loved not because of who you are, but *in spite* of who you are.

Now, I know what you're thinking. *That's not the kind of love we're talking about. We're talking about husband / wife love. You're bringing in religious love and that's something completely different.*

Wrong. Agape love is the highest form of love. It's wanting what's best for someone regardless of the cost to yourself. All other forms of love must aspire to this. Anything that doesn't aspire to agape love, isn't love.

Falling in Love is just a stronger dose of infatuation. It's Puppy Love concentrate. It's a more intense form of The Crush. It's great and wonderful and fun and all that, but it isn't real love.

Love isn't that fragile.

That's why Falling in Love can do so much damage to a marriage. If the connection between the husband and wife is made of that material, it will be very breakable. Falling Out of Love will always be a possibility.

True love does not submit to the gravity of circumstances. Real love is a choice. Many Married People would be so much happier if they understood this one small truth.

True love is weightless.

How the Mighty Became Fallen

Married People are susceptible to a variety of problems. Some of them are easily traced to modern misconceptions. But one problem in particular can be traced back to just before the Flood.

There was a reason for the Flood. It wasn't an arbitrary burst of anger. God was very open about His motivation for scouring the planet. "Then the Lord saw that the wickedness of man was great on the earth, and that every intent of the thoughts of his heart was only evil continually" (Genesis 6: 5). All sins are wrong, but the degradation was so prevalent and thorough, God destroyed the world. Only a few survived.

For our purposes, it's important we take a closer look at the corruption that led to the Flood. But in order to pinpoint the heart of the problem, we have to get past at least three misconceptions.

The first misconception involves mistaken identity. "Now it came about, when men began to multiply on the face of the land, and daughters were born to them, that the sons of God saw that the daughters of men were beautiful; and they took wives for themselves, whomever they chose (Genesis 6:1-2).

Some readers have concluded that this passage is describing angels coming down to earth and physically interacting with human women, who then in turn produced "Nephilim" a.k.a. "mighty men" (Genesis 6:4). Although the word "angel" is not mentioned, the phrase "sons of God" is indeed used elsewhere in Scripture to describe angels (Job 1:6). The conclusion would be that the Nephilim were a hybrid of angel and human. Many people suggest this might explain why we eventually read about such giants as Goliath.

However, there are several aspects of this passage which suggest this account has nothing to do with angels.

The phrase "sons of God" is also used in Scripture to simply describe people who belong to God. "For all who are being led by the Spirit of God, these are sons of God" (Romans 8:14). This is the more likely application here due to several other factors.

When the Sadducees tried to corner Jesus with a hypothetical dilemma, His primary counterpoint was built on a particular characteristic of angels. They don't get married (Matthew 22:30). One might argue that a lack of marriage doesn't automatically mean of lack of sex. Yet, at the very least, this verse draws attention to the lack of any Scripture that indicates angels are capable of this physical process.

Just the fact that sex is a physical process is an important factor. In Genesis, one of the distinctive traits God pinpointed about His newly created physical creatures was that they were capable of reproducing. There are no passages indicating propagation outside of the physical realm. The arrangement of propagation being exclusive to the physical realm makes sense in that this realm is notoriously temporary. With impending limitations to lifespans for each physical living thing, reproduction would be the one means to maintain each species. Such an arrangement for angels isn't necessary, being that their framework is already essentially eternal.

Throughout Scripture, during several direct interactions between the spiritual realm and the physical realm, there is a glaring incompatibility. The book of Hebrews emphasizes this contrast. Here, physical things are described as "those things which can be shaken, as of created things" and spiritual things are described as "those things which cannot be shaken" (Hebrews 12:27). This basic difference is emphasized in that the physical realm's fragile nature is made more stark when there is overlap with the spiritual (Exodus 20:19; Isaiah 6:4). The material from which spiritual beings are created far outshines any earthly ingredients (I Corinthians 15: 40).

Let's review.

First, a spiritual being has no need for reproduction and therefore has no physical DNA to pass along. Second, even though angels have taken on the appearance of human form, their inherent nature has great potential to damage flesh and blood. A tryst with a "shakeable" human would not result in an accidental upgrade in the form of baby giants.

The Nephilim were not the progeny of celestial beings. In fact, the significant nature of these "mighty men" had nothing to do with their DNA. Although they probably had the biceps and abs necessary to ravage battlegrounds, their mightiness was not simply due to genetics. We can deduce this with some simple math and a brief word study.

Simple Math: Before the Flood, there were Nephilim (Genesis 6:4). After the Flood, there were Nephilim (Numbers 13:33). There were no Nephilim on the ark (cf. ark passenger manifest—Genesis 7:7). The solution to this story problem is that although the Nephilim were certainly big and scary, they were more about character than breeding.

Word Study: The word "Nephilim" comes from a verb which means "fall, lie down, be cast down, or fail." In other parts of the Bible, the word is used to describe those who have fallen in battle (Judges 20:46) or who were defeated (II Kings 25:11). There are also indications that it is essentially a word associated with violent people. The Nephilim were mighty, but their name basically means they were the "Fallen Ones"—or to put it more simply, "The Defeated." At best, the etymology might present them as the ones who fall on their enemies, violently and without mercy. Still not an admirable legacy.

Now we can begin to see what all this has to do with the current troubles of Married People. During this prelude to the Flood, as men began to prosper, they made the bad decision of choosing women simply for their looks. Drawn to their beauty, men "took wives for themselves, whomever they chose" (Genesis 6:2). Their children grew up to be "mighty men," who in turn furthered the corruption instigated by their fathers. They were physically impressive but most important of all, they were spiritually defeated. When it came to spiritual strength, the Nephilim were by definition weak. This resonates with one of the most important commands God has expressed time and time again throughout Scripture.

Don't marry those who don't belong to God (Exodus 34:11-16; II Corinthians 6:14-18). As seen multiple times throughout Scripture, men have a tendency to compromise their spirituality through their choices about women. Solomon, Samson, and numerous others can testify to this.

If we conclude that this account is a record of angels interacting with human women, resulting in super-humans, we are left with merely an interesting tale. However, the Bible is designed to instruct and to give insight about our current circumstances. Everything recorded in the Old Testament is meant to have some kind of bearing on being a Christian right now (Romans 15:4). God's Word is filled with threads that can be followed through the passages which lead to truths designed to help us survive this world. Spiritual concerns always trump mere physical concerns.

The angelic explanation for Genesis 6 would be at best an entertaining blip. However, the conclusion that Genesis 6 is dealing with the danger of interacting with worldly people supports a prevalent lesson that God considers to be extremely important.

When the "sons of God" joined their souls to women who were not "daughters of God," this ultimately led to a widespread corruption. "Then the Lord saw that the wickedness of man was great on the earth, and that every intent of the thoughts of his heart was only evil continually" (Genesis 6:5). What these thoughts were in particular is not recorded, but it is important to notice that one of the key factors was that the men were letting themselves be swayed by the superficial aspects of the women. It was a chain of decisions and events warranting a vast execution with water. The account of the "sons of God" sets the stage for the Flood. But it wasn't about genetics, it was about spirituality.

The rain fell and the waters ruptured the ground, drowning the world, due to at least in part because beauty can make men foolish.

One of the most notorious low points of mankind was when men were defined by their violence and women were defined by their beauty. This does not make strength and beauty necessarily bad. But when Married People use these as their primary criteria in choosing someone, disaster is in the making.

When we let the world manipulate our ideas about what a man or woman should be, it never turns out well.

World Man, Real Man

Here he comes. Hurtling sideways, he slams his shoulder into the door and smashes it to splinters. Need those metal bars pried open? Here he is. Trapped inside burning wreckage? No problem. He's there—tossing aside that flaming debris and dragging you to safety. Done and done.

Not that most men are ever required to do any of these things. But they could. For some of us men, smashing a door down might require the door to be pretty old, but it's the thought that counts. In reality, the biggest opportunity a man will have to display his strength to attract a woman is to open a jar of olives.

Whatever feats he might tackle, God intended that men have some kind of strength. That strength comes in many forms. It can be biceps or smarts or wealth, or just some kind of talent. But when all is said and done, the male is powered by power.

When God designed man, He intended him to be a conqueror of the planet. "God blessed them; and God said to them, 'Be fruitful and multiply, and fill the earth, and subdue it; and rule over the fish of the sea and over the birds of the sky and over every living thing that moves on the earth'" (Genesis 1:28). Granted, man would be accompanied by woman, but it was the male who was given the birthright share of the strength, making him more capable of digging and constructing and all-around subduing. God gave man power and expected him to do something with it. Whether it's muscle or money, the male is measured by his ability to change the world. If he can't bench press it, maybe he can buy it. To a great extent, man equals power.

How that power is applied to the world makes all the difference. This is where you begin to see a distinction. You begin to see there are basically two kinds of men. We'll call them the World Man and the Real Man.

For the World Man, it is all about the show. Strength is a performance. Unfortunately, the demonstrations don't necessarily help other people. The man of the world uses his strength primarily to benefit himself. The World Man might very well have it in him to be a hero. But a great majority of his focus can be traced back to a basic agenda of using his strength so that he will be a viable attractor of females or of just public admiration. His strength becomes a tool to express his anger or to shove his way into a dominant position over other men.

Oddly enough, for the World Man, his power is often used to simply indulge his weaknesses. Here is where God and the world differ on their ideas about masculinity—how the power is used.

World Man doesn't control his temper. It is generally considered extremely macho if a guy completely loses it and throws a chair or punches a face. Whether or not the chair or face deserved it is almost beside the point. World Man is proud to be so powerful that even he cannot restrain himself.

World Man uses power to subdue women. In his eyes, sleeping with a lot of women means you are a real man. The greater number of physical interactions, the greater the man. On some level, the vanquished seem to understand. He is a man, and as such, is expected to make his way through a series of girlfriends. Most of the girls hope the buck stops here, but if he moves on, what can you do? He's a man.

World Man uses his power to express strong language. His crude vocabulary is often associated with his anger and his libido. But whatever the occasion calls for, he is ready to contribute foul language to demonstrate his command of words that are not burdened with intellect or any true wit.

Which leads us to the brutal truth of this brute. World Man has power, but he is always in the process of losing control of that power. He does not control his temper. He does not control his sex drive. He does not control his words. He is defined by his lack of self-control.

How typical of our enemy. To take something designed for power and shape it into something that becomes only a tribute to weakness. One might think that World Man is best symbolized by free weights and muscle shirts. But based on his tendency to lose control, a more appropriate icon might be diapers.

On the other hand, the Real Man controls himself. He keeps his anger under control because God said be "slow to anger" (James 1:19). The Real Man restricts his sex drive to marriage because God expects him to "abstain from sexual immorality" (I Thessalonians 4:3). The Real Man doesn't let his words run rampant, because he knows if he doesn't his "religion is worthless" (James 1:26). The Real Man has power, but he uses this power to build up his surroundings, not smash them. The Real Man is power. But he is power under control.

Married People often fail to realize this. A wife, who was so attracted to the Nephilim-ish nature of her husband, discovers that his lack of self-control is of no use when you're trying to build a home. His unrestrained weaknesses in his actions and words are one of the quickest ways to make marriage turn some pretty dark corners. A lot of the rubble surrounding us here can be attributed to the "hero" of the day—World Man.

He is weak in many ways, but his greatest weakness makes him just like the pre-Flood men. Lack of self-control toward women in particular has been the downfall of many a powerful man.

One Thousand Women

When it was time for Solomon to become king, there were conspiracies against him. Nothing less than drastic measures would be needed to keep his position and his life. So Solomon didn't mess around.

When his half-brother Adonijah tried to weasel his way into the crown, Solomon sent Beniah (essentially his personal hit-man) to take Adonijah out (I Kings 2:24-25). Joab, who had been a part of the same conspiracy, knew he was in big trouble. He ran into the temple and grabbed onto the altar, hoping to use it as a kind of sanctuary. But Solomon was done with this human thorn. He sent in Benaiah and had Joab killed right there at the altar (I Kings 2:28-34).

There was also a man named Shimei. Even though he had once thrown rocks at Solomon's father, King David, he was given a second chance. But when Shimei pushed his luck and asked for a third chance, Solomon sent in Benaiah. That was the end of Shimei (I Kings 2:44-46).

No doubt about it. Solomon was watching his back. If you tried to mess with him, you didn't last long. Solomon was keenly aware of conspiracies. He was a wise man. The wisest man who ever lived.

Sad to say, this wisest of men, who was so intently in tune with his situation, ended up being defeated by a completely different conspiracy. Shadowy, political intrigues did not cause his demise. He was not dethroned by spies and saboteurs. He was ruined by perfume and whispers. He was essentially assassinated by women. A thousand of them to be exact.

What Adonijah and Joab and Shimei could not do with swords and stones, one thousand women did with soft eyes and elegant embraces. They defeated the wisest, richest, and most powerful man on the earth. Solomon was able to stand up to espionage, but not estrogen.

Regarding Solomon's downfall through women, there were at least two key factors. First of all, Solomon defied God's standard for marriage. "Now King Solomon loved many foreign women along with the daughter of Pharaoh: Moabite, Ammonite, Edomite, Sidonian, and Hittite women, from the nations concerning which the Lord had said to the sons of Israel, 'You shall not associate with them, nor shall they associate with you, for they will surely turn your heart away after their gods.' Solomon held fast to these in love" (I Kings 11:1-2). This restriction about marrying foreign women was not a racial thing. It was a spiritual thing. Marrying a foreign woman who was spiritually foreign to God's commands, was one of the quickest ways to corrupt a man's devotion to God. The command was to not even "associate" with these women.

Solomon did more than associate with them. He married them. Notice Solomon "loved" these women and that he "held fast" to them. Even if some of the marriages were arranged to promote peace with another nation, ultimately it was about "love" or at least the world's version of it. Marrying a woman who does not belong to God has been the downfall of many, many men. But all it takes is one woman.

Just ask Adam or Ahab. But Solomon took things to a whole new level. Seven hundred wives and three hundred concubines (I Kings 11:3).

The second key factor that ensured Solomon's downfall was just sheer numbers. Solomon had a thousand Eves, a thousand Jezebels, all whispering, smiling, and gently dismantling Solomon's soul one caress at a time.

Once upon a time, he had been a man of integrity. He had been a man of insight. He had been so in-tune with the intricacies of this existence, the Queen of Sheba had made it a point to cross many miles to meet him face to face. She was stunned by his wisdom to the point of being "breathless" (II Chronicles 9:4). His wisdom and insight surpassed all her expectations.

But none of it saved him from the conspiracies of a thousand women. The swords, the chariots, his personal hitman Benaiah, and even his arsenal of proverbs did not prevent his progressive spiritual decay at the delicate hands of a legion of women who flowed in and out of his daily life. A thousand gentle voices, each with its own agenda, softly turning his heart.

Even as this king went about protecting his kingdom, looking over his shoulder for the next Adonijah or Joab, behind the scenes, in the intimate shadows, he embraced his assassins. Here, all his wisdom was useless. Many kings have appointed a fool to serve in the royal court. But Solomon was one king who eventually became his own fool.

This was how the wisest man in the world was ruined. There was no grand siege or breaching of the walls. The attack came from within—one thousand battles, leaving Solomon defeated a thousand times.

Today, no one has a thousand wives. There might be some sheik with a throwback harem in the Middle East, flaunting a dozen veiled courtesans. Occasionally a quasi-celebrity polygamist might surface on a tacky reality show with his cadre of sister-wives. But no one comes close to indulging the nuptial overload of Solomon.

Yet consider this. Almost every man alive—single or married—has a thousand women at his beck and call. These women are ready to be summoned onto the nearest screen, like temptresses flirting from their windows. The same tactics that destroyed Solomon are in full force today in the form of digital wives and virtual concubines. Research indicates at least one-third of the internet is devoted to porn. That doesn't even include the relatively milder allurements that are just as compromising to the male mind.

These are the modern temple prostitutes kept in binary shrines. Men everywhere are being destroyed as thoroughly as Solomon. Many Christian men would be wary of a woman of the night loitering at the front door, but he falls victim again and again to the smiling assassin who lives in the glow of his computer. Many husbands may have one wife, but he keeps 999 concubines.

The warning was posted a long time ago. Maybe it should be printed out and placed above every computer screen. "Do not desire her beauty in your heart, nor let her capture you with her eyelids" (Proverbs 6:25). A platoon of macho males pride themselves on being able to bench press their own weight, but these same bruisers fail to show any stamina when it comes to the power of eyelids.

In order to survive the strategy that took out Solomon, it will take more than strength and determination. The battle is won through a reliance on the wisdom of God. It is a matter of making a solid decision. "I will set no worthless thing before my eyes; I hate the work of those who fall away; it shall not fasten its grip on me" (Psalm 101:3). It is a matter of armoring yourself with the Word. "Your Word I have treasured in my heart, that I may not sin against You" (Psalm 119:11). It is a matter of constantly maintaining the focus of your heart. "For the mind set on the flesh is death, but the mind set on the Spirit is life and peace" (Romans 8:6). Without the strength of perspective, defeat is inevitable.

Married People suffer in this siege. In many cases, the soul of a man is drained away through his eyes. The danger of literal women is certainly a prevalent threat. But men of God need to also defend themselves and their homes against the infiltration of women made of pixels.

That Which Destroys Kings

We are drowning. Everywhere you turn, there is something implying sexual corruption. It's not just TV shows and movies. It's commercials, jokes, catchy tunes, billboards, magazines, internet pop-up ads, apps, tweets, posts, instagrams, texts.

We are drenched in the distraction of lust. Once it reaches our eyes, it infiltrates. The invasion is over quickly and the result is devastating. It finds its way beyond our gaze and lives in our brains.

For Married People, it's like having access to a self-destruct program. If left intact, it will destroy a family from the inside out. This comes as no surprise when you remember that it has also been known to destroy whole empires.

History is riddled with disasters that—when you remove all the discrete euphemisms—were caused by plain and simple lust. Everyone knows about the face that launched a thousand ships. There were far more many faces that *sank* a thousand ships.

Lust was the poison of Sodom (Genesis 19:5). It was Herod's kryptonite (Mark 6:22). It was the dark descent of the man Judah (Genesis 38:16). It was the sabotage of David's relationship with God (II Samuel 11:2-4). Not to mention Samson and Solomon. It wouldn't be unreasonable to suggest history is mostly a record of those who let their eyes linger.

Lust is the seed of many sins. Once it attacks through the eyes, it can run rampant inside your mind, infecting it with rationalizations and excuses which can then be used efficiently for lying, malice, and even adultery. Constant bombardment can chip away at the defenses of even the strongest Christian.

We've all been witnesses at the scene. A family abruptly disintegrates. Out of the blue, a solid Christian man seems to lose his mind. Sometimes a loving wife suddenly abandons her marriage. At the root of these and countless other tragedies, you will often find lust.

For Married People, lust is a saboteur, pulling the eyes of devotion away from the spouse. Pornography is the blatant culprit, but it doesn't even have to be that extreme. Some of the most tantalizing thoughts can start with a relatively mild image or suggestion.

It is an enemy that never completely goes away. Lust is always at the gate, always looking for an opportunity. It becomes even stronger than usual in a culture that fuels it and keeps it idling strong.

The "marriage bed is to be undefiled" (Hebrews 13:4), but it can be easily defiled if the minds of the husband and wife are conquered by lust. For the man in particular, God warns him about the enticement of women, describing that allurement as "that which destroys kings" (Proverbs 31:3). Unless he is on guard, any husband will be no match for such a destroyer.

Strangely enough, it was probably Solomon who was the voice of Ecclesiastes, inspired by God to say, "And I discovered more bitter than death the woman whose heart is snares and nets, whose hands are chains. One who is pleasing to God will escape form her, but the sinner will be captured by her" (Ecclesiastes 7:26).

Both men and women are susceptible, but it is well-known that the typical target is the man. He can be easily brought down through the gates of his eyes. But it is the woman who is often used as the instrument of his downfall. The enemy has achieved one of the greatest strategies possible against men and women. He has used them to hurt each other.

World Woman / Real Woman

Here she comes. Gliding into view and drawing every eye in the room. Every man's heart beats a little faster. Every girl's heart withdraws in humility. Her figure is perfect and her face is stunning. She is the very essence of love.

God designed women to have allure. That beauty comes in many forms. It can be cheek bones or grace or kindness, or just a steady confidence in some kind of talent, but the female is powered by beauty.

When He designed woman, God intended her to be a beautiful solution to loneliness. "Then the Lord God said, 'It is not good for the man to be alone; I will make him a helper suitable for him'" (Genesis 2:18). Angry agendas that demand we eliminate the differences between men and women will have to take it up with the Creator. This kind of thinking only succeeds in making women more masculine, defying a clear distinction made in Eden. The sad outcome is merely a race of mannish women. Such world-infused strategies miss the whole point. A woman is given an incredible amount of power. However, her power is a little less heavy-handed and for this very reason might very well be the more powerful power. A woman has just as much capability of changing the world, but if she's wise, she will set out to change it like a woman. If you will allow a deeper definition of "beauty," I think we can agree that to a great extent, a woman equals beauty.

How that beauty is applied to the world makes all the difference. Just as there is a prevalent distortion of the male, there is also a prevalent distortion of the female. There are basically two kinds of women. We'll call them the World Woman and the Real Woman.

The World Woman focuses on whether or not she is beautiful. Even though her design is meant to help people, the World Woman is of no real use in matters of importance, motivated only to help herself. The World Woman has it in her to apply a deeper beauty that could have profound and epic influences. But her agenda uses beauty to draw public admiration and to become a potent attractor of males.

There is nothing wrong with beauty, but it's easy to suspect a misguided perspective when the female half of the human race spends millions of dollars using products to alter their appearance. This alone is no universal failing, but surely something is off when so many females would consider it the greatest of travesties to be seen in public without makeup. The media takes great joy in photographing unpainted celebrities, exposing them as merely human. Men aspire to a certain standard of appearance, but the woman is hounded by merciless criteria.

The world's visual ideal for a woman has changed over the years. A certain weight, a certain hair style, a certain poise—these all shift depending on the decade. But once society has locked in on an image, a woman can find herself in a cruel world. She can feel as if she's always on display, always unable to just be a person. She has to be a person with a particular kind of veneer.

Distracted by her flesh, the female is reduced to trying to maintain the most temporary aspect of her humanity. This does not often bring out the best of the soul inside.

Jezebel was all about presentation. Her superficial nature culminated with one last session at her vanity. Sparkling with the ancient versions of Maybelline and Revlon, she was then unceremoniously thrown to her death. Her exterior beauty was doomed by her interior evil. All her beauty went out the window (II Kings 9:30-37).

Next time someone complains about a girl taking too long to get ready, someone should mention Esther. It took her a year (Esther 2:12). The beauty treatments were a cultural thing—along the lines of the Miss America pageant. Esther's outer beauty was used for good, but it was her inner beauty that was actually quite stunning (Esther 8:3-4).

God made women to be beautiful. If that beauty is just made of mascara and Pilates, then it will be brief and ultimately irrelevant.

The world limits beauty to the epidermis, demanding a specific image—which no real human woman can achieve. Women might briefly achieve this standard, but it is like a precarious spell, broken the moment she speaks, if she finds herself in bad lighting, or if she's just tired. This kind of beauty is a mirage. The world sparks this flickering image and then consumes it.

This results in the worst version of a woman. She is nothing more than physical beauty. All image and no substance. Her looks alone end up being a detriment to everyone around her and even to herself. "Charm is deceitful and beauty is vain" (Proverbs 31: 30). Charm is deceitful because it masks the true state of the soul underneath. Beauty is vain because all by itself, it does no one any good.

This deceitful, vain beauty is why men often spend women like matches. After a girl's appearance runs its course, she burns briefly and is then tossed aside.

On the other hand, there is a beauty that can become profound. "Your adornment must not be merely external—braiding the hair, and wearing gold jewelry, or putting on dresses; but let it be the hidden person of the heart, with the imperishable quality of a gentle and quiet spirit, which is precious in the sight of God" (I Peter 3:3-4). Notice this beauty is not "*merely* external." This implies there's nothing wrong with a woman being pretty or even complimenting it with make-up or accessories. But beauty was meant to reach "the hidden person of the heart." Any allurement that fails to reach this point is not the beauty God intended.

Beauty that includes significant qualities can accomplish incredibly good things. A godly woman does not ignore her beauty. But she is not defined by it.

Wearing the Pants

So as it turns out, the Bible says nothing about whether or not Eve thought Adam was hot. At first, I thought it did. "To the woman He said, 'I will greatly multiply your pain in childbirth, in pain you will bring forth children; yet your desire will be for your husband, and he will rule over you'" (Genesis 3:16). At first glance, "your desire will be for you husband" sounds like Eve looked at Adam and thought *hubba-hubba*. But that's not what this passage means.

The actual meaning is revealed when you notice the same phrasing is used in another part of the Bible. In fact, it's only a page or two away. In Genesis 4, Cain is premeditating murder. However, before he actually kills Abel, there is a key moment when God tells Cain he can still turn away from the darkness in his mind. He then describes sin to Cain in ominous terms. "If you do well, will not your countenance be lifted up? And if you do not do well, sin is crouching at the door; and its desire is for you, but you must master it" (Genesis 4:7). The phrase "its desire is for you" is the same one used earlier to describe the relationship between Eve and Adam. Sin desires Cain in the same way Eve desires Adam.

There are really only two possibilities here. Either sin thinks Cain is dreamy or sin has the potential to overpower Cain. I suggest it's the second one.

Rewinding back to Eden, we find that what God is saying to Eve is that she will *want* to be in charge, but she *won't* be in charge. Adam will be.

I'm not going to debate the woman's role. For the sake of brevity, let's cut to the chase.

"But I want you to understand that Christ is the head of every man, and the man is the head of a woman, and God is the head of Christ" (I Corinthians 11:3). "The husband is the head of the wife, as Christ also is the head of the church, He Himself being the Savior of the body. But as the church is subject to Christ, so also the wives ought to be to their husbands in everything" (Ephesians 5:23-24). "In the same way, you wives, be submissive to your own husbands so that even if any of them are disobedient to the word, they may be won without a word by the behavior of their wives, as they observe your chaste and respectful behavior" (I Peter 3:1-2). The husband is supposed to be in charge. Any disagreement with that basic premise will have to take it up with Scripture.

Over the years, I've seen a lot of men abdicate their leadership. It was mostly noticeable when a guy, shortly after getting married, would abruptly have a transformation of his ideals and even his beliefs. I'm not suggesting that any new ideas a husband may have can definitely be traced back to his new wife. But many times drastic transformations have suspiciously coincided with her arrival.

Before we get ahead of ourselves, we should point out that any man would have to be a fool to ignore his wife's insight. The very fact that the wife was designed to help the husband implies that he needs help. She will be more astute and perceptive about many things that elude him. No clear-headed Christian man would ever just shrug off the help he so desperately needs from his wife. Any man who blindly holds to his beliefs and is unwilling to listen to his wife at all is most likely to settle into a spiritual stagnation or even a decline. The problems come when she is the only primary input.

An embarrassing number of men don't step up to really lead. Husbands are eager to weigh in on finances and the car, but when it comes to things that actually matter—raising the children, strengthening the marriage, and making sure the family is spiritually secure—that all falls into the hands of the wife. Whether or not she actually pursues this arrangement, is beside the point. If the wife is calling the shots on the significant aspects of the family, then once again World Man has won the day, demonstrating an embarrassing lack of strength.

This emasculation probably happens so often and so quickly because men in general are spiritually wimpy even before they get married. Symptoms of this overthrow include an abrupt turn-around in Bible perspective, even to the point of ignoring guidance from those who are scripturally sound. Confronted with a wife who is substituting for the spiritual backbone, he quickly folds against her passionate beliefs, even if they are based more on her emotions than any solid stand on God's Word. Removed from being the true leader of the home, he becomes merely the voice, as guided by his wife. The wife ends up telling the husband what she thinks God wants.

Any husband should listen to his wife, especially on spiritual matters. But her voice is secondary to the voice of the Word. If the majority of the input comes from his wife, the husband is allowing her to have more influence in the matter than God. A wife who is a devoted student of the Word will be a priceless resource to a husband. But a wife who is mostly driven by spiritual fad books and a sincere heart is nothing less than dangerous. If the man is not fully established in the Truth, the whispering in his ear is unchecked and it will taint his perspective.

God pointed out this very thing just before telling Eve she wouldn't be in charge. He pinpointed for Adam the reason things had collapsed into sin. God told Adam it was "Because you have listened to the voice of your wife" (Genesis 3:17). Adam was accountable for his choice (Romans 5:12), but Eve was responsible for instigating it (I Timothy 2:14).

More than a few times, the measure of a husband was found in whether or not he was manipulated by his wife. "So Sarai said to Abram, 'Now behold, the Lord has prevented me from bearing children. Please go in to my maid; perhaps I will obtain children through her.' And Abram listened to the voice of Sarai" (Genesis 16:2). This choice resulted in Hagar giving birth to Ishmael. Even though God blessed this attempt to bypass His own plan, it led to many dark days for many people. When Abram let Sarai lead the way in this spiritual decision, it resulted in family turmoil and ultimately to global warfare.

You find the same male frailty in Jacob, when he became a pawn in a game played between his two wives (Genesis 30). You see it in spineless Ahab when he let his wife Jezebel indulge his selfishness to the extent of framing and murdering an innocent man (I Kings 21).

A whole world of trouble has been caused by men who withdraw from the responsibility of being the man, in the truest sense. This includes maintaining his role as the spiritual leader of the home. A man of God will listen to his wife. But only after first listening to God's Word.

Recipe for a Doomed Marriage

Okay, I'm about to make you mad. At least some of you.

But I'll refer you to the disclaimer in the introduction. Anything you can chalk up to this author's opinion, feel free to quickly discard as the ranting of a long-time bachelor. However, anything built on Scripture will still stand true, despite the disgruntled.

Ready?

One of the greatest mistakes a Christian can make is marrying a non-Christian.

It is very common. You find it everywhere. The fact that it is so widespread probably helps it appear somewhat benign. Yet, if you want a recipe for a marriage to fail, this is the prime ingredient.

In order to fully address this issue, we need to dig deep and get an accurate perspective. Fair warning—this is going to get ugly. For some it's going to get painful. But here it goes.

A Christian, by definition follows Christ. This in turn means that a Christian also belongs to God. A real Christian—not the pew hobbyist, but the real deal—is owned by the Creator. Everything about a Christian, every nook and cranny, every facet, every square inch of the heart and mind has been turned over to God. A Christian, despite sins along the way, is forgiven and therefore on the way to heaven.

A non-Christian is by definition someone who does not follow Christ. This in turn means that a non-Christian does not belong to God. They might be in the process of approaching that decision. They might be a "good" person. They could be nothing less than a shining Ghandhi-esque incarnation of love and kindness, but if they are not a Christian, they do not belong to God. This also includes the pew hobbyist who has deluded themselves into thinking that salvation is secured merely through attendance.

The truth is brutal but undeniable. Everything about a non-Christian, every nook and cranny, every facet, every square inch of the heart and mind belongs to Satan. You don't have to pledge loyalty to the enemy. All you have to do is reject complete devotion to God.

Jesus didn't pull any punches about this. Just having religious flair means nothing. Your actions demonstrate the truth of you. If you don't belong to God, you belong to the devil (John 8). There is no in-between. "You adulteresses, do you not know that friendship with the world is hostility toward God? Therefore, whoever wishes to be a friend of the world makes himself an enemy of God" (James 4:4). If you don't belong to God, you cannot claim the position of religious rookie or apprentice or even a pre-Christian. Until you belong to God, you are His enemy.

I know this sounds really mean—but stay with me.

Even though a non-Christian does not belong to God, they might very well (and often do) have admirable qualities and even godly characteristics that could put many Christians to shame. But since we know that all our righteous acts alone are merely filthy rags (Isaiah 64:6), any "good" person without Jesus is not on their way to heaven. How nice they are carries no currency in the salvation of their soul.

This is not cruel judgment. It is merely pointing out the emergency exit. The only way out of this burning building is through Jesus (John 14:6). You can't just hunker down and be nice.

This is not complicated. In fact, it is painfully simple. A Christian is on their way to heaven. A non-Christian is headed toward complete and eternal separation from God. A

Christian is a child of God (I John 3:1). A non-Christian is an enemy of God (James 4:4). No amount of pleasant reassurances or loving loopholes can alter the truth.

I am well aware that many readers will oppose this. But please believe me, I am not setting out to be unkind. I'm just trying to point out that the reason that so many Married People crash and burn is because the basic machinery of the relationship is built with broken pieces.

Since we're standing among the scattered ruins of thousands and thousands of annihilated marriages, maybe I can be given the benefit of the doubt, at least for a little while, as I point out the possible reason for the wreckage. Let's find the black box, so to speak, and see where it all went wrong.

The Black Box

Allow this basic premise. A Christian is completely saved. A non-Christian is completely lost. If these stark parameters are real, you begin to see why the union of marriage between two such people is a really bad idea.

When a Christian marries a non-Christian, they are not just headed in two different directions. They are headed in *opposite* directions. One of them claims to belong to God. The other by default is an enemy of God. It would be like marrying the sworn enemy of your family. This is not conducive to happiness.

Another basic premise to keep in mind is that marriage was invented by God. It is not an idea mankind thought up along the way. Marriage was invented by God in Eden. The very concept of marriage is built on the idea of joining two people who are spiritually unified in order to help each other get to heaven. It is the primary objective.

A Christian marrying a non-Christian is a defiance of the whole purpose of marriage. The Christian is uniting with someone who is the exact opposite of what a marriage partner should be. Marriage is not just the culmination of a fairy tale or the giddy ending of a romance movie. It is weaving two souls together to help them reach God intact. Everything else, by comparison, is fluff.

There is a passage in the Bible that opposes marrying a non-Christian and it seems pretty straight-forward. "Do not be bound together with unbelievers; for what partnership have righteousness and lawlessness, or what fellowship has light with darkness?" (I Corinthians 6:14). Lots of people will tell you this verse is probably dealing with financial decisions and / or other non-marriage partnerships.

However, this suggests that marriage is a lesser decision than choosing a business partner. Since the union of two souls through marriage is much more significant and intimate, compared to the very temporary and shallow connections in the corporate world, this inspired restriction is relevant *especially* to marriage. Any attempt to disqualify marriage here feels like a lawyer's ploy.

Let me add this gruesome analogy. There is a legend of an ancient punishment where a dead person was tied to the back of a living person. That person had to trudge through their days, hauling this corpse around as it rotted. The smell was horrific, but the worst part was that as decay ran its course, some of the disease would gradually spread to the living person. It was a burden that weighed you down and infected you. You and I both know lots of marriages that parallel this analogy all too well.

I can hear you gritting your teeth, but stay with me just a little longer.

In Jude, a non-Christian is described as someone who is inside a fire (Jude 23). The situation described is so dire, any Christian attempting to help could also put themselves in great danger. The idea is that your attempt at rescuing that lost soul could result in you bursting into flames. Marrying a non-Christian is like handcuffing yourself to a person who is in the process of catching on fire. Or it's like embracing a drowning person. Chances are you will both be lost.

When the people of God were about to enter into Canaan, one of the top priorities God emphasized to the people was a straightforward warning to not marry the people there. "Furthermore, you shall not intermarry with them; you shall not give your daughters to their sons, nor shall you take their daughters for your sons. For they will turn your sons away from following Me to serve other gods; then the anger of the Lord will be kindled against you and He will quickly destroy you" (Deuteronomy 7:3-4). It had nothing to do with race. It had everything to do with the spiritual condition of the souls. As far as God was concerned, to marry outside of the people who belonged to God was a deal-breaker.

Even though this is a constant theme throughout Scripture, a Christian will often choose to bind themselves to a lost soul believing that "true love" will find a way. But all the wreckage should at least make us pause.

We should address a prevalent argument that has already formed in your head. Please excuse any unintentional tone of facetiousness or sarcasm.

But I know lots of situations where a Christian married a non-Christian and it turned out just fine. In fact, the non-Christian eventually became a Christian.

All of us know about those situations. Let me go on record as saying, "Wonderful! Great! I'm so glad it turned out that way!"

However, for each one of these happy endings, we could easily find twenty more that didn't work out that way at all. The husband and wife remained spiritually divided. As a very important side note, these circumstances have the additional disaster of sons and daughters fractured on a spiritual level as their parents pull them two different directions.

Let's go ahead and elaborate on the opposing argument.

But if they hadn't gotten married, then that Christian would have not been converted.

Again, I am so thrilled to hear about these happy endings. But it's very important to know something about all events that occur in this world. The ends do not justify the means.

God will often take a bad choice and shape the results into a wonderful outcome. He used the murderous conspiracy of Joseph's brothers, the conniving immorality of Potipher's wife, and a selfish negligence of a cupbearer to bring about the rescue of a whole family (Genesis 50:20). But that doesn't mean any of these choices were in and of themselves good. To justify marrying a non-Christian with the hope they might become a Christian is like one of Joseph's brothers suggesting they stage his murder and sell him into slavery because it might eventually be a good thing.

To choose a path that defies God's consistent warnings and then suggest the decision is okay with God is an incredible assumption. Just about anything can be justified with that kind of reasoning.

God often uses mistakes to bring about blessings, but that doesn't mean we pursue mistakes. How much more will a person be blessed who stands by their devotion to God, even if it costs them someone they love?

The Ballad of Fred and Vanessa

I have a friend who met the love of his life in high school. We'll call him Fred and we'll call her Vanessa.

Fred really liked Vanessa. Vanessa really liked Fred. The only problem was that Vanessa was a Christian and Fred was not. Unlike most Christians in her situation, Vanessa decided to not make any compromises. She was all too aware of their spiritual differences and stood firmly on the other side of a very distinct line. She told Fred their relationship would not be going anywhere beyond friendship because he wasn't a Christian.

Just about any other Christian girl wouldn't have hesitated to choose romance. Just about any other Christian girl wouldn't have let anything as minor as the issue of salvation get in the way of "true love." After all, you can't fight destiny.

But Vanessa did not budge. She would not date a non-Christian, let alone marry a non-Christian. She made that very clear to Fred.

Fred of course was distraught and didn't understand. At this point, a lot of guys would have turned and walked away. Most would have pursued another girl. One that wasn't so complicated.

But Vanessa's adamant standard intrigued Fred. It didn't make sense. It seemed kind of over-the-top. But it was obviously incredibly important to her. It was so important, she was willing to walk away from him. A lot of guys would have walked away, too, but Fred didn't. He stuck around.

Fred and Vanessa settled into a friendship and nothing more. Eventually, because of college and job opportunities, they even grew apart to a certain extent. But the one thing that did not fade was Fred's admiration for Vanessa's morals.

This admiration was so strong that one day, Fred decided to start trying to find out more about her beliefs. At first, he was drawn to the search because he was interested in Vanessa. But it didn't take long for him to begin searching for God in a very genuine way. In fact, during much of this time, he visited a congregation Vanessa did not attend.

You know where this story is going, so let's jump to the end.

Fred became a Christian and he married Vanessa.

Everyone has the free will to choose God or reject Him. When Vanessa turned Fred down, if Fred had continued to live without God, that would have been Fred's decision. There would have other opportunities to find God other than through his friendship with Vanessa.

But his friendship with Vanessa had all the more of an impact on him because of her unwavering beliefs and what she was willing to sacrifice for those beliefs.

Vanessa could have convinced herself that marrying Fred would have been some kind of spiritual outreach. But because she was not willing to join her soul to someone who was headed away from God, *that* was the outreach to Fred. *That* is what saved him.

Of course there is always the possibilities of imposters. There is always the flake who will gladly go through the motions. He will tag along on the girl's arm. He will go to church. He will sit in the pew. He will bow his head. *Sit, Boyfriend. Sit.* Many a marriage has been sabotaged from the beginning by one of the people going into a marriage with a fake Christianity. It's important that both people know the true nature of the other person's relationship with God.

One last thing. Think about this issue from the perspective of the enemy. An outright effort to get a person to turn away from God rarely works. The attack has to come in the form of something you want or even love. What better way to sabotage a Christian's life than to pry open their standards with romance, so they end up linked to a dead person?

Whatever positive influence a Christian can have on someone they love is quickly smothered if they betray their standards. Anyone who is truly concerned about the soul of the one they care for as well as their own soul—and the souls of their future children—will be willing to trust God's ways of doing things.

Someone who walks away from you because of your devotion to God is not the one for you. To handcuff yourself to them and jump off a cliff, hoping for the best—the best you can hope for is a very long fall.

Pre-Nuptial Sabotage

One of the most creative sins we've ever come up with is "living together." It just makes sense. Before you get married, you try out a marriage-type arrangement for a while to see if you're "compatible." It's a kind of test-drive / trial-run before you actually commit to anything on paper or with rings.

It sure seems like a good idea, but there is more than one reason why it's a really bad idea.

First—it's a sin. "For this is the will of God, your sanctification; that is, that you abstain from sexual immorality" (I Thessalonians 4:3). This is where the conversation should end. Just the fact that it's something obviously condemned by God should just about wrap it up. He said don't sleep together unless you're married. But apparently for many people, this isn't enough.

So here's an additional, lesser reason. People who live together before they get married have a higher divorce rate than people who don't. There are polls that say otherwise. There are studies that claim the percentages are improving. However, there is enough research that should at least make people have second thoughts.

You can line up all kinds of rationalizations as to why it's a good idea, but the results are in. If you live together first, there is something in this approach that often taints any future effort for a permanent relationship. By living together, people essentially sabotage their hope for a marriage that will last.

It comes back to one particular strong possibility—that God knows what He's talking about. He designed us. He designed love and how we connect through love. Maybe He has some insight on the matter.

Marriage is meant to be a commitment. Everything in Scripture about marriage assumes a life-long devotion that defies time. Two people living like Married People without actually being married are counterfeit creatures. They are imposters, masquerading as united souls. The truth is felt in the ambience of instability. It is a door left slightly ajar. It is the ultimate unresolved chord. It is conditional love. With the intimacy of sex involved, it is an insult to both souls who have given each other everything except devotion.

Living together is like having children, but only letting them remain with you depending on how difficult they become. To see if they're compatible. Can you imagine the child trying to develop any kind of closeness with their mother or father if there was always the option that Mom and Dad might at any moment decide to just call things off?

Life would be lived under a grim shadow. No matter how many lullabies, or loving words, or warm hugs, there would always be the sensation of something held back. The relationship would be reduced to mere superficial maintenance. No matter how much you might "try to make it work," there would always be a horrible temporary nature to the relationship.

Even if the mother or father said "Okay we think this will work, we'll keep you." The stigma of that initial lack of commitment would remain. Everyone involved would be offering only conditional devotion. They would be a person who is in it for the long run, as long as things don't run too long.

Let's be honest. The truth about living together comes down to some very basic issues. The underlying concern is whether or not the two people will remain sexually attracted to each other. Whether or not the everyday mundane aspects of personalities will get annoying. Whether or not someone more attractive might come along. Let me offer some answers to all three of these basic issues.

No, there will be times when you will not be sexually attracted to each other. In fact, if you're doing marriage right, sex will ultimately become less than the primary force that connects you. Sex does not have to fade or even decline in significance, but there are actually other more important things that make two people resonate on a deep level.

Yes, there will be a whole bunch of things about the other person that will drive you crazy. They will annoy you in a way that only they seem to have a knack for doing. They will push your buttons and make you grit your teeth. But good luck finding someone who doesn't.

Yes, you will come across someone else who is attractive. The world is filled with eye candy, but if you're only living life for candy, be ready for a sad and lonely ending.

Let's just leave it as this. Living together has a horrible track record. It indulges the worst of both people and it is an insult to the relationship.

The Law of Amusement Parks

There's another world-idea that has crept into our thinking. You can find it in the subplot of many romantic comedies and it seems to haunt a lot of real Married People.

The idea is that the only way to maintain love in a marriage is to make sure sex remains wild and fulfilling. If for some reason, that physical act wavers or wanes, that love is doomed. As a result, when sex becomes less than fiery, many couples call it quits. After all, "they have needs."

I have to be honest. When I hear that tired phrase, I want to say, "Yeah, I agree. You do have needs. In fact, you have one particular need. You need to grow up." (I just think it—I don't actually say it.)

It's a subtle but prevalent idea that love is all about maintaining that physical spark. Don't get me wrong. Some of the wiser and spiritually strong Married People I've talked to have emphasized how important it is to keep romance alive. What a sad story it is if the husband and wife settle into being only platonic roommates.

Let's hear it for the old man who still writes poems for his wife. Let's hear it for the old woman who goes out of her way to greet her husband dressed in elegance and a smile that belong only to him.

But there are many, many stories out there of a desperation to sustain some kind of guttural, artificial passion. As time goes by and familiarity comes into play, there is apparently a kind of panic. In service to selfish libidos, there are even ventures into degradation.

Creativity in the bedroom notwithstanding, there is a tendency for shallower solutions. Motivated by insecurity, the wife will look to implants and Botox, not to just look better, but to "save the marriage." Feeling the same insecurity, the husband will scramble for various tactics to look and act young. There are even Married People who resort to pornography to dredge up one more flicker of desire.

If that's all there is—if the only thing connecting two people is their physical attraction, then nothing can be done for them. Eventually, all the procedures and treatments will be defeated by time.

Love is not just chemical fireworks. We are more than cascading hormones. We are more than our containers and hopefully, there is something attractive about the soul inside the body.

Trying to build a relationship mostly on sex is dooming yourself to the Law of Amusement Parks. Consider Disneyland, Six Flags, Worlds of Fun, and every little state fair conglomeration of contraptions that seem designed to reveal what you had for lunch. It's all based on the thrill. Almost every year, in order to draw the crowds, an amusement park has to build a new ride. There has to be something new, something that can provide a bigger hit of excitement, or the people will start losing interest. You can only ride The Twister or the Mind Eraser so many times before the experience declines toward ho-hum.

Running a marriage according to the Law of Amusement Parks is a doomed enterprise. You can only play that game for so long. Eventually it will degrade love into a circus of stimulus and response.

Married People don't fall deeper in love by desperately attempting to match the expectations of the world. Real love and solid marriages don't happen through desperation to maintain one small part of love, but by growing every aspect of love.

Adultery at Ground Zero

It would be somewhat irresponsible to discuss the pitfalls of marriage without addressing the deepest pit of all. Nothing less than an abyss.

Adultery.

There are numerous marriages that have survived this sin. Adultery always causes damage, but it is very possible for

Married People to fully recover. They can shine just as bright as before and reach the blessings waiting for those who fully belong to each other.

From what I understand, for marriages that have survived this devastation, the best thing to do is to completely forget it. Once there is repentance, once there is forgiveness, it can never be used as leverage during an argument. It has to fade. It has to be like something that happened to someone else—a couple you once knew, but have since lost contact with.

Many Married People have dealt with adultery and recovered completely. Let's not talk about them. Let's allow them to move on to the bright future.

But as far as the sin itself, we need to pause and take a look. As we do, it's important we don't allow the world to have any influence on our perspective. It's important we see the truth.

Without belaboring the obvious, adultery is wrong. God ended any debate about it on Sinai. "You shall not commit adultery" (Exodus 20:14). Sin is sin, but adultery under the old covenant was punishable by death (Leviticus 20:10; Deuteronomy 22:22). Under the old covenant, God allowed capital punishment as an appropriate response. The fact that the new covenant does not allow execution for adultery, does not make it any less serious. Jesus actually made the condemnation even more adamant by holding anyone accountable who even considered adultery in their heart (Matthew 5:18). Total spiritual separation from God waits for anyone with "eyes full of adultery" (II Peter 2:14). Although there is no loss of lives under the new covenant, there is still loss of souls. It is a sin that causes incredible damage not only to the one who committed it, but to countless others.

Like many of you, there have been times when I was hit with the news. The preliminary, ominous silence said everything. I knew what I was going to hear. Whenever there was "something bad" to be disclosed, it was obvious what it was going to be. When someone has committed adultery it has the same shock level as hearing someone diagnosed with a terminal disease. Even if you are not directly affected, the indirect impact leaves you speechless. The impact for those directly involved must be almost impossible to measure.

It's vital we emphasize the disastrous nature of this mistake. Not to dig up dead memories, but to counteract society as it tries to make adultery seem small. If more people saw adultery as it really is, they might be less likely to even go near it.

There are so many analogies that might work for us here. But I'll use only one.

Maybe the most appropriate comparison is a nuclear bomb. When something gets nuked, it doesn't just destroy the target. Those who are within a certain range, even if they survive the initial blast, will die of radiation poisoning.

Plus, there's something called fallout. After such an explosion, radioactive particles infect the weather system, and depending on the severity of the blast, the range and damage of its effect is frightening. The full effect of such a bomb is impossible to predict, but it is always far more severe than expected.

Adultery can destroy a marriage as thoroughly as Hiroshima. After the explosion, there might be nothing left of the Married People involved—just a faint resemblance of who they were, like two shadows burned on a wall. Those in the vicinity of the marriage also suffer. The fallout of the sin can be as widespread and poisonous as radiation. Even if everyone ends up spiritually surviving, it can take a long time for full reconstruction.

The world doesn't think of adultery in these terms. The world spins marital betrayal as something minor. The world calls it "cheating" or "slipping" or that oldie but goodie: "an affair." Our culture has gotten very good at romanticizing this particular sin. The potential for this sin is nestled in the heart of every person, but for men especially, adultery is treated as almost unavoidable. It's considered the nature of the beast. The world says everyone just needs to understand that a man isn't designed for monogamy. Given such a license to fail, it's no wonder so many men do.

There are probably a thousand reasons why someone might choose this mistake. It can be the culmination of a series of selfish decisions made by incredibly selfish people. It can be a sudden snare that appears between two friends who never would have dreamed of even going near such a catastrophe. It can begin with a premeditated search or even a simple comment. Not everyone sets out to fall.

But here's a thought. If a person has moved through the dating process like most people do, that means they have already crossed the line into sexual immorality more than a few times. Since sex was not honored as valuable and not restricted to marriage before the fact, that broken line becomes easier to cross after the fact.

Someone who has delayed intimacy strictly for marriage will have a much more difficult time even considering pursuing that same intimacy with someone other than their spouse. Sleeping together and even living together, along with all the other compromises the world promotes, make adultery much more likely. In fact, for some it probably just feels like the next step.

People are convinced that sleeping around can be shut down by the exchange of rings. But this alone is a precarious arrangement. A consistently sinful heart is not so easily restrained. When things go wrong and the timing is right, someone will "slip." Their footing was never reliable. Just saying "I do" often does very little to make them more sure-footed. People who approach marriage through a series of sinful relationships are primed for adultery.

Once more, a thousand cheers for the survivors. But here and now, before the next person makes such a dumb mistake, we should all see adultery for what it is. Perspective is always a good thing. So for the sake of clarity, to anyone who might ever even consider adultery, do yourself and everyone around a favor. Set off a nuclear bomb instead. You'll do less damage.

Love and Amputation

I don't remember when I first heard about it or even saw it, but I eventually learned that Married People can end up not being married anymore. It's one of the darkest words you'll ever hear: divorce.

I had a friend who only had one parent. No one died. It's just that one of his parents left. Technically, my friend still had two parents, but not in the same house. My friend had two households. Two childhoods. My friend was broken into two smaller versions of himself. He had two houses, but no home. Not really.

Typically, the children are with the mom. On occasion, the dad appears to take his turn. Neither one of them can be parents at the same time anymore. Now, it's lop-sided love. Most of the "quality time" is spent doing damage control. Holidays and weekends aren't vacations anymore. They're bargaining tables.

Hollywood chimes in to try and make it sound like kids are especially resilient when faced with this particular difficulty. Some even imply the children are even better off for it. After all, it would be worse for the children if two people stayed together if they don't love each other, right?

As always, it's best to jump right to the hard truth. Here's what God thinks about it. "But I say to you that everyone who divorces his wife, except for the reason of unchastity, makes her commit adultery; and whoever marries a divorced woman commits adultery" (Matthew 5:32). He braces up this hard and fast standard by referring back to the original marriage. "But from the beginning of creation, God made them male and female. For this reason, a man shall leave his father and mother and the two shall become one flesh; so they are no longer two, but one flesh. What therefore God has joined together, let no man separate" (Mark 10:6-9). As far as He's concerned, the nature of the union between Adam and Eve has everything to do with the union of Married People today.

He then leads us to the truth about divorce. The nature of the union between Married People determines the nature of attempt at disconnection. "Whoever divorces his wife and marries another woman commits adultery against her; and if she herself divorces her husband and marries another man, she is committing adultery" (Mark 10:11-12). There is one and only one reason given that can authorize a divorce. Any reason other than adultery is not authorized. Since the union is drastic, the reason for any disunion must also be drastic.

Using the concept of "one flesh" established in Eden, we can suggest that divorce is nothing less than amputation.

The first rule of amputation is don't do it unless it's absolutely necessary. As far as God is concerned, adultery is the only circumstances that might lead to such a decision.

You don't amputate your arm unless it becomes a threat to the rest of the body. In the same fashion, don't even consider divorcing your spouse unless they are corrupted to the point of committing adultery. Even then, there might a way to avoid such brutal surgery.

If we take world-thinking and apply it to this analogy, it might help reveal how far we've come in our thinking.

Sure, sure—don't amputate the arm unless it becomes a threat to the rest of the body. *But what if the arm hurts? What if the arm doesn't always do what you want it to do? What if the arm is not as strong or sleek as it once was?* Take those reasons to your doctor and note his response. The look on your doctor's face might be a good measure of how messed up our thinking has become in regard to divorce. In all these instances, amputation is a ridiculous option.

There are many cases of abuse and it would be more than logical and spiritually responsible to choose separation. But there is a difference between divorce and separation, in the same way there is a difference between restraining your arm and amputating it. The bottom line is that divorce should only be considered as a last resort as guided by God's Word.

Even those who have been trampled by adultery have often found the means through forgiveness to salvage the limb, so to speak. Just like you doctor would tell you, there are other options to consider before amputation. Divorce is emergency surgery done only in the most extreme circumstances—to possibly escape the gangrene of sin that has led to adultery. It is not a break-up. It is the equivalent of lopping off a limb. It is trauma and blood loss. It is a gruesome procedure that leaves half a person. Even the most complete person is left undone when the union of marriage is severed.

Most of the time, the woman is the one who is abandoned. God points to the man as the typical guilty party. God uses the book of Malachi to show that when men leave their wives, it isn't just an indicator of irresponsibility toward marriage. It is irresponsibility toward God. He also emphasizes that He has been quite aware of how they have treated their wives. "The Lord has been a witness between you and the wife of your youth, against whom you have dealt treacherously, though she is your companion and your wife by covenant" (Malachi 2:14). God will hold accountable any man who abandons his wife.

For many a man it's almost standard procedure. He fuels the marriage with world-thinking and when he burns up whatever good was in the relationship, he seeks to undo it—to set himself free so he can pursue another woman. Using rationalization and veiled selfishness, the "wife of his youth" is quickly and efficiently discarded. Whether she was a shrew or a shrill nag, it doesn't change the fact the man failed to stand firm. Any macho posturing is a lie. He is no man.

The woman who ventures off to find "true love," abandoning her husband and children is no princess. On the fairy tale landscape, she has become the one who coldly leaves her loved ones in the dark forest.

I know it's pretty easy for someone like me to sit back and calmly ramble on about divorce. I realize that every single situation has its own unique complications. But the bottom line is this. Marriage is made to last a lifetime.

The world's version of marriage is counterfeit. The world is eager to make divorce seem relatively benign. But God feels the exact opposite. "For I hate divorce" (Malachi 2:16). That alone should make someone pause before they get out the bone saw.

WorldSpeak 3—You Deserve to Be Happy

I know of a man who had a wife and four sons. He was a leader in the church. After twelve years of marriage, he abandoned his family.

A guy and a girl I knew in college got married right after they graduated. Within a few years, she left him. They even had a child, but she walked away from both of them and never came back.

I was friends with a young couple who attended the same congregation as me. Out of the blue, the girl decided she was going to leave the marriage. Several Christian friends met with her, pleading for her to reconsider. She still believed in God. She knew it was wrong to leave, but nothing anyone said could change her mind. She left.

There are lots of others. You know all too many yourself. It's a tired tale. Everything seems fine. You see them at church. You see them smiling. From where you're standing, it all appears very stable and secure.

Then the shocker. Someone tells you the news. One of them left. They just—left.

I've often wondered about them. It was always hard for me to imagine how someone could just suddenly open the door and walk away. The ones who really astounded me were those who left children behind as well as their spouse.

To me, the most surprising thing about all of these decisions was how sudden they seemed. For those of us on the outside (the crowd gawking at the wreckage) everything up to that point had seemed to be running so smoothly. These happy people were living their married life. They had a spouse and children and jobs and routines. But then all of the sudden, they became this other person. They went rogue.

Some of them were never real. They were fakes the whole time. They never were ever really what they pretended to be. They were imposters, posing as a husband or mimicking the image of a wife. This is not to say there was never any affection or love, but they were never truly present in the marriage. Even as they said "till death do us part," they had one foot out the door.

They went through the motions for a while, possibly hoping the marriage would make them more real. Maybe they were thinking it might make them be good. But the veneer chipped away and the real person surfaced in a calamitous burst of selfishness. And poof—they vanished in a puff of car exhaust.

For others, it was different. When they said "till death do us part," they really meant it. On every level, they really did mean it. Saying "I do" rang true for them. They jumped in with both feet and were ready to stay for good. So what about them? How does someone like that become the person taking off their ring and then taking off?

It eventually hit me. I was seeing it all wrong. I had misread everything. Something like that didn't just happen overnight. No one just wakes up one morning and decides to uproot from everything that once mattered so deeply to them. There had to be some kind of gradual lead-up.

You can bet they lay awake at night, thinking it over. As they went about their day, brushing their teeth, eating lunch, waiting at stoplights, the plan began to grow. Even as they said "goodnight" to their family, they were figuring out how to say "goodbye." There had to have been some stuff in their head for some time.

I think I know what it is now. Maybe not in all cases, but in most of them.

It's a direct result of yet another bit of WorldSpeak.

"You deserve to be happy."

This is spoken by well-meaning friends. It's not necessarily a horrible thing to say to someone who might be down on themselves. But when you get right down to it, it's kind of a lie.

The truth is, you *don't* deserve to be happy. You actually deserve to be nailed to a cross and left there until you suffocate to death.

Fortunately, even though every single one of us deserves such a thing because of our sins, God has made other arrangements. He sent His Son to go through that horrible experience in our place. We now can have the privilege of continuing to live, despite our mistakes.

When it comes to what we deserve, it's important to put some light on the matter. Each one of us is worthy of execution. "For the wages of sin is death" (Romans 6:23). It's called the Law of Sin and Death. The only price for any sin is death.

One sin kills us spiritually (Isaiah 59:1-2). God has postponed our physical death for an undetermined amount of time so that we can recover from spiritual damage. In light of the fact, that we are all on death row, it seems kind of silly to campaign for what we "deserve."

I know it sounds harsh, but no one *deserves* to be happy. It's not something owed to you. It's not something you earned.

It's fine if you end up being happy. That's great. It's even better if you hope that someone else has happiness. But no one deserves it.

The reason I'm being so hard-nosed about this is because I believe it is this particular bit of WorldSpeak nonsense that is the culprit. This is why those people walk out the door.

It's easy to imagine the thought process. A man finds himself struggling through the challenges of being a husband and father. His job is exhausting and all his responsibilities drain him of any passion for life. All the images he once had about his future are trampled by the mundane march of everyday drudgeries.

At this point, instead of seeking to salvage joy in the current circumstances—instead of standing firm by his responsibilities, he begins to consider a new perspective. Life has robbed him of the happiness he deserves. He deserves to be happy.

So he leaves.

A woman is discouraged that marriage has fizzled into something less than the passion of her adolescent daydreams. She drinks in movies and sips romance novels. Slowly, but surely, she becomes convinced there is a better life "out there" with someone different who will understand her. Life is going by and she isn't fulfilled. Instead of holding to her commitment, she decides to "follow her heart." She deserves to be happy.

So she leaves.

The idea that we deserve to be happy thrives on one of the core flaws of all human beings. We are selfish. If it is nurtured, we think anything standing in our way needs to be cast aside in honor of "being true to ourselves."

Even if you make good choices, the idea that you deserve to be happy can hide in the shadows. Your spouse becomes nothing more than an acquirement on your wish list. Children ultimately serve the purpose of making you complete as a person. It's kind of startling when you fully begin to realize how insanely selfish you are. Every sunrise is about finding a new day in which you can serve the self.

With the lie firmly embedded in your head, you set out with expectations about the future and how it will all play out so that you find the happiness you deserve. But things don't go as planned. Tough times can wear away your optimism. Your spouse falls short of what you imagined. Marriage becomes an effort and raising children seems mostly an exercise in punishment and scowls. Life becomes blah.

So some husbands begin to linger at other doors. Some women gaze out the window a little too long. They've seen enough movies to know that an adventurous romance is waiting out there, just beyond the end of the driveway. Home is where the heart has yet to be.

They begin to rationalize. They justify themselves. They make everyone around them the bad guy. It's not them, it's their circumstances or their spouse. Anything but them.

A basic rule of thumb in writing a novel or a screenplay is to make sure the bad guy doesn't know he's the bad guy. A legitimate villain doesn't know he's the bad guy. He perceives everything in such a way that his selfish motives are only common sense.

This is what happens. The husband is disillusioned by his marriage and his home. The wife is heartbroken because her happily-ever-after only turned out to be only ever-after. So they panic. As they hit mid-life, they become keenly aware that time is passing by and that life has not turned out the way they wanted. Maybe there's still time to find the original dream. The current dream is certainly not working out. Time for a re-do. I'm not happy here, so it must be out there. Whether or not the abandoned spouse or children might be happy is irrelevant. They are merely collateral damage.

I realize I'm probably oversimplifying here. I'm sure there are situations that make things complicated. There are many people living in horrible situations, resigned to a darkness you wouldn't wish on anybody.

What we're talking about here is the person who lets selfishness justify sin. Not one of us *deserves* to be happy. The sooner more Married People realize this, the happier they would be.

Fool in the Water

Once upon a time, there was this really handsome guy. He was extremely handsome. He was so handsome that every woman who saw him, immediately fell in love with him. Wherever he went, females gazed adoringly.

He was so insanely handsome that one day when he went to the river to get a drink of water, when he looked down at the water, he saw his own reflection for the first time, he thought it was some lovely girl, and fell in love with himself. His name was Narcissus.

I know, I know. How do you confuse yourself for another person? For that matter how do you confuse yourself for another gender? It also makes you wonder how he could come this far in life without ever seeing a mirror before. How does a guy who wows the girls like this maintain any kind of style without ever having checked to see if his hair was sticking up or if there was food in his teeth?

Regardless, the story says Narcissus saw his reflection and became fully infatuated with the image. He sat there on the bank of the river mesmerized by himself. But, whenever he reached for the image, his fingertips would disrupt the surface of the water and his beloved would disappear into meaningless ripples.

Unfortunately, he never snapped out of it. In fact, his obsession became so overwhelming, he tried to embrace the image and ended up drowning—a victim of his own good looks. He fell in love with himself.

This mythological character is now part of our language. This is why when we are talking about an extremely self-centered person, we can call them narcissistic.

The moral of the story is don't fall in love with yourself. But there are other possible insights here.

Married People have a lot of things to overcome. They have to take on bills and sickness and plain old exhaustion. However, one of the most significant obstacles I have observed in Married People is selfishness. We're not just talking about people who are arrogant or uppity. Even a soft-spoken recluse can be selfish by indulging in self-pity. Granted, Single People can be just as selfish, but if you combine two selfish people in a marriage, the sum is worse than the parts. Marriage can be a collision of two people with intensely selfish agendas.

The results are similar to Narcissus. People think they are reaching out to someone else, but they are actually only wanting to reach for a reflection of themselves—or at least their expectations. When the other person inevitably fails to meet these expectations, the image ripples and they are disappointed. Love ends up being forever out of reach, shimmering and shattering at a touch.

If I had to pick one culprit that is the most responsible for the most wreckage in this landscape of marriage, it would have to be selfishness. This is why, just like Narcissus, so many marriages are doomed. As long as both people are intent on pursuing their own happiness, there will be no happy ending.

Backward Planet

Something's wrong with the system. As far as all the things we do in order to become Married People, there is a lot that needs to change. There are definitely some flaws in the system. But as far as marriage itself, there is nothing wrong with the system. It's perfect.

You can't blame a car for not running well if you treat it badly. If you pour honey in the fuel tank or you drive over the "severe-tire-damage" spikes, you can't stand beside the incapacitated vehicle and claim the car was badly designed.

We have allowed the world to have too much say. Instead of relying on God for guidance, in all things romantic, in all things concerning married life, we have let the world call the shots. And the world has gotten it all mixed up.

God set up the system. Then the world turned it around. The truth is easy to see. God expects certain things to occur in a certain order. The world expects the same things to occur in a different order.

Discounting some minor exceptions, here is the order God expects:

Attraction
Love

Marriage
Sex

The world has severely mixed things up:

Attraction
Sex
Love
Marriage

This is typical of the world. When it comes to right and wrong, the world will get everything turned around. "Woe to those who call evil good, and good evil; Who substitute darkness for light and light for darkness" (Isaiah 5:20). The world can corrupt anything, tangling up ideas of right and wrong—even to the point of getting everything completely backwards.

For Married People, the world has caused major havoc adding such things as "living together" and an indulgence in chronic lust. And that's just the trip there. Once people are married, there are so many other threats.

People who become Married People might actually go through a ceremony that gives a token nod to the Creator, but after that, the marriage is primarily built on world ideas. This can be easily seen in how husbands and wives typically treat love. It's all backwards.

According to I Corinthians 13, love is patient and kind and not selfish and doesn't remember wrongs and is not jealous. The world has a different approach. Although the world will allow this to be read at the wedding, as far as putting those things into practice every day during marriage—not so much. In fact, the world promotes the exact opposite of God's criteria about love.

A brief corruption of the text proves the point. *Love is impatient, unkind, selfish, remembering wrongs and it's jealous.* Just about any romantic will deny these, but behavior says otherwise.

According to the world, love doesn't wait—it will defy any obstacle to serve desire. Love is unkind—it indulges some of the most spiteful snippiness. Love is selfish—it wallows in self-pity or passion. Love is jealous—it undermines trust and suspected impurity.

It's all twisted. When this twisted thinking infiltrates the connection between Married People, it causes a whole lot of damage.

Another example of backward world-thinking can be found by analyzing another passage. According to the Bible, a wife is supposed to focus on her husband. She's not supposed to pine after the knight in grimy armor that never graced her pristine palace. Every day is about devotion to her husband. "But as the church is subject to Christ, so also the wives ought to be to their husbands in everything" (Ephesians 5:24). A wife is meant to be devoted to her husband with the same daily devotion of the church toward Jesus.

A husband is supposed to focus on his wife. He is not supposed to be daydreaming of a slinky soul-mate who understands him better. He is supposed to be incredibly busy making sure his wife is okay. "Husbands, love your wives, just as Christ also loved the church and gave Himself up for her" (Ephesians 5:25). Christ did not love the church in a hit-and-miss fashion. Every single moment of every single day was designed to serve the church. A husband is meant to have the same intense devotion toward his wife as Jesus does for the church.

But the world has it all quite backwards. The wife is focused on herself. The husband is focused on himself. They have brief bouts of interaction, followed immediately by withdrawing to separate corners to measure their own happiness. However, if they did it the right way, they would be so busy serving the other one, they wouldn't have time to ponder whether or not they were getting the happiness they "deserve."

Ironically, one of the worst possible ways to get happiness is to pursue it. I realize the US government gives us the earthly right to chase after happiness, and the gesture is much appreciated in that it protects our efforts to make the most of our physical life.

Yet, the point still stands. All the health or wealth or laughter or beautiful moments are bonuses that none of us deserve. Don't get too caught up in the "rights" provided by a generous nation. On an earthly level, that freedom does ring true. But when it comes to the nitty-gritty truth of existence, we deserve nothing.

Any happiness that has any real duration or depth comes from serving others. This is not a Christian hobby. It is built into the fundamental nature of every human being who ever lived. If husbands and wives are focused on making each other happy, they will discover their own happiness.

Looking around at the wreckage of so many marriages, you can clearly see something is wrong. To blindly swoop into a wedding with giddy grins, thinking you'll be the exception just because you think you're the exception is foolishness.

Love will find a way.

Nope. It won't. Look at the ruins. This is what "love" found.

It's God who will find a way. His ideas of love are the only reliable ones. The rest is candy and poison.

The only hope any Married People have is to go the Word every day for clarity. Both of them have to let the Word shape their thinking to fight the world's input. This is how they can counteract the world tampering with their minds. This is how they can keep it from sabotaging their marriage.

A refined perception through the Word makes all the difference. It helps Married People see love as a choice and not as an affliction that comes and goes. It helps them see that their own happiness will be found in securing the happiness of the other. It helps them see things as they really are.

It's not as complicated as we might think. The only way to do it right is to include God. Until the husband and wife both belong to God, there will always be something missing. If God is kept at arm's length, relegated to a brief visit on Sunday, the marriage is still doomed.

Going into marriage without God is like taking off in a plane and then shoving the pilot off. Things will cruise along just fine—for a while.

The take-off went really well. There are blue skies ahead and the excitement of the trip is in full swing. But eventually, no matter how hard you try, without God, you will begin the descent, and it will not be a good landing.

This is why we stand here in the rubble.

But I'm happy to say, there are some Married People who are doing just fine. They are a rare species, but they do exist.

PART 5

THE
FOR-REALS

Cautionary Tale

When I was in college, I met a guy who was engaged. I had met other people who were engaged, but the reason I remember him so well is because I saw him fall apart. Let's call him Ryan.

He and I and a handful of other guys traveled together to a Christian youth camp. All of us were unattached except for Ryan. He was attached. He had given a ring to a girl back home. Let's call her Alice.

Ryan and Alice were engaged. That meant that he had asked her to marry him and she had said yes. They planned to eventually complete a ceremony that would result in them spending the rest of their lives together. At the time, even in my college years, the idea of me asking a girl to marry me sounded as bizarre as asking a girl to join me in a padded cell—forever.

But once in a while, I could imagine getting married. I knew that I wouldn't be pursuing it any time soon.

When we pulled into the campground, everything seemed great. We got out of the van and we were made to feel welcome. But within an hour, Ryan had a kind of meltdown.

I remember very clearly watching him break into a sweat. His eyes were wild and he couldn't seem to get his breath. It was sort of like a cross between a panic attack and a seizure. It took us a while to get him to tell us what was wrong. Finally, after much coaxing, he explained.

It just so happened that an old girlfriend of his was at the campground. He had no idea she was going to be there and when he bumped into her, he was totally caught off guard. Years ago, they had dated pretty seriously. Let's call her Brenda.

Ryan said he was shocked to discover he still had feelings for Brenda. He had made a commitment to Alice with the engagement ring, but now here he was—faced with Brenda—and suddenly he wasn't so sure Alice was the right choice.

Ryan was a mess.

The end of the story is that Ryan went home, broke up with Alice, then proposed to, and eventually married, Brenda. I guess you could call it a happy ending—except for Alice. I suppose she ended up marrying someone else and found her own happy ending.

But at the time, none of this matters to me. What I remember most from that incident isn't Ryan, the-guy-engaged-to-Alice. It isn't Ryan the-guy-who-married-Brenda. The image burned into my brain is Ryan the-meltdown.

It wasn't like I hadn't seen wreckage of love before. I had strolled the ruins long enough to have seen plenty of couples crash-and-burn. I had seen more than a few marriages gone bad—real bad. I had seen enough to develop a healthy share of disillusionment.

But Ryan was different. He had been so sure. He had been 100% positive he had found the girl for him. He was so confident, he proposed to her. Then, he had been pulled into a turmoil of emotions with all the violence of someone yanked into a tree shredder. After he recovered, he unproposed to the first girl and proposed to the other one.

I made a vow to myself that day. (I'm not kidding.) I would never ever propose to a girl unless I was absolutely sure. I was not going to be the next meltdown.

When you walk the landscape of broken people, it's hard to not become cynical.

But that's not all there is. Believe it or not, there are those out there who are doing just fine. They are not just putting up a pretense. They're for real.

General Characteristics

Before we take a closer look and observe the behavior of Married People in their natural habitat, we should go over a few things.

Married People are not born married. They start out as a

Single Person. As we have already discussed, there is typically a transition period called "dating." This often leads to two of them making the decision to become "married."

Although marriage is an incredibly powerful transformation, Married People look just like everyone else. Even though there are profound differences, it's not always that easy to tell them apart from other people. There is nothing drastically unusual about their appearance. They do not glow. They do not necessarily smile all the time. However, one of the few distinguishing features is a ring on the fourth finger of the left hand.

This ring indicates that the Married Person is connected to another Married Person. The other Married Person is called the "spouse." The male of the species is called the "husband." The female is referred to as the "wife."

Although they are two separate individuals, they are joined together through a ceremony called a "wedding." From then on they are to exist in a condition called "marriage." They still retain the ability to think and speak and act on their own, but they also demonstrate behavior indicative of an intense unity.

Physical proximity is not essential to their survival. They can be separated for hours or even weeks without complications. Regardless of considerable distances of extended duration, their connection is often said to be uncannily strong.

They mate for life, but disconcerting research suggests this particular trait is on the decline. Environmental factors are the likely cause.

Despite this trend, in many cases, Married People sustain a powerful connection that resonates on many levels, even to the point of having eternal advantages. This two-in-one nature of Married People is mysterious and profound.

My field work took place over a period of approximately fifty years and during that time I was able to observe the Married People in their natural habitat.

Rules of Engagement

I don't know a lot about cars. But from what I understand, somewhere in the machinery there are gears. When these gears mesh and turn, they are said to be engaged.

Something similar occurs in the realm of the Married People. When a Single Male and a Single Female have dated long enough (duration varies) and they have weathered complications (intensity varies), they can also become "engaged." Just like the gears in a car, once they mesh in this way, things typically move forward.

Even though in the old days, "going steady" was initiated with a class ring and even though a "promise ring" can imply commitment, there is much more significance in the engagement ring. This is why an engagement is usually accompanied by an official announcement. This is why my friend Ryan spiraled into a meltdown.

An engagement usually begins with the Single Male purchasing the engagement ring. The ring is placed in a small box. He then arranges for a time and place to present the ring to the Single Female. In many cases, he will attempt to surprise her.

He might suggest they go for a walk. When they reach a park with a bird bath or an apple tree, he gets down on one knee and presents the ring along with a question. "Will you marry me?"

There are times when the Single Female knows it's coming. Many girls have often been frustrated that it hasn't happened sooner. But all in all, the engagement is famous for catching her off guard.

With the advent of YouTube, it has become fashionable to attempt more creative approaches. Proposals have included everything from skywriting to skydiving, flash mobs, professional football games, horses, and parades. The only constants are the kneeling and the ring. Whatever the fanfare might be, the finale is a hopeful fellow on one knee, holding out a piece of jewelry perched on a tiny cushion inside a small box.

The Single Male is essentially risking everything. He is not unlike a condemned prisoner placing his head in a guillotine, counting on a generous pardon. For if the girl declines, he must close the small box and skulk away, the debris of his daydreams trailing behind him. Many romantics have arranged their own public execution on a Jumbotron. I suspect some of these guys are actually manipulative creeps who try to use the pressure of the situation to force the girl's hand, apparently hoping she will accept the ring just to avoid humiliation. Such weasels probably deserve the grim outcome.

If the answer is "yes," the Single Male and Single Female are officially engaged. They tell their family and friends (at least those who weren't at the stadium) and set about pondering how long the engagement will be.

The length of time varies. Some proposals are open-ended and the wedding ends up becoming a fuzzy probability in the blurry future. Some proposals quickly lock onto a specific time frame almost immediately. Many factors come into play, but the proposal is meant to be an "engagement," and just like gears, everything begins to move forward with a real purpose.

The Wedding

A time and place are selected. Wedding invitations are sent out. Family and friends are invited to gather to watch the Single Male and Single Female declare their love through a ceremony.

After family members are ushered to their seats, the groom stands at the front with the preacher and attempts to look calm.

The procession enters the back of the auditorium, carefully organized, moving at the rate of a parade. There is musical accompaniment.

A cute little girl decorates the aisle with flower petals. She must be old enough to master the art of consistent floral distribution. A cute little boy is given the task of ring-bearer. The job description consists of being able to walk and to grip a small pillow. Given that little boys are notoriously less responsible than little girls, it seems odd to me a little boy would be entrusted with the most significant items in the ceremony.

The flower girl and the ring-bearer can provide an adorable photo op. If there is lack of good parenting, they can also provide minor sabotage.

The bridesmaids and groomsmen arrive by twos, some perfectly at ease, others looking quite uncomfortable due to awkward pairing or a hideous dress. At the end of the aisle, the temporary couples go their separate ways and find their preassigned spot. Here, they smile and wait for the bride. Their job is to make sure none of the decorations are falling over or catching on fire. They are also useful when it comes to wrangling feral flower girls or rogue ring-bearers.

The groom is usually dressed in a black suit. Other than the occasional kilt or throwback coattails, the suit is simple and straightforward. The groomsmen are dressed a lot like the groom. Sometimes, it is even difficult to tell which one is actually the one getting married. However, when the wedding party is in place for the ceremony, he will be the one closest to the center, next to the bride. Identifying marks of a groom also include wide eyes, restlessness, and excessive perspiration.

The bride is attended by her maid of honor and assorted bridesmaids. All of them, except the bride herself, wear matching outfits. If you look closely at their expressions as they come down the aisle, you can sometimes tell whether or not they actually like the outfits. Among those involved in the wedding, the bride is the easiest to spot because her appearance is unlike anything to be found within a twenty-mile radius—except once in a while, she might bear a remarkable resemblance to the cake.

Traditionally, the bride's father will give her away. This is to indicate that she is no longer a tax write-off. It also helps the groom remember there are those who are intent that the bride be safe and happy. This is often expressed through a grim smile and a gleam in the eye, not unlike the gleam off the barrel of a shotgun.

The preacher leads the male and female through the ceremony, describing their love and their devotion and all the things that marriage is meant to be. He will talk about the nature of love. He will emphasize the significance of their decision.

One of the dumbest things a preacher might say (mostly in movies now) is asking the audience if there is anyone who knows of any reason why they shouldn't get married. There is a token moment of silence—apparently just in case there is a person there ready to stand up and say, "Stop! I love you Edna!" or "He can't marry her! He's married to us!" It seems to me that if these naysayers have a legitimate gripe, they aren't going to wait until they have an aisle paved with flowers to speak up.

Numerous wedding ceremonies include the lighting of a candle or even numerous candles. These add to the romantic atmosphere. They also provide additional tension, in that everything and everyone is flammable.

Rings are exchanged. The preacher reads vows which the bride and groom repeat while putting the rings on each other's ring finger. Just as the bride's dress is more extravagant than the groom's suit, so her ring is also much more beautiful than his.

After a little bit more talking, the preacher says, "I now pronounce you man and wife" followed almost immediately by "You may kiss the bride."

There is more music and the procession proceeds out. This time, the parade is led by the bride and groom. It is also much faster.

At the reception, there is cake. The bride and groom feed each other a small piece. Depending on the nature of the couple, this might be a delicate exchange of dessert or an all-out food fight. Either way, the rest of the people are then able to eat some cake and some butter mints and possibly even a meal.

At one point, the bride throws her bouquet over her shoulder into a crowd of Single Females. Whoever catches the bouquet is supposed to be the next one to get married. Some of the single women calmly wait, prepared to catch it with finesse and grace if it happens to come their way. Some might even avoid it. Other Single Females suddenly become linebackers, snagging the bouquet out of the air like an interception.

After some time, all the people form a gauntlet, armed with bird seed or bubbles. In the old days, it used to be rice, but rumors have it that birds eat the rice and somehow explode. Personally, I think it would be pretty cool to rush to a stretch-Hummer while birds exploded overhead like fireworks.

The male and female run arm-in-arm while being attacked by bird seed or bubbles, to a waiting car (anything from a motorcycle to a limo). The groomsmen and other friends of the groom have tied empty pop cans to the rear bumper. On the back of the vehicle there are two words: "Just Married."

Whether this means Recently Married or Merely Married is debatable.

Weird History

Some of what happens at a wedding comes from the Bible. A whole lot of it comes from traditions collected over the years. The origins of some of these traditions are enlightening.

The cake idea comes from Ancient Rome. But back then you held a much smaller cake over the head of the bride and broke it. At another point in history, there was a wedding pie with a ring inside. It was the equivalent of a bouquet, because any Single Girl who found the ring in her piece of the pie might be the next to marry, or the next to get emergency dental work.

The cake was later accompanied by a shower of rice. All of these edibles were meant to imply plenty of food for the future. Since we have upgraded the finale to bird seed and bubbles, now the implication is plenty of birds and baths—or maybe birdbaths.

Historical records also describe the bride throwing a piece of the cake over her shoulder. No one caught it. But the groom would also throw the plate over his head. If the plate broke, that was supposed to mean a very good future.

Tasting the cake before the wedding was considered bad luck—like the groom seeing the bride in her dress before the wedding. It was believed that eating some of the cake too early could result in loss of the husband's love. Saving a piece of the cake meant he would be faithful. Plus, saving a piece of the groom's cake and putting it under your pillow meant good luck.

Also in the olden days, it was considered good luck to tear off a small piece of the wedding dress. The idea became so prevalent and borderline violent, someone came up with the idea of throwing a garter as an offering to the luck grubbers—to keep her dress and propriety intact.

Demons were an issue. Superstition has shaped much of the wedding tradition.

People believed the bride was a prominent target of supernatural forces. As far as they were concerned, demons might very well come after her and abduct her during the ceremony. If that was really the case, you can imagine the extra tension in the air. There wouldn't be as much worry about the candles staying lit or there being enough plates for the guests. There would be more worry about demons bursting into the procession and carrying off the screaming bride.

Since she might very well be abducted, she would ask her best friends to risk their lives and dress up as decoys. That way when the demons or malevolent spirits or whoever came to take off with the bride, they would be confused, unable to definitely pick out the bride, and abandon the mission. The

5 – THE **For-Reals**

groomsmen were also meant to be decoys. This was the original purpose of the wedding party—demon patrol.

Even the veil came from the idea of warding off evil spirits. It was thought that the bride was exceptionally susceptible to supernatural spells and such. The veil was meant to protect her—like an ethereal knight's visor.

The veil also played a key factor in arranged marriages. This way the groom was not able to determine his imminent wife's hotness until he had fully committed to her for life.

The best man dates back to the tradition of actually kidnapping a woman to be the bride. It makes you wonder if this nuptial kidnapping is connected to the desperate measures used to salvage the tribe of Benjamin (Judges 21). At the very least, it probably has some connection with Roman legend, when Romulus threw a big party for the Sabines and then kidnapped the women.

But it wasn't that long ago when the groom would pick his target and then go get her. There was no sipping lemonade on the porch swing. There was no awkward meeting of the father or a curfew. The groom just went in and abducted the girl.

There wasn't time for invitations, registering at Target, or choosing colors. The guy just kicked down the door and took the girl.

Back then, the groom had to worry about angry soon-to-be in-laws, who might try to stop the wedding. While he was vowing his endless love to his girlfriend / captive, her family could very well burst in and try to shut it all down. It was also very possible other suitors might show up to try and steal her for their own frantic wedding. The reason a bride now stands to the groom's left is because once upon a time he needed his right hand to fend off these other suitors. As you can imagine, back then the officiator did not ask if anyone had any objections. Any objections surfaced in the form of fists and blood.

Being that she might put up a fuss and that the family would be equally opposed to the removal of their loved-one, the groom would need his strongest and most capable friend—his *best* man, to fight off the family while he made off with the bride.

In some cases, after everything was over, the groom's family would throw a party for the bride's family as a kind of apology. *Sorry about the kidnapping thing, so here's a feast.* This was later reduced to pop cans tied to the back of the car.

I'm not making any of this up.

Confessions of a Groomsman

I have been a groomsman several times. Not once did I ever realize that I was essentially a decoy. I had no idea that when I was asked to be a member of the wedding party that I was putting my life on the line. Mostly, the other groomsmen and I just enjoyed watching the groom fidget. I remember often thinking how glad I was to not be the guy waiting for the bride to come down the aisle. The whole idea seemed terrifying.

When the ceremony was over, I would get back in my car and drive back to my carefree life of bachelorhood. But the new husband would be dragged away into a lifetime contract. To me, his ring looked more like a shackle.

I have to admit, it was an honor to be up there, dressed like a chess piece. It was cool to share some of the attention and you couldn't help but be curious about which bridesmaid would be your parade partner. You got to walk down the aisle with a girl without actually marrying her. There was at least the passing thought that someday I might be the one actually standing in the hot spot. The spot where you said things that last forever.

I have been the singer at a wedding or two. Waiting for the cue, playing guitar and harmonizing with my sister or other people as the proceedings proceeded. It was nice to provide the ambiance.

I have also been the officiator more than once. I had to make sure I had my notes prepared and that I said the right things. I was the one who had to speak the most so there was the pressure of making it all come together in an organized fashion. But even though I said, "I do" twice during the ceremony, when it was over, the fourth finger on my left hand remained comfortingly bare.

Several of the weddings had at least a faint ominous moment for some of those in attendance. During one particular wedding, one of the preliminary songs for the ceremony was a recording of "Unforgettable," sung by Nat King Cole. During the rehearsal, one of the groomsman started singing along, except he changed the words a little. He sang, "Irreversible… in every way…Irreversible…that's how you'll stay…" We all laughed, but I found it unnerving. The groom himself seemed oddly at ease—even with this clumsy jibe at his permanent decision.

I have heard horror stories of people setting the date and then having second thoughts even as the ceremony is in motion. I've seen grooms that look like deer transfixed by a semi. One girl told me that as she walked down the aisle she questioned whether or not she even loved her soon-to-husband.

With all these horror stories drifting around my head, I often pondered the philosophical question, "If you change your mind before the wedding, how late is too late?"

Just before you say, "I do"?

While the bride is walking down the aisle?

The rehearsal dinner?

When the first invitation is sent out?

It was a frightening concept. To make a decision that ultimately was indeed thoroughly and resoundingly irreversible.

I literally had at least two dreams in which I was the groom and the wedding was pending. One dream was about sending out the wedding invitations and me having second thoughts. The other—the ceremony was actually beginning and I was telling my dad I had changed my mind. We both were desperate about what to do next. Not fun dreams. More like nightmares.

But as a groomsman, I stood at attention and watched one guy after another go down the tubes.

I even caught two garters at two separate weddings. According to tradition, catching the garter is like catching the bridal bouquet. I was supposed to be the next one to get married. But neither of the garters led to anything. Either they don't work or they canceled each other out.

The Honeymoon

Immediately following the wedding, there is something called the Honeymoon. This is also rooted in historical oddities.

After the abduction of the bride, since her family would be out looking to retrieve her, the groom would take her into hiding for thirty days. During every one of these days, a family member or friend of the groom would bring the newlyweds a cup of honey wine. That's how we ended up with honeymoons.

The reason a groom carries his bride over the threshold goes back to the idea of protecting her from demons. These particular demons lived in the floor. A fact the real estate agent neglected to mention. But after the groom set the bride down in their new home, it was all good.

Whenever a friend of mine got married, he and his new bride disappeared for about a year. The official honeymoon didn't last that long. It was just that all the new complications of being Married People took them off the grid for a while. During that first year of marriage, I might catch glimpses of my friend, but these were brief and sketchy, like sighting an urban legend. [Interestingly enough, under the old covenant, a newly married man was given a year off to be with his new wife (Deuteronomy 24:5).]

Eventually my friend and his wife would reappear.

He didn't seem any different.

The honeymoon is considered to be a stretch of time during which everything is relatively easy or even blissful. But

I have also heard stories of arguments that happened while the happy couple is driving away from the wedding. As it turns out, there are some wedding nights that are difficult and even embarrassing.

But at least they're not having to hide out from the bride's family for a month. In fact, more than likely, her father or someone else representing her family openly surrendered her at the wedding. So there's that, at least.

Rumor has it that the honeymoon does eventually come to an end. After they're settled into their home and they have sorted through the wedding gifts, they begin to adjust to the reality of living with each other every day all the time.

The duration of the honeymoon is unclear. Although there is a ceremony to begin the honeymoon, there is no ceremony to end it. The end arrives gradually. Whether the honeymoon lasts a week or two or the standard month, it is assumed the fun eventually comes to an end and everyday mundane drudgery moves in.

Slowly but surely the newly married couple are transformed into average Married People. It's not that they become sad or disillusioned necessarily. But they are no longer the blissful couple that dashed away in the car trailing cans and bird seed.

The piece of wedding cake is frozen. The wedding dress is stored away.

Now begins reality. All the romance novels and chick flicks withdraw. This is when the bride and groom begin to see if the relationship is built on anything real.

I heard tales of those who were dazed, wondering, "What have I done?" "Do I really love this person?"

I assume these thoughts appear in some form in the minds of just about everyone. The sheer permanence of the arrangement has to strike some kind of profound chord. It just makes sense.

If their relationship only has momentum, things begin to coast. If everything up to this point was made of just chocolate and flowers, the truth of their connection is discovered over meatloaf and pop—TV and monthly budgets—colds and clutter. The little cute habits begin to trigger pet peeves. It takes a little while for the dust to settle, but eventually the days reveal the exact nature and dimensions of this particular happily-ever-after.

However, even after these slight blips, many couples discover that marriage is filled with blessings far beyond what they hoped for.

The Naked Truth

With much discretion, we will now approach one of the more delicate matters surrounding Married People. Research confirms and evidence suggests that when they are alone together, Married People do not necessarily always wear clothes. It is one of the more intriguing elements of their realm—a state of nudity can exist between husband and wife without moral compromise. This is one of the more striking characteristics of the arrangement as designed by God. When it comes to Married People, fabric is optional.

Very early on in your life, one of the first lessons learned is that it is vital to keep yourself clothed. You must say goodbye to the carefree au naturel infant you once were. It is a standard rule of propriety—the greater majority of your skin must be covered. Mortifying embarrassments await the person who overlooks a zipper or button. The recurring nightmare of finding yourself in school wearing only your pajamas—that alone is enough to make many of us sit up in a cold sweat in the middle of the night. Discounting those who disdain modesty—every day, we make sure to cover up our bodies.

However, Married People occasionally forgo this particular restriction. Marriage removes the stigma of removing clothing in the presence of another person. Most of the time, a Married Person will be fully dressed, but when the world is reduced to just the husband and wife, nakedness is a strong possibility.

This very arrangement occurred between the first husband and wife. "And the man and his wife were both naked and were not ashamed" (Genesis 2:25). Despite a complete lack of apparel, there were no averted eyes. In fact, the concept of clothing would have initially seemed silly to these two Edenites.

But all that changed when they sinned. "Then the eyes of both of them were opened, and they knew that they were naked; and they sewed fig leaves together and made themselves loin coverings" (Genesis 3:7). Very soon, they would both be kicked out of the garden, but there was another more immediate side-effect of their mistake. From then on, they and all their descendants would be starkly aware of being starkers.

Being naked was a brand new concept. It's not that Adam and Eve didn't notice the lack of clothing before this point. It was just that now, the concept of nudity took on a whole new level of meaning. Nudity was abruptly associated with the shame of sin. From then on, the ever-present potential embarrassment of being seen naked would be connected to the ever-present potential embarrassment of sin.

God was making the point that their innocence was gone. Sin should cause shame. You know that intense feeling of humiliating disgrace you would feel if you found yourself unclad for all the world to see? That's the appropriate response we should have towards our sins. Whenever we sin, we make the same choice Adam and Eve made. We oppose God.

When sin is new, we feel shame. But over time, if we continue to sin without regret or repentance, we can become numb to this feeling. We are like someone who blatantly removes clothing in public so many times, they lose the ability to feel shame. As the Bible puts it, we can lose our ability to blush. "Were they ashamed because of the abomination they have done? They were not even ashamed at all; they did not even know how to blush" (Jeremiah 6:15). When it comes to sin, shame is a good thing.

To lose the connection between sin and shame is to lose connection with reality. This is detrimental. Our perception of what pleases or displeases our Creator is essential to our interaction with Creation.

It's not that God is eager for us to feel shame. He was the One who provided the much more effective animal skins that replaced the pitifully ineffective and out-of-fashion fig leaves. This alone taught the first Married People and their descendants, that attempting to handle sin without God is a pathetic undertaking. "Their cobwebs are useless for clothing, they cannot cover themselves with what they make" (Isaiah 59:6). Any attempt on our part to spiritually clothe ourselves always fall short. Even at our best, all our good deeds are just so much "filthy rags" (Isaiah 61:6). The only way to cover our shame is by putting on Christ in baptism. "For all of you who were baptized into Christ have clothed yourselves with Christ" (Galatians 3:27). It isn't just a metaphor; it's the one and only solution to dealing with the repercussions of Eden and the man and woman who suddenly found themselves blushing.

All of this, oddly enough, is why it's more than appropriate for Married People to follow the dress code of pre-sin Eden. God thinks of the husband and wife relationship as a parallel with the relationship between Jesus and the church. There are no pretenses between the Savior and those who belong to him. Nothing to hide. Mistakes are removed by His sacrifice. There is no sin here. Only vulnerable forgiveness.

Despite strategic posturing and blurry lenses, nudity is mostly an awkward state. When it comes down to it, without clothes, in all our unclad lack of glory, everyone kind of looks silly.

Married People navigate this precarious condition in ways that no one else can. Shame is upgraded to mere vulnerability. There is no room for animosity here, so any kind of armor is out of place. Any kind of clothing is unnecessary. They have an intimacy that speaks of complete vulnerability—the kind that imitates the incredible love that originates outside this dimension.

Married People are a potent synchronization of two selves. If two souls are to be truly united, there can be no barriers. There can be no dishonesty. There can be no agendas. And sometimes, almost as a tribute to all this, there doesn't necessarily have to be any clothes.

This arrangement can certainly lead to attraction, but there's more to it than just physical enticement. Eventually, everyone's hotness declines and all too quickly, naked becomes cute familiarity that belongs only to the one who truly loves you for you and not just the container you inhabit. There is no humiliation here. There is comfort and peace. There is love that does not need stunning abs or perfect curves to survive.

This exhilarating multifaceted bareness is profound. If these two people can truly be one on such an intimate level, they can access significant blessings of this existence others cannot. They are the ultimate synergistic presence. They are nothing less than a walking analogy of the meaning of life—Jesus and His church. They are a constant reminder that there is a connection that transcends all obstacles and pitfalls. There is a love that defiantly survives no matter what.

Married People can stand completely unclothed before each other and still be loved. Their imperfections are irrelevant. It doesn't matter how beautiful or handsome they happen to be on that particular day. Photoshop, flattering light, not even stylish clothing or any clothing are necessary here. Just the plain and simple naked truth.

What the World Thinks the Christian Thinks about Sex

There are a whole lot of movies about people sleeping around. Believe it or not, a whole lot of them are comedies. With clever writing and pop music, the film treats sexual immorality as just so much wacky antics. Tee-hee.

Inevitably, if there is a religious character in the story, this person is adamantly opposed to the antics. They are naïve and uptight. But this "Christian" is not just opposed to the idea of general infidelity. The character is written in such a way that suggests this moral person actually despises the very idea of sex.

This reveals an interesting truth about the world and its ideas about Christians. The world thinks that Christians think sex is bad.

This is a pretty ridiculous assumption for at least two reasons. 1) Christians are notorious for having children and 2) God was the One who came up with the idea in the first place. The world seems to think that Christians think of sex as an evil necessity at best, and yet God instigated it and even promotes it.

He gave the green light to Adam and Eve. "And God blessed them; and God said to them, 'Be fruitful and multiply, and fill the earth'" (Genesis 1:28). Populating the earth would require Adam and Eve to have sex.

When Noah and his sons walked out of the ark with their wives, God gave them the same instructions. "And God blessed Noah and his sons and said to them, 'Be fruitful and multiply and fill the earth" (Genesis 9:1). Again populating the earth would require these couples to have sex. Probably a lot of it.

A Christian does not look down on sex. A Christian looks up. In other words, God intended sex to be held in high regard. This is the heart of the issue. God considers sex to be valuable. The world considers it to be cheap.

Whereas God adamantly restricts sex to marriage, the world has broken down those walls, dragging sex out into the dirt. The world throws sex to the whims and indulgences of dating and even down to shallow, crude trysts. The world is wildly unrestrictive about sex. As long as it happens between two consenting adults it's all good. The Bible says otherwise and the world mocks this standard in practically every movie, sitcom, pop song, and commercial. What was meant to be treated like valuable china is treated like paper plates.

Christians don't think sex is bad. They think it's valuable. Sure, there have been religious people who have promoted a dark stigma over sex—that it is an evil necessity strictly for the purpose of propagation. But anyone who knows their Bible, knows that Christianity is not anti-sex. Proverbs 5:18-19 is very pro-sex. Virtually the whole book Song of Solomon is filled with honorable, yet blush-worthy material.

The stuffy schoolmarm or the grimacing, cloistered clergyman are easy targets. The world uses such straw-man tactics to promote indulgence. The truth is, Christians are not ignorant or naïve about sex—they have insight. They understand that what has value is valuable because it is rare. They are more aware of the lifelong consequences that follow, when treasures are squandered.

This conflict between the world and the Word is measured in ridicule. "And in all this, they are surprised that you do not run with them into the same excess of dissipation, and they malign you" (I Peter 4:4). Here, we are provided with some clarity. The true Christian will not make the descent toward degradation. Oddly enough, it is the ones wallowing below, who point at them and laugh.

Happily Married People know the value of the physical connection that God intended to only occur between them. They protect this treasure and keep it valuable. This is one of the main things that keeps Married People married.

Arranged Marriages

In the olden days—or in places that still live like it's the olden days—there is an approach to becoming Married People that is quite shocking to those of us living in the modern days.

The arranged marriage.

You don't choose your spouse. Instead, your spouse is chosen for you. Typically, your parents meet with the parents of your spouse and all you have to do is show up for the wedding. Sometimes you get to meet each other and even chat a little before making a vow to love each other the rest of your lives. But sometimes you don't even see each other until just before the rings are on your hands. For the groom, the veil serves as a sort of "ta-da!" for the moment when the groom discovers how attractive he might find his now sudden wife. One can imagine the officiator being a game show host.

To those of us living in modern times, this concept is downright horrific. It's bad enough to risk a blind date. But a blind marriage? No way.

I felt the same way. But I was surprised when I heard about how countless arranged marriages have worked out pretty well. Somehow, a system in which two strangers were united in matrimony, turned out to have a decent success rate. At least as far as simply staying together.

This is not to suggest that we bring it back into prominence. We have to admit that many of these arranged marriages were in truth merely business transactions or political treaties.

The arranged marriage completely eliminated the dating phase. There was no shopping around or social mixers or online matching. The parents made the decision.

Take out the trash, mow the lawn, and after you're done, get cleaned up. Because you're getting married.

The great majority of First World countries—at least those in the so-called Western civilization—would not even consider entertaining this wildly obsolete idea. Opposition to arranged marriages from those of us entrenched in the smorgasbord approach to finding a mate basically comes down to a very simply question.

What if I don't like them?

5 – THE For-Reals

We are mesmerized by the idea of love at first sight and as far as this arranged marriage thing, there is the strong possibility of not-love at first sight. Just as you can instantly be in love with someone the moment you see their eyes and bone structure and hair and basic flesh paradigm, you can also instantly eliminate someone as a candidate for your love—at a glance. If the eyes and bone structure and hair and basic flesh paradigm of your arranged spouse fall short of your hopeful specifications, there you are—stuck in a loveless imprisonment.

On the other hand, technically, you could argue that all marriages are arranged. The only issue is who exactly is doing the arranging.

If it's a financially desperate father intent on using you to pave the way for a business deal, then he's probably not your guy. If it's a well-meaning mother who is only driven by the fear of you ending up single the rest of your life, then it would probably be wise to say no thank you.

But let's not jump to conclusions. It would also be foolish for you to go to the other extreme, shutting out your father and mother, along with the whole family, all your friends, and anyone who doesn't blindly endorse your whims.

We have a tendency to assume that when it comes to marriage, the Single Male and the Single Female should be the only arrangers. However, based on their current track record, I would suggest that the lovebirds on their own have not proven to be very good at arranging much of anything.

And yet that's the typical scenario. The Single Male and Single Female are "in love" and they latch onto each other with a romantic death grip. If anyone expresses any concern about their relationship or suggests caution in regard to their future plans, these naysayers are immediately shut out.

The determined couple can then fall back on the cliché of "no one understands us."

Only we get it. Our love will conquer all.

The problem is, this kind of approach doesn't work. In these cases, the only thing love conquers is your ability to think.

You can't blame anyone for not wanting to be pawns in an arranged marriage as brought to you by old-world customs. But if the people who love you are waving their arms in the air and anxiously urging you to reconsider, it seems just as foolish to ignore them. If there was ever a person going into marriage blindly, it would be those who insist on being the only ones giving input about the decision.

At the very least—it's just plain common sense to make sure you find out God's thoughts on the situation. Yet, His Word is the usually the last source of advice to be consulted on the matter.

Believe me, I get it. It's hard for a couple in love to not want to pull away from everyone if they are being only negative and seem intent on undermining their happiness.

But God has proven over and over that He has your best interests in mind. Plus, He knows you better than you do and He even knows the future. Lovebirds who shrug off God's help in arranging anything, especially marriage, will have a very short flight.

So maybe arranged marriages aren't such a bad idea. It just depends on who's doing the arranging. You should certainly be involved, but why not get the input of those who love you? Knowing that infatuation is notoriously unreliable, it would serve a lot of people well to listen to at least some outside input. Instead of whispering sweet nothings to each other in the dark, enabling each other toward bad decisions, let it be sweet somethings. Let it be wisdom from the ones who love you. Let it be wisdom given by your Creator in His Word. If God isn't involved in such a decision, good luck with that.

Many of the Married People I know took advice from loved ones. They also listened to God's Word. Then the two of them decided to make a lifelong commitment. In a sense, it was an arranged marriage. And guess what—it's going extremely well.

The Dowry

If you think arranged marriages are weird, get a load of the dowry. This is also an outdated concept. When the groom married the bride, he didn't just get the girl. He also got some money and possibly even some property.

What's up with that? The girl alone isn't good enough? She has to come with some kind of finding fee?

When marriages were degraded down to being business transactions, the dowry was used to sweeten the deal. That way, when the potential suitor and the potential suitor's family considered the possibility of a marriage, this dowry might sway the outcome. It wasn't always romantic but it was good for finances.

Here you go. Here's my daughter's hand. Plus you get a thousand rupees and half the goat farm. Congratulations.

It's hard to imagine a modern equivalent in our sophisticated culture.

Congratulations. Here's your wife, a 401(k), and the Laundromat on 8th Avenue.

Let's shrug this little custom off right away. But not before using it as a platform to learn something about Married People.

In a sense, every marriage comes with a dowry. You don't just get the girl—and for that matter, you don't just get the guy.

There's baggage.

It could be good, it could be bad. But when you marry someone, in some respects you also marry their family. If they are the kind of family who was involved before, then get ready for them to be involved after. This can bring definite blessings and it can also bring definite complications.

One thing I've learned during my observations of Married People is that they need to be portable. This is mostly noticeable during Thanksgiving and Christmas. The husband and wife have to establish a trade agreement. If they spend Thanksgiving with her family, they have to spend Christmas with his family. The following year, they switch. Distance to respective families can be a factor.

When you get married, you also marry your spouse's habits and shortcomings. These can ultimately improve or get worse, but whatever tics and quirks they own—these are part of the "dowry" as well. The dating process can reveal some of these odd facets of their personality, but not all. There are always interesting surprises, from the way she scrimps to the way he snores—or vice versa.

The dowry can include pleasant surprises as well as unpleasant ones. To make things even more interesting, some of the very things you found cute or attractive before can end up being a primary source of annoyance.

After the vows and possibly even after the honeymoon, the dowry begins to make itself known. Married People who thrive are the ones who have a special kind of love. They don't just love the glamorous semi-hunk or quasi-model. They love the zombie who trudges through the morning gloom to find clean clothes to wear. They love the sick, pathetic flu victim wheezing on the couch. They love the stubbly shadow with the bad breath strong enough to make the dog crawl under the house.

I'm also glad to report that the dowry includes many wonderful things. This includes the in-laws, who end up being bonus fathers and mother and sisters and brothers who make you wonder how you lived life without them. The dowry includes all the things that make your spouse shine, but even more so when allowed to thrive in the light of real love.

The point is this—no matter what, no one goes into a marriage without carrying something. It could be a decent bank account, but more than likely it will be a credit card debt. When you see a wedding you are often watching a merger of debts.

The dowry is made of burdens and blessings. But happy Married People have the kind of love that turns all the former into the latter.

The Mystery

Once in a while, when God tries to help us understand something, He will make a comparison. He used the lamb to explain the innocence of His Son (John 1:29), He used our respiration system to explain inspiration (II Timothy 3:16), and He used fire to explain the destructive capability of our words (James 3:5). When He makes these parallels, it's important to keep in mind that since He is omniscient and omnipotent, when He designed and created the lamb, He had Jesus in mind. When He fashioned the intricacies of our lungs and circulatory system, He had inspiration in mind. When He crafted fire, He had gossip in mind.

God didn't just create a bunch of stuff and then browse for something that sort of worked for His analogy. He didn't simply search through the various nooks and crannies of Creation hoping to find something useful that would kind of work for his object lesson. When He made the objects, He had the object lessons in mind.

That being said, God also has an analogy to help explain Married People. Anyone who wants to even begin to grasp Married People has to consider this analogy. In a sense, this allows you to see marriage through God's eyes and that alone can be very revealing.

He thinks the relationship between a husband and wife is just like the relationship between Jesus and the church (Ephesian 5:22-33). This alone is a pretty solid reason why any marriage that does not include two Christians is going to be severely crippled when it comes to pursuing the truest connection intended by the Designer.

When God designed husbands and wives, He designed them with Jesus and the church in mind. It was very intentional.

That alone tells us that as far as God is concerned, He considers marriage to be a very big deal.

But He also realized it would be something difficult for us to grasp. Despite the fact that marriage seems so straightforward, there are elements to it that remain difficult to understand.

"This mystery is great; but I am speaking with reference to Christ and the church" (Ephesians 5:32). Since it is a mystery, venturing into marriage without the Bible to help map out the way will only make it more mysterious. It's no wonder that most Married People are entangled in heartache and confusion. To them, the mystery remains unsolved.

But when marriage is done right, it is incredibly powerful. These two people are attached on a powerful level that outshines all other connections. Even the protective mother instinct toward her child, even the self-sacrificing nature of the father for his family run a distant second to what is going on (or should be going on) between Married People. They are accessing aspects of eternity. It is not some faint supernatural vibe. It is a resounding replication of the machine that runs the universe.

It's no wonder we write songs about it. This explains why we like to see movies about it. It makes sense now that the number one best-selling genre of books is romance. We sense something powerful—something mostly unreachable yet necessary.

This also explains why people tend to latch onto something they hope will contain the mystery. They want the love that makes existence hum. But when they search for it without God, their hopes wither, corrupted and degraded by their own desperate clinging.

To most, the mystery remains a mystery. Even those who shine in their marriages as far as laughter and happiness will ultimately learn that something essential is missing. Understanding a mystery requires investigation and study and thought. You can't fall into the answer. If you want to understand marriage, you have to understand Jesus and the church.

True Love and Truer Love

God and the world are clearly at odds. There are many instances in which it is obvious they are not on the same page. One of the best ways to see this drastic conflict of perception is in their perceptions of love. What the world thinks of love is in direct opposition to what God thinks of love.

To gain some clarity, it doesn't hurt to refer one more time to those wacky arranged marriages. As wacky as they are, they reveal something pretty significant about the true nature of love. Something that the world adamantly denies.

Love is a choice.

Think about it. If you were one of those lucky couples where you didn't meet until just before you were holding the rings, at that point there would be some profound options for you. You could stumble along into your wedded "bliss," hoping that love might just sort of take hold, along the lines of the flu. But another possibility would be to simply decide to love.

The world doesn't believe this is possible. As mentioned before, the world believes love is a pit that defies gravity. You can fall into it and you can also fall out of it. It's out of your hands. No one can promise to love and cherish another person any more than they can promise that the unity candle won't set something on fire or that the ring-bearer won't leave the flower girl. It's all up in the air. You can give it your best shot, but love is as reliable as the weather. The trick is to try and live somewhere warm.

Not so. You don't fall in love. You don't fall out of love. You choose love. You choose not to love.

It's funny how people will talk about "true love" in such a way that makes it sound so powerful and yet allow for the idea that it can so easily fall apart.

Which is it? Is true love something strong? Or is it something frail that can crumble in your hands even if you don't want it to?

If love comes and goes like a flu bug, then marriage and dating and romance is all balanced on the chemicals that jitter through our body, at the behest of stimuli. We are rats manipulated by shocks and cheese. Nothing more than mindless creatures wandering a maze.

God thinks love is a decision. That goes for Married People too. Sure, they can find each other attractive. Sure, there can be that wild magic that makes them gaze into each other's eyes. But if this true love isn't upgraded to truer love, then rings might as well come with an expiration date.

How much greater it would be if two people who were attracted to each other and then "clicked" personality-wise went into their marriage with the idea that love will be a choice. That way, when one of them veers toward being unloveable, the other one can step up and love them anyway.

God thinks love is a choice. The thrills may wax and wane, but the truest kind of love has a lot more staying power.

The main problem with the world is that it tries to degrade stuff, including love. That's why someone can say they love nachos and they love their truck and say it with a straight face. It's because the world has tampered with the definition of love. The world has created lesser versions of it.

One of the most powerful secrets Married People have is that love is a choice. That there is something higher than "true" love.

Most people will wallow in the lower regions, thinking they have found another dose of "true" love in the flashes of infatuation. But when that last hit fades, they will venture off to find someone else, trusting that the next one will have something more.

The world has turned everyone into love junkies addicted to artificial love.

This is not to completely condemn infatuation. God provided that thrill as part of the adventure for Married People. But if it remains only at the level of "true" love, it will end up being very temporary.

Married People who choose to love their spouse are the

ones that last. Although there are other kinds of love—friendship and brotherly / sisterly love, it is the love between a husband and wife that is held up as the earthly standard with a heavenly resonance.

This is why it's important to not let the world chime in about the love between Married People. The love between Married People is the love most damaged, most corrupted, and most misrepresented by the world.

The attack makes sense. After all, if the relationship between Married People parallels the relationship between Jesus and the church, that would be the best target—the most vital connection possible.

Imagine if we measured the love between Jesus and the church by the standards of the world. Jesus could fall in love and out of love. It would be constantly precarious. It would have been a disastrous factor as He approached the cross. When the mob came to arrest him or even when he was standing before Pilate and could have summoned legions of angels to rescue him—if there were ever reasons to fall out of love, those would have been more than legitimate. But Jesus chose to love.

It makes all the reasons people use today to "fall out of love" seem pretty pitiful.

Worldly love is a fragile thing. Real love (a.k.a truer love) overcomes obstacles, including waning hormones and anger and annoyances and fears.

This is one of the main things that keeps Married People happily married.

Living for Someone

There is a lot of singing about dying for someone. Dying for someone seems to be the standard of love.

I would die for you.

The idea seems to be that if it came down to it, that person would sacrifice themselves for the other person.

Maybe the guy is dying of a disease and a girl offers her

own blood for a transfusion that will save his life. The story is better if the transfusion threatens her own life.

Mostly, though, it's a guy thing.

I would die for her.

The best case scenario involves bad guys who are about to shoot the girl for some reason. Just as they pull the trigger, the guy heroically throws himself in front of her. He takes the bullet meant for her and she weeps over him as he dies in her arms. His last words—"I love you."

Whether it's a stray bullet or a rogue bus, the man is always ready to die for her.

But let's take a closer and more objective look at this.

Dying for someone is certainly a big deal. I don't want to belittle such a powerful sacrifice. There is indeed something to be said for someone who does something so self-less. All of us hope we have that kind of quality in us. There are probably a lot of us who might reach the same decision—if we had time to weigh the circumstances. Those who don't hesitate to put their lives on the line, the ones who make that split second decision—they are amazingly heroic.

Dying for someone might involve you having very little time to think it over. The danger approaches. You don't have the luxury of reviewing your bucket list. You either hesitate and let her be killed or you take action, taking her place so that she can go on living with tearful memories of you as her one and only true love.

I would die for you.

Incredibly admirable.

But brief.

Living takes longer.

Merely saying that you'll die for someone isn't as impressive as it sounds for two reasons.

First, it doesn't last that long. Second, it's not likely that it will ever happen.

The best a modern hero can hope for today is to leap in front of her to open the door or to courageously carry her purse.

Unlike Jesus' death, dying for your true love probably won't have much of an impact as living for them.

Plus, don't forget that Jesus not only died for us, He also lived for us. It was vital that He did. By living for us He was "tempted in all things as we are, yet without sin" (Hebrews 4:15). Without his life, His death would not have met the qualifications of a perfect sacrifice for our salvation.

For Married People, (and the husband in particular), dying for someone sounds great—from a distance. But the substance of love will be seen in living for someone. Their daily and consistent determination and example has a much more long-lasting effect.

A husband, even though he is exhausted from a long day at work, drops by the store for eggs, so that his wife doesn't have to do it. A wife, even though she is overwhelmed by financial worries, summons up a smile for her husband's peace of mind.

These seemingly mundane things are more significant than you might think. They are indications of patience and kindness and most of all, a love that endures.

Not to burst anyone's bubble, but Married People rarely have to die for each other. Most of the time, they are doing something that requires much more time and effort—living for each other.

A Collaboration of Superpowers

Men and women are different. Yep, it's true.

I know this seems pretty obvious, but I think it actually takes quite a while before many of us fully grasp this truth. It might even be possible that none of us ever *completely* grasp this truth.

When you're little, you have to process the idea that boys and girls are physically different. It dawns on you that the body of the opposite gender has some major differences. It takes some time just to process that.

Your own body is familiar to you. The other kind of body is bizarrely unfamiliar. At first, there is a mixture of revulsion and fascination, but when the smoke of childhood clears, it's primarily fascination. The other kind of body becomes very, very interesting.

Then one day, you make the other discovery. It is possibly the more profound revelation. Your bodies are not the only thing different about you. Your minds are extremely different too.

When childhood was far behind me, I thought I had it all relatively figured out. Men and women have different bodies of course. But they also think differently.

But it took many years before it really sunk in. We don't just think differently. We perceive and interpret and comprehend differently. It's not just that our thoughts are different; our brains our different. Not just slightly different, but wildly different. As the bestseller said long ago, it's like we're from different planets. Women and men have completely different kinds of brains. In fact, I'm pretty sure my male brain still fails to grasp the depths of these differences.

The world pushes for the idea that our brains are essentially the same. People talk as if you could just trade brains and things could just keep strolling along without any problem. If it was up to us, men and women would be almost virtually indistinguishable.

There are some problems with this idea.

The first is that males and females are males and females on a genetic level. Every cell is either XX or XY. That means ever single cell is a particular gender. Those troubled souls that alter the exterior change absolutely nothing about their true gender.

It's sad to see the world clamoring to try and erase the differences when God was so determined to establish them. God wanted men and women to be different. "Male and female He created them" (Genesis 27). This was not an afterthought. He intentionally made two versions of humanity. Not just in body but in mind. We don't just look different. The way we think is different.

This difference is a source of great frustration for both camps. First as a man, you become irritated that women don't think correctly. Of course, women are thinking the same thing about men. But the difference is intentional and when these kinds of minds are combined through marriage, it provides years of interesting interaction. The discrepancy is not something that needs to be fixed. It isn't a mistake. It's actually something that can be used to our advantage. It needs to be nurtured. It needs to be harnessed.

I know it sounds strange, but one of the most profound realizations that will hit Married People is the fact that men and women are not the same. The nature of each gender's mind is intentionally and wonderfully different.

I have a friend who read up on this whole issue. He said that according to one book, men are like lasers and women are more like an all-encompassing glow. That's why inventors tend to be men, since they can focus that laser on one specific thing to the extent he breaks new ground. But this is also why the same guy can be so focused on something that he does not notice that the world is falling apart around him.

A woman can be simultaneously aware of the doorbell ringing, the baby crying, and a song playing in the background, while the man sits clueless about all these things because currently his laser mind is zeroed on ESPN.

But this is perfect. Marriage can be like a partnership between superheroes. When Glow Woman sees trouble, she can urge Laser Man to direct his attention to it. The partnership is quite effective.

This is one of the many reasons why Married People can be such a powerful influence on the world. Not by trying to remove the differences, but by using them to their fullest extent.

Contagious Faces

There has been a lot of research done on Married People. I'm sure there have been thousands of studies that have shed some insight. There have also been thousands of studies that achieved articulate nonsense. But there was one study in particular that really caught my eye.

The researchers took individual photographs of a bunch of Married People—just one picture of the husband and one picture of the wife. The study involved a wide spectrum of Married People. The photos were of men and women who had been married for only a year, for several years, all the way to photos of men and women who had been married for several decades. But keep in mind—none of the spouses were photographed together. This was important to the study.

Once the researchers had collected the photographs of these Married People, they put all of them together and mixed them up. Next, they gathered together a whole new group of people to get to work. They brought the group in and confronted them with the pile of photographs.

Their assignment? Try to match the right man with the right woman. In other words, try to figure out who belonged to whom just by looking at their faces.

You might be thinking there were a few lucky guesses, but mainly a lot of mismatches. You might suspect that because of mere chance, there were some accidental matches, in which the right husband was matched with the right wife.

Not so fast. The researchers actually discovered something a lot more interesting than that. A surprising number of the matches were spot on. Plus, they noticed that the longer the couple had been married, the greater the chance of them being matched correctly.

The results suggested something pretty significant. The longer you're married, the more you look like each other. The ones who had been married a short time did not necessarily resemble each other. However, the ones who had been married for some time actually had certain details in their features that made it possible for a discerning eye to match them together.

So what's up with that?

One decent theory (but not very likely) is that deep down on a subconscious level, we tend to be attracted to certain subtle facial nuances that are similar to what we see in the mirror every day. It might not be narcissism, but it could be we are just drawn to what is familiar.

That theory doesn't really work. It doesn't explain why the similarities are more prevalent among those who have been married longer.

The answer is actually quite simple and quite startling.

Marriage transforms you. When you are married for an extended amount of time, your face actually begins to take on certain features of the other person's face.

It's not magic. It's just a matter of proximity to personality.

If you marry a grouch, eventually you both start looking like a grouch. Living with someone who scowls most of the day and grimaces from one obstacle to the next makes their face take on a certain arrangement. As you spend more and more time with this grouch, you will inadvertently and at least subconsciously mimic their expressions. Moods can be contagious. Even if you pride yourself on being an optimistic soul, constantly being in the presence of a human Eeyore can gradually sculpt both of your expressions into a matching set. If the default setting is pessimism, you can eventually see it quite clearly. The crow's feet and furrowed brow fall easily into frowns, mapping out tales of anger and complaints. Whoever is married to this will take on a similar topography.

If you marry a happy person, you can both end up looking somewhat more pleasant. Living with someone who smiles most of the day can have just as big of an effect on your face. Someone who tries to face obstacles with optimism or even laughter will also transform you. As you spend more and more time with them, you will find yourself automatically matching their cheerful expressions. The laugh lines and happy wrinkles mapped out on your face tell a completely different story.

Here's some advice. Marry a happy person. Be a happy person.

Married People are contagious—to each other. Even though they both have drastically different brains, their unity does begin to smooth out the seam between them. They still maintain their own unique male and female perceptions, but these two incredibly different ways of seeing the world can be fused together into something horrible or something wonderful.

I can sure appreciate the fact that some people have been through the darkest of trials, but it seems there are also those who almost enjoy languishing. To settle into a perpetual loop of sadness is not a good plan.

God indicates that we can choose the course of our thinking. "For those who are according to the flesh set their minds on the things of the flesh, but those who are according to the Spirit, the things of the Spirit. For the mind set on the flesh is death, but the mind set on the Spirit is life and peace" (Romans 8:5-6). It's pretty easy to see that God expects us to have the capability of "setting" our minds. In fact, how we "set" our minds can be a deal-breaker, "because the mind set on the flesh is hostile toward God" (Romans 8:7). How we "set" our minds is definitive. "Set your mind on things above, not on the things that are on earth" (Colossians 3:2). One of the greatest blessings God ever gave us was the ability to "set" our minds.

That doesn't mean it's always easy. But, God goes even further in helping us find the right mindset. "Finally, brethren, whatever is true, whatever is honorable, whatever is right, whatever is pure, whatever is lovely, whatever is of good repute, if there is any excellence and if anything worthy of praise, let your mind dwell on these things" (Philippians 4:8). Grouches would feel so much better if they did this. So would their spouses.

If you're not happy, then learn to be. It can be done.

Marry a happy person. Be a happy person.

Buddy System

As far as I was concerned, all Married People were at least a little strange. The whole idea that they were living their lives attached to another person just seemed so bizarre to me. But Jerome and Jane were even stranger than most Married People.

Most of the Married People I observed from day to day seemed at best to sort of put up with each other. Some seemed like lab partners, willing to go along with the pairing, but not holding much hope for a very good grade. Some seemed like bickering siblings on a long road trip, only able to keep some fashion of peace by staying on their side of the backseat. Some actually seemed like two countries sharing a precarious border, but always on the verge of declaring war. At best, most Married People were putting up with each other.

But Jerome and Jane were different. It was almost as if they were friends.

More than that, it was almost as if they were best friends. I'm sure they had their marital spats. They might have even had full-fledged arguments. But there was something about the way they treated each other which indicated something that kind of blew my mind.

I could tell that even if they hadn't gotten married, they would have still been good friends. They might have even been best friends.

Given that the greater majority of Married People appeared to maintain a fragile détente, Jerome and Jane were fascinating to me. Married People who were friends.

Who would have thought?

Most Married People can often be spotted together, but their side-by-side proximity is simply because that's how it all played out. It's momentum and inertia. The rings are on the fingers. *That means we have to move in this direction, together.*

Married People who are friends are different. As I noticed with Jerome and Jane, if there was another dimension in which they were not married, both of them would still enjoy being around each other. They would have been friends.

Jerome and Jane were friends because they had history together. That's also true of all Married People, but Jerome and Jane learned to like each other's stupid stuff. They didn't just have the lub-a-dub factor going. They liked each other's bodies probably, but they also liked each other's minds. Each one tried to find out the appeal of the things that fascinated the other one.

They may have had some things in common before they were married, but they continued to go to the trouble of finding more in common even after they were married. If Jane loved to ski, Jerome gave it his best shot to ski. If Jerome loved Star Trek, it wouldn't be very long before Jane could quote Spock.

It didn't have to be fanatic devotion to their interests. Jerome didn't have to take on Black Diamond slopes. Jane didn't have to go to a Trekki convention. But at least there was a little effort in both directions. They found new ways to connect. They grew their friendship.

That led to more laughs and more smiles. Even when they argued or went through tough times, they had the simple fact that they were pals. It sustained them through some pretty serious challenges.

It's not that they had to be around each other all the time. They had other friends. But there's something to be said for doing the silly, stupid stuff with your spouse too.

I guess you could say they had another level of love. They didn't just have the romantic partner. They also had a buddy. And there are plenty of days when that's exactly what all of us need. A buddy. Your best friend.

Jerome and Jane made me realize, when it comes to partnering up and going to the altar, friendship is underrated. I remember thinking. If marriage can be like that, then maybe it's not so bad.

Burning the List

Married People were once children. They too ran the gauntlet of elementary school romance. They too faced the brutality of the List.

For me it was Mary's List. But everyone confronts their own version of it. Whether it's Melvin's List or Madeline's List, all Married People are haunted by criteria which determines whether or not they are attractive.

Even though elementary school is long past, the List stays with them, nestled into the back of their mind, sometimes assuring them they are not at the bottom of the List, but more often reminding them they are nowhere near the top of the List. There is always someone more attractive than you.

This unofficial rating system follows Married People into the marriage. Even after they are joined to their spouse in marriage, I've learned that many Married People are still quite distracted by where they might fare on the List.

Especially women.

Our culture brutally holds women to a much more strict and prevalent standard, that can only be met by a Photoshopped un-human.

More Married People than we might suspect remain hung up on their looks. They have specific physical features that might rate low on the List. Everyone must admit to having features that rate high, but it's the flaws and glitches that keep us insecure. Even if a Married Person's spouse has loudly proclaimed them to be a 10, it's not enough to exorcise that stupid List.

I have often heard that Married People who make the effort to remain attractive to each other can benefit greatly. But it has often been obvious to me that there is much more concern about personal appearance as seen by outsiders. Many

Married People don't aspire to please their spouse. They aspire to rate higher on the merciless, unappeasable, ever-irrational List. Many Married People have compromised their modesty and even their behavior, all for the sake of gaining a higher rating on the List.

However, the biggest problem happens when a Married Person lets the List start to affect how they rate their spouse. My guess is that mentally holding up a husband or wife to the standards of the world is one of the quickest ways to make both people unhappy. When you compare a spouse to a standard made of glamor shots, they are bound to get bad ratings. Even the glamor people can't maintain that dazzle.

Married People have it much easier when they ignore the world's whispers. Married People who let God set the standards tend to be quite happy. But it's not that God considers physical attraction to be irrelevant. I think a lot of people think that God seeks to arrange some kind of passionless partnership that will be pleasantly unfulfilling.

We need to give our Creator a little more credit than that. Don't forget. He's the one who came up with physical attraction in the first place. So He's certainly not opposed to it.

I think the trick is for Married People to realign their focus. When you get married, God expects the wife to focus on the husband and the husband to focus on the wife (Ephesians 5:22, 28). Married life is a challenge in which two people compete to put the other one first.

That means both of them stop leering at other people. Every time they linger over the sex appeal of someone else, it adds another tiny drop of poison into their marriage.

For husbands in particular, this is a vital issue. As men, our eyes are constantly snagged on the milling of women parading past our lingering glances.

That's not the way it should be. For the husband, his wife is the new standard. It's like Good Morning America or Project Runway suddenly announced that his wife is the woman to which all other women aspire to resemble. If she's short—

short is in. If she's tall—tall is in. If her hair gets gray, gray is so in.

Seems to me that this would help a lot of husbands. If they simply realized that they have married the woman that just happens to be at the top of their List.

The Excellent Husband

In elementary school, we learned some mythology. We were all fascinated by creatures such as the Gorgons, the Minotaur, and the Hydra. Even though we all knew they didn't exist, I suppose we spent time talking about them because they had at least some influence on reality, even if it was just to fill us with a sense of wonder.

Along these same lines, I would like to briefly draw your attention to another mythological creature—the Perfect Husband. Even though there are rumors of sightings, he is as real as Sasquatch or Slenderman. It's important that we dismiss him quickly so that we can approach an analysis of the husband. There is no Perfect Husband.

On the other hand, Bad Husbands have been confirmed. More than a few witnesses have verified even Horrible Husbands. But don't let cynicism convince you to believe there's no such thing as an Excellent Husband. Many consider him to also be mythological, but he *does* exist. He is simply a rare species.

In order to accurately classify the Excellent Husband, it will help to consult the Designer. The Word will help us slough off the world's input that often distorts our ideas about him. "Husbands, love your wives, just as Christ also loved the church and gave Himself up for her" (Ephesians 5:25). Since Christ lived and died for the church, this means a husband is designed to live and die for his wife. "So husbands ought also to love their own wives as their own bodies. He who loves his own wife, loves himself" (Ephesians 5:28). Based on this passage, a husband is designed to treat his wife with as much attention and care as he does his own body.

Yes, the husband is supposed to be the bread winner. One of the assignments he has is to go out there and victoriously acquire loafs. Yes, he's supposed to protect his family, making sure to lock up at night. Yes, he's supposed to be the voice of reason, maintaining a stability when it comes to the financial future of the family.

But to limit the design of the husband to mere physical concerns is to fall far short of what the Designer intended. Not just as a husband, but as a man.

Jesus explained that "Man shall not live on bread alone but on every word that proceeds out of the mouth of God" (Matthew 4:4). An Excellent Husband doesn't just sustain the physical welfare of his family. His priority assignment is to sustain the spiritual welfare of his family. If he never provides the bread of life (the Word), then he's no bread-winner. That's nice if he brings home paychecks to make sure the family is fed. Maybe he even puts in some tough, extra hours. But there's more than one way to starve to death.

Since the Word is the only source of spiritual sustenance for any soul, an Excellent Husband is going to make sure his family is fed with Scripture. Anything else means he is no better than the man who ignores justifies an empty pantry. He is like the man who lounges on the couch while his family has nothing to sleep on.

An Excellent Husband makes sure his family is safe from intruders. He's the guy who locks up at night. He might latch the windows and turn the bolt. But there are intruders much more dangerous than the ones who might try to slip into the house. An Excellent Husband will also watch out for the things that will compromise the spiritual safety of his wife and children. Any solid man will make sure his security system goes deeper than just house security. That's all temporary safety. He will also make sure his family is safe, both body and soul.

5 – THE **For-Reals**

He is the voice of reason. But just because his voice is deep and loud doesn't accomplish anything unless it is shaped by biblical wisdom. Without the Truth in his heart, he will merely be another blustering tyrant. The Excellent Husband doesn't just demand respect, he expresses it. Even when he is firm and adamant, his motivation is driven by an unwavering love for those under his care. His power is gentle.

The Excellent Husband puts God first. His wife comes second. Unless he puts God first, he will never be the husband his wife needs. Unless he puts God first, he will never be the father he could have been. Without that essential connection with the One who invented husbands, he will remain only a shadow of the idea.

Despite the male's tendency to be chronically oblivious, the Excellent Husband makes the effort to notice little things. Little things might include his wife's new hair style, the full trash can, or even the little things known as his children.

The Excellent Husband listens to his wife talk about things he doesn't care about. He summons one more ounce of strength to play with the kids or to handle the kitchen. The easy chair and the remote have him only after everyone in his family is done with him.

The Excellent Husband makes mistakes. But even in his flaws, he shows a great depth of character in handling his mistakes. He faces the music and apologizes when necessary. He allows his wife and children to see the real person he is. He shines even as he stumbles.

The Excellent Husband tries to do better. He is not only ready to wrestle assassins, he also protects his family from himself. From his grouchiness, from his lack of self-control, from his scowls. He is man enough to take on the world because he loves his family. But he's also man enough to take on himself.

However, in order to truly define an Excellent Husband, it would help to see what God considers to be an excellent man.

"How blessed is the man who does not walk in the counsel of the wicked, or stand in the path of sinners, nor sit in the seat of scoffers. But his delight is in the law of the Lord, and in His law he meditates day and night. He will be like a tree firmly planted by streams of water, which yields its fruit in its season and its leaf does not wither; and in whatever he does, he prospers" (Psalm 1:1-3). This seems to capture the essence of it all.

An Excellent Husband will fight entanglements with sin. He will be a man of the Word. His devotion to God will be as steady as a tree planted by water. Any husband who does not aspire to these cannot be an Excellent Husband. He will merely be a husband.

The Excellent Husband is rare, but he does exist.

The Excellent Wife

Believe it or not, my research has also revealed there is also no such thing as a Perfect Wife. You might as well try to find a wood nymph or unicorn.

There are plenty of Bad Wives. There are also Horrible Wives who methodically dismantle their husbands one nag at a time. There are wives who undermine a man's attempts to lead. There are wives who let their role as mother overshadow their role as wife.

However, do not despair, evidence confirms the existence of the Excellent Wife. She also is quite rare, but she does exist.

The Designer in this case also has some insight. So we must look to God for clarity.

The wife is designed to be "a helper" (Genesis 2:18) to the husband. This is no small assignment in that both God and the Spirit are described in similar fashion (Psalm 115:9-11; John 14:16-17). She is not a token sidekick, but a partner who makes all the difference as each challenge approaches.

An Excellent Wife support her husband as the leader of the home. In other words, the Excellent Wife is patient with his struggles to be the Excellent Husband.

Yes, the wife shines as the mother of the children. Yes, she has insight that often escapes her husband. Yes, she points out things to her husband that he could improve.

But just as with the Excellent Husband, the Excellent Wife doesn't just concern herself with the physical level. Her main concerns reach a spiritual level. And without the Word, any woman becomes merely a shadow of the wife God intended.

The Excellent Wife puts God first. Her husband comes second. Unless she puts God first, she will never be the wife her husband needs. Unless she puts God first, she will never be the mother she could have been. She makes sure her family is fed spiritually as well as physically. Just making sure everyone takes their vitamins and doesn't eat too much candy isn't of much value alone. There are greater concerns when it comes to souls.

The Excellent Wife can be beautiful on the outside, but if it stops there, her value fades quickly. She is adorned with "excellent works, as is proper for women making a claim to godliness" (I Timothy 2:9-10). Her beauty is sustained and powerful because of her relationship with God.

The Excellent Wife points out things to her husband, but always with love—not just because she's annoyed. She supports him when it's easy. She supports him when it's not easy. As long as he does not oppose God, she stands by her husband's decisions. She lets him be the voice of reason as guided by the Word.

The Excellent Wife treats her husband like the church treats Jesus—with respect and honor and love. She does not belittle him or bring him down.

The Excellent Wife may want to be in charge, but she goes to great lengths to support her husband being in charge (Ephesians 5:22). The Excellent Wife puts herself last so that the Excellent Husband must make a real effort to put himself first.

The Excellent Wife holds her tongue when there's malice and speaks openly with kindness. She is the one who notices the pain of others, to point them out to her husband. Then together, they do something about it.

The Excellent Wife does not let her own self get in the way. She focuses on others, finding her happiness in the smile of those she loves. She rocks the cradle and rules the world. The world doesn't rule her.

Proverbs ends with wisdom concerning wives.

"The heart of her husband trusts in her" (Proverbs 31:11). The Excellent Wife doesn't sabotage her husband's position as leader of the home with under-the-table politics with their children. She is his confidante and advisor.

"Strength and dignity are her clothing, and she smiles at the future" (Proverbs 31:25). The excellent wife maintains a positive perspective, helping her husband laugh through life and the troubles that come their way.

"Charm is deceitful and beauty is vain, but a woman who fears the Lord, she shall be praised" (Proverbs 31:30). Most of all, the Excellent Wife fears the Lord. Because her relationship with her Creator is where her excellence comes from.

An Excellent Wife is rare, but she does exist.

Buying Canaan

There's an odd part of the Bible that in the midst of God's grand design, seems to be an obscure fragment. It involves a grave.

Everything has been moving along according to God's promises. Despite both of them being well along in years, Abraham and Sarah have had a son, who will father a nation, which in turn will serve as the stage for saving the world through Jesus. Then Sarah dies.

I would have thought Scripture would merely mention her death and then move on. After all, many other deaths are recorded in the Bible and they are sometimes mentioned almost in passing as the next profound event looms.

But here, in a sense, the Word pauses.

Abraham's love has passed away. He and Sarah have been through so much together. They traveled strange deserts. They survived the edge of annihilation—within sight of the smoky ruins of Sodom and Gomorrah. They rescued their nephew, when he was kidnapped by kings. They laughed with doubt and then joy over a son that should have never been born. Now their story as a couple has come to a close. Sarah lies silent before Abraham.

In the midst of the book laying out God's eternal purpose—the grand design to rescue a whole planet of souls, everything stops briefly so Abraham can bury his wife.

It becomes more than just a simple, touching moment because there are complications. In particular, there's one specific problem. Abraham is a nomad. That means this widower has nowhere to bury the body of his wife. He has no land.

So Abraham does something most nomads don't do. He sets out to buy some land.

Since this completely goes against the very definition of nomad, it's a big deal. Besides, he's not even staying. He's going to be moving on soon. That's the plan. Buy some land, bury Sarah, move on.

Abraham talks to the locals and expresses interest in buying some real estate. He picks out some land that belongs to a man named Ephron. But when Abraham suggests a transaction, there's a slight glitch. Ephron doesn't want to sell it to Abraham. He wants to give it to him. Ephron said, "No, my lord, hear me; I give you the field, and I give you the cave that is in it. In the presence of the sons of my people I give it to you; bury your dead" (Genesis 23:11). Seems like a good deal. It's actually an incredible deal. If someone offered to just give you a house or even just some land for free—no strings attached—most of us would jump all over that. When it comes to real estate deals, it's hard to beat free.

But Abraham insists on paying for the land. "He spoke to Ephron in the hearing of the people of the land, saying, 'If you will only please listen to me; I will give the price of the field, accept it from me that I may bury my dead there'" (Genesis 23:13). Abraham doesn't just want to have the land. He wants to own it.

Ephron relents and allows Abraham to pay 400 shekels, which was the standard going price—and the deal is closed. "So Ephron's field, which was in Machpelah, which faced Mamre, the field and cave which was in it, and all the trees which were in the field, that were within all the confines of its border, were deeded over to Abraham for a possession in the presence of the sons of Heth, before all who went in at the gate of his city" (Genesis 23:17-18). At that moment, Abraham becomes a nomad who owns some land.

Abraham insists on paying not because he's worried about being indebted to Ephron. It also isn't some kind of final, grim anniversary present. This is not Abraham just enshrining his wife.

Abraham is simply thinking ahead. It's easy to miss, but some of you were paying attention.

Abraham just bought a piece of the Promised Land. When he handed over those 400 shekels, he was thinking back on the promises of God made and he was thinking ahead to the promises God would eventually fulfill. Abraham now owned a little patch of land with a suitable cave to honor his wife. He was fully confident his descendants would someday own everything in every direction as far as the countless eyes of his descendants could see.

Abraham wasn't setting up a graveyard. He was buying the door of the house he would someday own completely. As he walked away from this newly purchase place to head on his nomadic way, he knew he had just secured an investment in the Promised Land. It was yet another act of faith by a man of faith, proving that he fully believed God, when God said that someday all of this would eventually belong to his countless descendants, the current grand total being one and only one son.

Years later, Abraham would also come to the end of his earthly life. I'll give you a million guesses where he wanted to be buried (Genesis 25:9). Guess where several other members of his family were also eventually buried. In this same obscure, little spot. The land that Abraham the nomad owned.

Abraham and Sarah being buried together was more than a romantic gesture. It was a suitable and symbolic end for two people who would also have a beginning in the eternal Promised Land. In a very real way, they had a small piece of the symbol of Heaven—until they reached the real one.

That grave was a layover.

Most happily-ever-afters kind of smooth over the fact that eventually the handsome prince and the beautiful princess are going to move onto the rest of their lives together. Sure, they will get the upgrade to being a handsome king and beautiful queen. But there can only be so many fanfares of the trumpets. There can only be so many times they can waltz the night away. The magical moment of standing on the balcony together watching the sunset is available for a limited time only. All of it is headed toward an undeniable and unavoidable and kind of unroyal ending—death.

Happily Married People have a death plan. This is not as gruesome as it sounds. Think of it along the lines of the husband and wife agreeing to meet somewhere for dinner. One of them might get there before the other one, but either way, they'll see each other again.

Unless a husband and wife have this, there will always only be a semblance of a happily-ever-after. In truth, it will merely be happily—for a while—after.

Married People who are Christians belong to God. They have been buried into Christ through baptism. This is a lot like Abraham and Sarah buried in the Promised Land. The brief grave of baptism and even the slightly less brief grave of physical death are interruptions, not conclusions.

When Jesus returns, Abraham and Sarah will be reunited.

The adventures they had together will seem like children's toys compared to what waits for them in their new lives. It will be far more than marriage. They will share the thrill of exploring the incredible paradise God has prepared for those who belong to Him.

So yes, in case you're wondering.

There is such a thing as happily-ever-after.

PART 6

High-Impact SOLITAIRE

The Cards You're Dealt

Everything I've been rambling up to this point, has simply been so I can now ramble about this section. As mentioned, I have a lot of experience being a single person. This has possibly allowed me to reach objective conclusions about Married People. It is has also allowed me to have a deeper appreciation and empathy for others who have been single for some time.

Before I get to the issues surrounding Single People, I want to do some preemptive apologizing for anything that might come across as unfeeling or flippant. It's not easy being single when it seems like most of the world is not. Even a lot of Single People are "with someone." So if you are completely unattached, it can feel downright unnatural. When you don't have what everyone else seems to have, you become intensely focused on having that. Making sure you are "with someone" might be the central preoccupation of virtually every creature on the planet.

A solitary person is in a unique position. If you're a Christian—the real kind who pursues the standards God has set down in Scripture—then that puts you even more at odds with your surroundings. Not only are you struggling to remain moral, you are to a certain extent struggling on your own. Enough time goes by and you feel like you're the one and only one and only.

The only circumstances I know really well are my own. After that, if I take even one step in any direction, I realize I am out of my zone. Scripture can serve as a means to find insight. But anything else—the world, my perspective, and yes—even your own perspective—are highly susceptible to subjective opinion.

You might be very happy with your life. You might be very unhappy with your life. As they say, we all have to play with the cards we're dealt. But make no mistake. Don't let that analogy imply that all of this is left to chance. Before we venture on safari among the Single People, don't be fooled into thinking existence is left to chance. Before we move on, it's important to remember there is a Creator and that He is deeply involved in His Creation. He is very interested in your particular set of cards. You have not been left to the mercy of the odds.

One of my favorite verses might be very appropriate at this point. "For the eyes of the Lord move to and fro throughout the earth that He may strongly support those whose heart is completely His" (II Chronicles 16:9). God sees the world and He sees you. He is also very eager to support you if you turn your heart over to Him.

I don't know how many times you've been the odd man out. I don't know how many times you've been a bridesmaid and never the bride.

One thing I do know. There is a Creator and He is eager to bless you. How that plays out, might very well be determined by the cards you're dealt. But make no mistake. Whatever the outcome, you will win.

Men are Stupid, Women are Insane

After a few decades of being on my own, like a lot of people in my position, I began to feel a little cynicism. Then a little more. When it came to matters of romance, I became more and more skeptical of the system. After all, how good can the system be? From where I was standing, it seemed like everyone had gotten married but me.

I settled into a life that showed no sign of me ever becoming anything other than a Single Person. I was happy. Definitely happy. But the cynicism still murmured in the back of my mind. In fact, it eventually convinced me to believe in a classification system for men and women that was not flattering to either. But as far as I was concerned, sometimes it summed up the whole situation.

Men are stupid. Women are insane.

Now, I realize there are probably more tactful ways to put this, but at least it feels equally offensive to both sides. Plus, even though this bitter epiphany was born in solitary confinement, I would suggest there might be a glimmer of truth here.

Let's consider men first. They are not very good at communication. When it comes to subtle cues they are clueless. They can remain quite oblivious for days or even weeks to something that has changed. A girl's shoes might as well be invisible. Hurt feelings can be remain equally unnoticed. When it comes to interacting with people, men are usually one step behind women.

Men will boldly pursue an idea, reluctantly admitting it was a bad idea, only after he is standing in the rubble of his decisions.

This is not to say men are the bumbling fools of sitcoms. The husbands and fathers of those insipid shows are only paper-thin characters to scribble third-rate jokes on. They are unfair, exhausted clichés.

However, if a man is allowed to descend into his natural state, unchecked by himself or any friend, he will descend into a state of stagnation distracted only by the sight of a remote or an attractive woman.

In a very real way, men are essentially stupid.

Women on the other hand, have their own flavor of mental complication. They are so much the opposite of clueless, so in tune with the world around them, that this often serves to almost disable them. It's as if their highly-tuned sensory and emotional capabilities overload and become too much for them.

Faced with problems, they will shrug away logic and trust in their feelings. They then ride the wave of these feelings into the situation, convinced that the heart will win the day. Apply anger and/or tears and no amount of legitimate facts will be able to stand against them.

If they allow this maelstrom of emotion to run feral, it quickly goes bad. If they do not restrain themselves, they will fall into a mindset of indulgence and entitlement. They

inevitably descend into a state which by the loosest of definitions might be accurately described as crazy.
Women are insane.
I'm not handing out ammo here. To dismiss either gender as just "stupid" or just "insane" would probably only confirm your own label. In others words, if you bitterly sum up the opposite sex based on the flaws of the few, this would probably only prove that you are either stupid or insane.

There are levels of course. Some men are not as stupid as others. Some women are not as insane as others. And we're not talking literal stupidity or literal mental instability. You get the idea. But I think most of us would agree. Both sides have a propensity for their own special kind of wackiness and I stand by my opinion—dumb as I may be.

I would suggest each side allow for something. These sloppy labels could help identify the differences between us and maybe even help us understand each other better. If a woman is patient with men when they're doing something a little stupid, maybe men will be patient with women when they're doing something a little insane.

I know, I know. This is clearly exaggeration. But you have to admit that these titles carry at least a faint validity.

Men are stupid. Women are insane. It's not that catchy and you probably won't find it on a T-shirt or a bumper sticker. But still—it has a certain ring of truth.

The Circling Flame

One of the most drastic changes anyone faces in college is the sudden increased potential for social connections. Even if you stay in your dorm and study all the time, you inevitably encounter a whole new variety of personalities and ideas.

The most exciting change is the sudden increase in prospects. Girls have more guys to choose from. Guys have more girls to choose from. Something long-term begins to feel much more feasible.

I realize college is often a time for some to merely "sow their wild oats." Eager to wallow, they find others to share in the corruption and then spend the rest of their lives "reaping their wild oats." I'm not talking about them.

There are also those who wanted to just play games. The game seems to be called Date as Many People as Possible. I saw plenty of those who seemed to be constantly entangled in some romantic drama of some sort, one after the other. I'm not talking about those people either.

I'm talking about those of us who were genuinely searching. Sure we were all there for the education. We planned on walking away from there with a degree. But I suspect that the number one priority in a lot of our minds was the strong hope that we would "find someone."

There was a standing joke that a lot of the girls just went to college to get their MRS, but there probably were just as many guys there looking for a wife.

You went to class, but your romance radar was running all day, every day. Homework was merely the means to strike up a conversation. The library was nothing more than a quiet mixer.

As I did my time at college, I became acutely aware that there were many girls there who were hoping to not only graduate with a degree, but also with a ring. There were more than a few guys who were haunted by the same anxiety.

At the college I attended, there was a tradition. I don't know how prevalent this ceremony is at other schools. But at this school (at least during my stretch there) there was a ceremony among the girls called a "candle-lighting."

This is how it worked. If a girl got engaged, she would not necessarily go around telling everyone. To make things a little more fun and suspenseful, she would only share the news with a close friend or two. They would set up a time for several of the girls to gather in the dorm at night.

Once everyone was gathered, they might sing a little. I'm not sure. I was never actually present for one, being that I am male. But I do know the girls would sit in a circle. At one point, a candle was brought out. It was placed in a nice little holder with some sort of flowery garnish around it. Tied to the garnish was a ring. An engagement ring.

Maybe only two or three girls in the circle knew who it belonged to. All the other girls only knew it was someone in the circle.

Then the ceremony began. The girls passed the candle around the circle, one girl to the next. I suppose it went around more than once in order to build the suspense. But eventually, when the time was right, one of the girls would keep the candle. She would not pass it on. She would smile, lean forward, and blow out the candle. Then everyone would know it was her. With much chattering and excitement, the circle would break up into a congratulatory mob. Another girl had found her man.

I don't know if there was any real equivalent among the guys. At least I never heard about it. I doubt there was. That's probably a good thing. The man-version of a candle-lighting would have probably involved a torch. Or even better—a grenade. They could pull the pin and start passing it around. They would definitely have a circle that was a little more on edge. I would almost be up for that.

But during my time at that college, toward the end, I began to notice something about the candle-lighting ceremonies. They tended to happen during the final quarter of the year. It wasn't just that spring was in the air. Actually I think the main reason they happened then was because people were running out of time. Graduation was looming. That meant if some guy had cold feet, he better get them warmed up or use them to start walking.

Not only did the candle-lightings happen during this final quarter. They tended to increase in frequency as the quarter drew to a close. This was so much so that by May, it seemed there was a candle-lighting every week.

There was an atmosphere of urgency. I'm sure that wasn't always the case. But from my perspective, several of the engagements didn't seem that well thought out. Many of them smelled of desperation.

I'm going to graduate and I'm still single!

For some, getting engaged was a panic move. Faced with the post-college possibility of still being alone, many guys and girls compromised on their choice of a spouse as far as spirituality. It was a decision that haunted some of them for many years to come.

Though unspoken, the idea was well known. *It's better to be with almost anyone then to end up alone.*

I'm happy to report many of these candle-lightings led to some happy Married People. The ceremony was no curse.

However, every now and then, I can't help but think back to that circle of girls. There was much laughter and happiness, especially for that one girl. But there also had to be one or two or more girls who passed that candle along, wishing they were the one about to extinguish that little flame and claim the ring.

The candle approached, was briefly in their hands, and then it moved on. Not for them.

One candle-lighting and then another and then another.

That circling flame was the beginning of something wonderful for some. That ring would soon meet its partner ring and yet another two Married People would walk the earth.

But there were many who watched that flame go by and they graduated ring-less.

Old Maids and Spinsters

Let's take a minute to establish an important distinction.

When it comes to being single, someone might argue that both the male and female can be equally lonely. However, in many ways, the state of being unmarried is undeniably tougher on the female. Case in point: when it comes to describing an unmarried girl, there are at least two terms hovering over them, both with highly negative connotations.

Old Maid and Spinster.

Compare these to the male equivalents. An unmarried guy doesn't become an Old Man or a Weaver. He gets the relatively neutral and possibly stylish terms Bachelor or Eligible Bachelor. On their own, neither of these titles carries the slightest stigma.

Women however must pretend to carry on calmly waiting for a prince to step onstage, while their own grim titles wait in the wings, waiting for their cue.

The guy can remain single for some time and never have to worry about the biological clock. The girl however hears it ticking every day and every time the sun sets without "finding someone," the next day can feel a little more hopeless. The clock is striking midnight. She's dropped her slipper and as far as she can tell no one will be picking it up.

Today, again, she is an old maid. Today, maybe tomorrow, maybe forever, she is a spinster.

With a handful of words, the world has trampled the elegance of the single woman. But I would suggest, before we look at the lives of single people, that we pause to see that there is a glimmer of respect (however unintentional) in how the world sees the unmarried woman.

"Maid" is short for "maiden," which is synonymous with "virgin." To be given that title is no insult. It indicates something incredibly honorable. Here is a woman who treasured purity. While the world has mocked such a standard, she has avoided degradation, enduring years of temptation. She is a rare champion who has refused to compromise her body for the sake of brief poisonous comfort.

Regardless of the stigma of the term, any woman who has maintained her integrity in this regard is not only rare, she is honorable.

"Spinster" actually has to do with a specific occupation. In the olden days if a girl remained unmarried by a certain age, it was considered necessary for her to find some kind of work, since there would be no husband to support her. In many cases, a woman in her position would be able to make money spinning thread. It was one of the few jobs a woman could take on that provided some kind of decent income.

But again, there is something honorable in this etymology as well. Spinsters who remained single weren't necessarily in that circumstance just because they had been overlooked or rejected. When the term was first used in this regard, a spinster was a woman of high standard who was unwilling to abandon her standards for a husband. Instead of lowering her criteria in order to acquire at least some kind of consolation prize husband, she did not budge. She did not sell out her standards, even if it meant being single forever.

Here, in this 21st Century world of sexual corruption, a woman who has maintained her purity is of greater rarity and deserving of greater admiration. Countless women have fallen into impurity. They have found their way through many grimy relationships, only to find that the journey has left them with just a shadow of their hopes. Many of them would give anything to start over.

Before we venture off into my observations of Single People living among Married People, I feel like it's important to at least give a brief nod of admiration to the 21st Century Old Maid or the Modern Spinster.

I know the world seems to turn smoothly without you. The candle has moved on and it never came back round again.

But I would point out (not with any satisfaction or joy) the married girl who was so afraid of being single, she now goes home to a lout who fills her home with stress and anger. I would draw attention to the girl crawling out of the wreckage of yet another divorce.

I wish these girls well. But I wouldn't wish their lives on anyone.

For you Single Girls who have yet to "find someone." I also wish you a hundred lifetimes alone, rather than even one lifetime of being trapped in a miserable marriage.

But here's a thought.

You spinsters out there. You're spinning threads.

(Stay with me here. This is no message of patronizing consolation.)

I know the songs and the movies and the books haunt you daily. I know that the world has whispered promises of some boyish rogue or rugged hero to come along and sweep you off your feet.

And here you are still. Your feet remain unswept. Your ring-finger remains ring-less. Your daydreams of rocking your child to sleep have dissolved into traces of daydreams.

There's a play called *Cyrano de Bergerac*. The hero has a huge nose. He lives his life in secret agony over the fact that no woman will ever love him. But one woman, even though she did not become his wife, had a profound effect on his life. Cyrano put it this way. "But you—because of you I have had one friend not quite all a friend—across my life, one whispering silken gown."

Among Christians in particular, you are that "whispering, silken gown." You are the "sister," the "mother," the "wife" that was missing for so many people. You spin thread. You quietly go about untangling lives and reweaving them back together again.

The days can be brutal. The ticking of the biological clock can be deafening. But you sit before the spinning wheel. Most likely, you will not prick your finger and fall into a deep sleep. A handsome prince will probably not be kissing you awake.

But spin on. When this very brief life is over, when all spinsters gather with the moms and wives and everyone else to prepare for paradise, that moment will put things in perspective. It will make pining away for a knight in shining armor seem petty. It won't matter at all.

I promise. It won't matter.

How to Win at Musical Chairs

After college, it wasn't like there were no more prospects. I knew there was still a chance I might bump into someone.

But as time went by, I began to waver. Every time I walked back to my car alone, every time I stood up as a groomsman, I wondered if I was going to be the last single.

It was beginning to feel a lot like musical chairs. Except in this version, you *want* to get out. The music plays and everyone marches in a circle. Every once in a while, the music stops and someone gets married.

Then back you go into the circle, your smile just a little smaller than it was the last round. As time goes by, there are less and less people. Pretty soon, it's just you and a few others trudging around and around waiting for the music to stop. But it doesn't.

For a while, it's not a big deal. A friend of yours gets married. Another friend gets married. Your brother gets married. Your sister gets married. It seems that every few months you're attending another not-your-wedding.

But it's not just the weddings. There is an ever-present atmosphere throughout society that everyone has to "find someone." The radio sings it to you, the movies preach it to you, and sometimes it seems you are surrounded only by couples.

For me, I mostly kind of enjoyed being the guy who got to leave still unencumbered. Walking back to my car alone sometimes felt a little stylish. I would get in and crank up the music as I drove back to my bachelor pad (a.k.a. small, cluttered apartment). I became an uncle and enjoyed that upgrade very much. I always had a great time being an uncle. I would drop by my sister and brother-in-law's house, wind up their kids and then go home.

I kept thinking there was plenty of time. I had seen enough bad situations to almost fear the idea of heading toward marriage. As a result, I was mostly at ease with being on my own. I knew I would probably get married someday, but I was in no hurry.

But time continued to pass by and I finally noticed that sometimes it seemed I was the only one left in this game of musical chairs. I was the only one walking around in a circle, waiting for the music to stop. Once in a while, I would meet a girl and we would go out. But due to my own immaturity, any romantic aspects of these relationships did not last. Fortunately, many of them continued on as friendships.

Plus, the whole idea of until-death-do-we-part still kind of terrified me.

But I continued to march in the circle, not sure how this was all going to play out.

There's hope for a while. You hold onto the possibility that maybe you're one of those eleventh-hour stories, like you're a protagonist in a movie.

He had given up all hope. He had watched one friend after another get married. But just when it seemed he would end up alone, suddenly—

Nothing.

Suddenly nothing.

You get up each day wondering if this is the day. But as far as romance, it's just like yesterday. Clear to partly nothing with scattered nothing, probably continuing throughout the week. Throughout your life.

You still take the time to make yourself presentable. Just in case an opportunity happens along. But the music hasn't stopped in a long time.

And as far as you can tell, it looks like this circle will soon be made of one.

Boaz and Ruth

Once there was a girl who found someone and then lost him. We don't know much about her husband except that he died and his name means "weak." Whether this means his health or just his general strength, it's hard to say.

But here's what we do know. Ruth had no reason to hope.

In fact, when we first meet her, we overhear a conversation between her and her mother-in-law Naomi, who has confidently mapped out a very dark future for herself and anyone foolish enough to tag along (Ruth 1:14). Naomi even reminds Ruth that keeping her company is not likely to lead to a new husband (Ruth 1:11). Everything about this situation indicates there is absolutely no reason for Ruth to continue on in the company of Naomi. According to Ruth's mother-in-law, things are bad and they will only get worse.

Ruth's best bet is to go back home. If she continues along this path she's currently on, it will only lead to hardship and grim companionship with a destitute pessimist.

But there's more to Ruth than meets the eye. She has spiritual depth. She tells Naomi, "Do not urge me to leave you or turn back from following you; for where you go, I will go, and where you lodge, I will lodge. Your people shall be my people, and your God, my God" (Ruth 1:16). She's sticking with Naomi. She's choosing to follow Naomi's God.

With no possibility of a man in sight, Ruth continues on with Naomi, who is heading back home to get about the business of giving up. Back to Square One. Here's the plan—be miserable.

When they enter Bethlehem, Naomi is not at her best. She is down on life. But there's Ruth, walking next to gloom incarnate, sticking close.

It gets worse. Bethlehem may be home to Naomi, but home is not in good shape. For a single woman like Ruth, there is no social scene. Everyone is mostly focused on just trying to survive. There's a famine going on so the priority is food, not whether or not someone Like-Likes you. At the top of just about everyone's list in Bethlehem is *#1 Find Something to Eat.*

Ruth doesn't mourn her descent into poverty. Despite Naomi's frowns, Ruth gets up and goes to a field to begin the humiliation of gleaning. This meant going to a field that belonged to someone who was better off than you and collecting the scraps of the harvest.

That's what Ruth does. "So she departed and went and gleaned in the field after the reapers; and she happened to come to the portion of the field that belonged to Boaz" (Ruth 2:3). This is where it gets good.

Boaz spots Ruth and finds out about her admirable decision to stay with her mother-in-law and her devotion to God (Ruth 2:12). It's not long before Ruth finds out Boaz is an admirable man.

There's no real matchmaking. Ruth catches Boaz's eye and there are a few conversations. There is mutual respect. But as far as I can tell, it all comes about because of kindness toward people and devotion to God.

There isn't much potential. He's older. She's is a widow with zero prospects. Her life is headed toward subsistence living.

But God arranges something beautiful. It works out. It works out rather well.

Don't jump to the moral of the story.

This doesn't mean there's someone out there for everybody. That's missing the point. The point is that God is on the job. He is aware and active and involved in your life as much as you allow Him to be. That may or may not mean you "find someone."

But here's something I think we can take away from the love story of Boaz and Ruth. Trying to map out your future by using your current surroundings is a pretty useless endeavor. Everyone's assignment is to do what Ruth did. Put the past behind you and get busy following God. Where that might lead is up to your Creator. But one thing you can count on. He's really, really good at blessing your life.

Solitary Confinement

Our culture likes to sort people. Your age, marriage status, and profession determines your corral. If you are young and married, your group is called the Young Marrieds. If you are married and have been married long enough to have kids—even if you don't have kids—your group is called the Young

Professionals. The older people get more creative names like the Keenagers.

We call it demographics. Everyone has a place. If you are out of high school and unmarried , you are part of the Singles. It's short, sweet, and appropriately only one word long.

Since I was out of high school for a long time and single for a long time as well, I had the opportunity to be part of this demographic for quite a while. I also benefited from being part of many singles groups connected with various congregations.

Singles groups are a relatively new idea. In the early 1800s, the average lifespan was 37 years old. So there wasn't much time to play the social scene. If you were going to settle down and have a family, you had to settle down pretty quick.

On the average, people live a lot longer nowadays. Because of this and because of career issues and such, people are getting married later than ever before.

The end result is a lot of single people.

A whole lot of this particular demographic squanders its integrity in decadence. However, there were many of us who would simply get together as a matter of solidarity. Kind and loving people would open their homes so that we could gather together, in a sense defying our very nature of normally being alone.

In my experience, a Christian singles group would gather on a Friday night at someone's house. The house would typically belong to Married People. Girls brought the snacks, guys brought the beverages. My understanding is that you never switched those around because the girls would automatically bring diet soda—mostly nasty concoctions. This also prevented scary, male-inspired snacks.

After a little preliminary conversation, we would have a devotional together, including some songs, a lesson, and a prayer. Done right, this can't help but be good for anybody— single or married.

Then we fell into small talk and games, drinking non-diet soda and safe snacks. After a while, all of us would go home—still single.

Part of the reason for singles groups is encouragement. When it seems like everyone on the planet is married except for you, it's nice to spend some time with other people who also sometimes feel like everyone else on the planet is married except for them.

But to be honest, deep down, everyone was hoping for the possibility of "finding someone." When you first walked in the door, during those first few seconds, you weren't wondering how tasty the snacks would be. You were not anticipating whether or not someone brought Dr. Pepper or Cheetos. Phase one was scoping.

I don't mean to be crass. But I'm willing to bet that this was the case for most of us. You can't lose if you sit down and study the Bible with a group of Christians. Fellowship with chips and Pictionary has often been the recipe for some of my favorite memories. But whenever there was a singles activity of any sort, when a single person rang the doorbell, their radar was set for even the slightest ping. They were wondering if this would be the time they "found someone."

This doesn't mean there was always an agenda. Almost all of the devos I participated in with other singles meant spending time with some of my best friends, who to this day remain people I still look forward to seeing—hopefully still sharing junk food and games.

But the theme was always in the back of your mind. Singles groups were often the opportunity to "meet someone."

It actually happened several times. I know of more than a few Married People who owe their introductions to a singles devo. It was kind of humorous. Once a couple formed, they would collide and then vanish. It was a lot like witnessing atomic fusion.

But for those of us who continued on as a herd of singles, sometimes there was a tone of pessimism. Who knows? It might have been just me. But occasionally I had the distinct sensation of a cloud hanging over everyone.

Once again, I don't have anything to do on Friday night, so here I am. With all of the rest of you who don't have anything to do on a Friday night.

But after years of various singles groups, I finally figured out something. Whenever I quit being so focused on "finding someone" and turned off my radar, I started enjoying myself more. I got more out of the devotionals. I got more out the fellowship. I laughed more and had a better time. I enjoyed regrouping and recovering from the week. I had fun.

The downside of singles groups is if they become collective pity parties. Or if they merely serve as thinly veiled dating services. Some congregations are too caught up in meeting the needs of the squeakiest wheel. Groups end up becoming quarantined, self-serving support groups.

The secret is to do things in such a way that are pleasing to God. "Do nothing from selfishness or empty conceit, but with humility of mind let each of you regard one another as more important than himself; do not merely look out for your own personal interests, but also for the interests of others" (Philippians 2:3-4). This would include singles groups. As long as it's a search to make you happy, you never will be. The trick is to walk in the door and put yourself last. It's the only way. Doritos are optional.

Expiration Date

We've probably all had friends who drove clunkers. Maybe you *were* that friend. Whenever you got behind the wheel and turned the key, you braced yourself for nothing to happen. Or worse, for something to happen—something fiery.

But even if the car rattled to life one more time, you drove with your fingers crossed. You got to where you ignored the "check engine" light so long, you didn't even notice it anymore.

Dating is a lot like that car.

By now you might suspect that I don't hold the process of dating in high regard. Once you've seen it trample its way through high school and watched it thrash a college campus, it's hard to still believe in it as a good thing. Sure, we all know lots and lots of people who are now happily Married People because they went on a bunch of dates. But I'm willing to bet a box of Valentine Day chocolates that the path there led through some heartbreaking territory, either for them or for those they left behind.

In most cases, it seems that dating contains a self-destruct device built into it. At the very least, it's a lot like driving a car notorious for its bad craftsmanship. You can almost count on it leaving you stranded or involved in some kind of heartbreaking collision. Almost every time, one or both of the people involved will be damaged in some fashion. Then when it's your turn to crawl from the wreckage, collecting whatever pieces of your heart you can find, you actually looked shocked.

Look at it this way. The roads are littered with abandoned cars, all the same make and model. There are a few of them who took two people where they wanted to go, but most of these vehicles have failed.

So why do we get in?

I suspect the biggest reason is because it's so shiny and new. It's the fun and buzz of "finding someone." It's the dazzle of flirting. It's the whirlwind of physical contact.

I suggest that the debris of hearts along this particular stretch should make us at least pause. The body count alone should convince us there's something not quite right here. Dating has some serious flaws.

One of the primary flaws is that dating promotes the concept of disposable people.

Meet someone, try someone, leave someone, meet someone, try someone, leave someone. We live in a culture stuffed with disposable products. It seems that this mindset has even effected how we deal with people.

We would also have to admit that the great majority of dating involves physical compromises, which progressively destroy purity. Dating has become an indulgence in desire, burning up and discarding people like matches.

For most people this pattern gains momentum. They date several people one after the other. Then the next one and the next one. Then this hurtling mess hits marriage.

Date, break-up, date, break-up, date, break-up, date—stay!

Two people exchange rings and repeat words of commitment, but it often carries the ominous undertones of nothing more than a prolonged date. They might convince themselves they're in it for the long run, but deep down, they know they can always just "break up."

It's doomed from the start. Life has been lived without commitment through numerous relationships. Such a life will find it incredibly difficult to suddenly have staying power. That kind of loyalty and steady character doesn't just switch on with the "right one."

I don't know. Dating seems to be the best way to make sure you experience lots of disasters. No one realizes that all those stunned, shuffling, broken older people, trudging through their dark days were once on the dating circuit. These were the party people. These were the ones who thought dating would lead to something wonderful.

It just makes sense to consider other possible approaches. Dating, at the very least, needs some adjustments. As is, things are not going very well.

However, anything other than standard dating is typically thought to be suitable only for homeschoolers and the Amish. I can smell the skepticism from here.

But consider this. God invented marriage. We invented dating. I'm not suggesting we go back to hanging out at wells or arranging marriages, but maybe there are some better options. Let's be honest. Just about anything would be better.

Shipwreck Etiquette

I went to a singles retreat in Montana. There were probably about 30 or 40 assorted solitary people who spent the week enjoying Bible classes, games, and outdoor activities. The underlying theme of course was "Boy, I Sure Hope I Find Someone," but I'm happy to say this distraction didn't get in the way of some spiritual growth. Also we just ended up having a lot of fun. It was a great week.

Some of us decided to go whitewater rafting. We divided up into two separate rafts, each holding about six of us, plus one river guide. It was really fun, for a little while. I was in the raft leading the way, so as we took a bend in the canyon, we were the first to see the trouble up ahead.

There was a snarl of water that no one—not even our guides—were expecting. The river dropped into a bowl-shaped cluster of rock, the water sort of curling back on itself before continuing on in a wild rush. Before we could even think about navigating around it, the snarl pulled us downward then suddenly upward, flipping the front up over the back. Just like that, we were all scattered in the freezing water.

Our river guide quickly coordinated an effort for us to boost him up on top of the overturned raft, so he could then pull us out of the water, but we couldn't do it. The water was too turbulent and we couldn't get any leverage.

So we hung onto the raft and each other. At one point, I tried to help a friend stay close to the raft and to this day I think he thinks I was trying to use him as a floatation device.

At the urging of our guide, we abandoned the raft and tried to reach the bank. This was harder than it sounds because the water was moving fast and the water was incredibly cold. It seemed no matter how hard I swam, I stayed right in the middle of the river.

But little by little, I made progress, snatching at passing leaves and branches until I was able to finally crawl ashore. I ended up not too far from one of my other friends and we sprawled on the rocks, trying to catch our breath.

I found out later we almost lost three of our group. One of the girls was briefly trapped underneath the overturned raft. Another girl was swept far downstream before the other raft rescued her. One of the guys was overcome by hypothermia and they pulled him from the water unconscious. But because of our lifejackets, we all lived to tell the tale. Which I'm telling you now.

You might think the moral of this story is to avoid singles groups—they can kill you. But let's try another angle.

Although most of us had never met before that week, our near-death experience quickly transformed us into a unified group. Even though the roar of the water was deafening, even though we were confused and disoriented, we did our best to help each other. Just knowing we weren't alone in the situation was a huge encouragement. When we all went into the water, we stopped being singles. We started being survivors.

When our raft flipped over, one of the guys approached a girl while she was gasping and struggling to keep her head above the water. He smiled at her. "So how's it going? Would you like to go out to dinner sometime—maybe catch a movie?"

She batted her eyes and said, "Why yes, you husky rogue. I would be delighted."

Can you believe it?

Of course you don't. Because when you're busy trying to stay alive, all the flirty stuff just doesn't seem all that important. Any handholding going on that day wasn't about making hearts go pitter patter. We were more focused on making sure hearts just kept beating at all. We were very hopeful of "finding someone," but it was more about simply finding them breathing. On that day, if we had acted like singles, that particular bend in the river in Montana would probably be named after us.

When it comes to life in general, a solitary person doesn't have much of a chance. Two people are better off (Ecclesiastes 4:9), but I bet you can guess which number is better than two (Ecclesiastes 4:12). The point is this: survival works best as a group activity.

So here's a thought. Since this life is primarily about spiritual survival—that our souls are in as great a predicament as a dozen singles in a Montana river, there might be room for reconsideration as far as the whole dating thing. Since two people "going out" almost always leads to bad things, maybe it would be better to consider going out as a group.

Married People are like two people together in a raft wearing lifejackets. Most of the time, dating is like two people out of the raft with no lifejackets, clinging to each other while floundering in the rapids. The embrace can be comforting at times, but usually it goes badly for one or both of them.

Until you're married, a group makes much more sense. In addition to having a better rate of survival, there are also other significant benefits.

A group of singles doesn't have to worry about the awkward, initial moment at the door. You just meet and go.

A group of singles doesn't have to worry about the even more awkward goodnight at the end of the evening. You just say tell everyone you'll see them later.

Group conversations are much easier. There are less lulls and the lulls are less painful.

I know what you're thinking. The door moments can be nice. Having time alone is nice too. I hear you.

But there's something to be said for getting to know someone in a group. Not to suggest anyone is intentionally deceptive, but people on a date typically do not behave like they usually do. In other words, dating is one of the worst ways to try and get to know the real person. Eventually the facades and filters do come down, but it takes quite a while. In the meantime, you're pretty much hanging out with an imposter.

In a group, you not only get to see how a person interacts with you; you also get to see how they interact with other people. That can tell you a lot more, believe me.

How do they act when they get annoyed? What happens when they lose at Pictionary? What happens when someone spills Dr. Pepper on them? What kind of slang surfaces when they're joking around?

You can also learn more about a person at the assembly than on a date. Do they have time to speak with the elderly members? How do they react to annoying children? How involved are they in the work of the congregation? Or how about whether or not they have the spiritual fortitude to walk in the building, actually carrying a Bible?

These might not be deal-makers or deal-breakers but they can certainly tell you a lot. These are the things that don't show up right away when you're dating. But they are the very things that you'll be dealing with if you marry that person.

It would be nice to know about them as soon as possible. So I'm thinking that for the most part, the dating game has failed as the best means to "find someone" to marry.

Instead of dating, try something much more simple.

Survive with them.

Girl and Friend

Is she a girl?
Yes.
Is she your friend?
(pause) Yes.
Then she's your girlfriend! (maniacal laughter)

Almost everyone has been a part of this bit of fun. With lawyer tactics, the adults or a giggling friend corner you into culpability. You are framed and convicted.

Everyone knows it's meant as innocent teasing, but it also helps pinpoint a common misunderstanding that took me years to overcome.

For a long time, in my mind, eligible, single girls fell into two categories:

6 - High-Impact Solitaire

1. Girls I Don't Like
2. Girls I Like

If you liked a girl, you tried to decrease the distance to her. You didn't necessarily hate the other girls; you just didn't concern yourself about decreasing the distance. On occasion, it was kind of important to maintain a platonic distance or there might be misinterpretation. People might think you like her or worse—she might.

When I got to college, my roommate George and I adapted the categorization. We noticed that among the eligible girls that were attractive to us, there were two subcategories. We upgraded the taxonomy.

1. Girls I Don't Like
2. Girls I Like
    a. Girls That Are Attractive
    b. Girls That Are Attractive and Marry-able

We had noticed that among the girls we found attractive, there were some that seemed somewhat plastic. Although we appreciated a girl getting spiffy as much as the next guy, there were several girls that seemed to be barely held together with L'Oreal and Maybelline. We found ourselves more interested in the attractive girls that you could picture actually dressing sloppy once in a while or having a water balloon fight. You know—someone real.

This classification system shaped my brain for several years.

It wasn't until I was in my thirties that I really began to grasp that there was actually yet another category. It was something I would have openly admitted to as far as its existence, but for the most part, I had lived my life virtually ignoring it as applied to any eligible single girl.

1. Girls I Don't Like
2. Girls I Like

    a. Girls That Are Attractive
    b. Girls That Are Attractive and Marry-able
    c. Girls That Are Friends

There had been many girls who were my friends, but not really. Especially as time went by and my single status became the prominent trait of my existence, I found that I tended to maintain a comfortable distance from most girls, subconsciously assuming that when it all came down to basics, there were only "girls" and "girlfriends."

Girlfriends were one thing. But it wasn't until relatively late in the game that I discovered the incredible blessing of the girl / friend.

My sister and I have been friends our whole lives. When I didn't understand girls, she would often translate things for me. She was my source of inside information. Many times, when I expressed interest in someone, she would do a little reconnaissance work for me. I am deeply in debt to her.

But a whole new world opened up for me when I began to develop real friendships with eligible girls. I may have very well been romantically interested in her, but she wasn't romantically interested in me. Or vice versa. But I found that once we got past the romance discrepancy, there was a lot to be said for just the friendship.

Part of the misunderstanding comes from the worn-out breakup phrase, "I just want to be friends." The truth of this statement is actually, "I just want to stop dating you and maintain a more comfortable distant interaction with you, but if that means never seeing you again, that would be fine too." With that kind of thing hanging over every romance, it's easy to believe that friendship is the consolation prize.

Thanks for playing and here is a small parting gift—a vague friendship that will most likely fade into polite acquaintance.

I'm proud to say I ended up with more girl / friends than girlfriends. And believe me—girl / friends are a lot less complicated. Sometimes we could meet for dinner and even go out to a movie, but our friendship became something incredibly valuable to me that would have been destroyed if we had made the mistake of automatically trying to twist it into "dating."

To this day, there are several girls who I consider my good friends. I would be a much lesser person if I had never figured out the opportunity of making them like extra sisters. They helped me understand women more and they even helped me understand me more.

So while, I have the opportunity.

Thank you, girl / friends. I am deeply in debt to you too.

A Tribute to Tricycles

Let's bring out that chaperone one more time.

Here she is, folks. The one who ruins everything. The sour biddy in the black dress whose sole purpose is to smother any romantic possibilities. Like a malicious spider, she lurks in the corner, ready to drain the life out of love.

Thank you, Ma'am. But you are dismissed. Be gone!

It has taken some time, but we have thoroughly shaken off that nuisance. No more disapproving stares. No more intrusive interruptions. Love can proceed unhindered. She might appear in the form of a parent or another authority figure when you're in your teens, but after you're on your own, the very idea of a chaperone is laughable.

It feels a lot like graduating from a tricycle to a bicycle. The childish times of the third wheel are over. We only need two wheels from now on, thank you very much.

Now a Single Male and Single Female can indulge whatever attraction they have for each other and destroy their futures without anyone getting in the way.

I know this sounds a little extreme, but we don't have to search very long to find people who can trace more than a few regrets back to a time when they were chaperone-less.

We need to remember we have an enemy. It's easy to see how two people being alone together are easy targets for Satan and his agenda. He is very good at using good for bad. All the romantic ambiance of sweet nothings in the shadows have mostly led to severely damaged lives. Some souls have never recovered from those "magical" nights. Our enemy will use every opportunity he can and he is very astute with the innocent attraction between two people. He will take what could have ended up being love and twist it into yet another cliché of degradation.

When did accountability become a bad thing?

When a girl and a guy are pursuing a romantic relationship, there is something to be said for placing yourself in the company of others. There have been many sincere Christian couples who have ended up causing spiritual damage to each other, all for sake of having some time alone together.

If you believe in God—I mean really believe in Him—then that's going to affect your behavior. You will be aware that God is observing your life. That's the very factor that determined Joseph's decision when he was faced with a dangerous opportunity.

When his master's wife tried to seduce him, Joseph refused on the grounds that it would be an insult to his master. But Joseph knew that the sin would ultimately be an affront to his God. When Potipher's wife drew closer to him, Joseph asked her a key question. "How then could I do this great evil, and sin against God?" (Genesis 39:9). Joseph awareness of God's awareness was enough to make him run away from the temptation.

I mention all this because I believe there are many who do actually consider the fact that God does expect us to live by a higher standard. As such, this same person will possibly make better choices—especially when it involves the soul of another person. I know of some couples who were actually engaged and yet refused to be alone together in order to maintain the highest standard of purity until they were actually married. Wishing to protect the gift of their purity until the perfect time, they made sure they were always with other people. They made sure their happy ending was intact. They not only believed in God, they lived like they believed in God.

Despite their ridiculous reputation, chaperones served a good purpose. They controlled behavior. They prevented mistakes. They kept the shine of the romance shiny.

Tricycles might seem childish, but there's one thing about them that makes them better than bicycles. They have much less tendency to fall over.

The Hug Drug

When you mix chemicals, sometimes you get a reaction, but people are different. When they interact, there is *always* a reaction. The intensity of the reaction is determined by a variety of factors, but for the most part, it depends on the amount of physical contact. We're not just talking romantic situations. We all know that even something as mundane as the intensity level of a handshake can determine the final outcome of the encounter.

This is true even more so of course for interactions of a more intimate nature. God designed us to interact with people, but the level of interaction depends on the circumstances. There is an extensive number of possible interactions and it isn't always easy to pinpoint where each of them might fall on the spectrum. For instance, let's take the hug.

Married People hug. So do football players and enthusiastic game show contestants. However, as a general rule in our culture, a hug is typically reserved for people who know each other relatively well, such as family members or friends. But the hug also has enough complexity in relation to the romance arena, that some reconsideration should be given as to its distribution.

The group hug is technically more of a huddle than a hug, so we will immediately dismiss this version and go straight to the two-person hug.

An actual hug can be initially identified in two forms.

1. The One-Armed Side-Hug
2. The Two-Armed Embrace

(This is not to say that arms are a necessary component. Hugs can be "thrown" a short distance in the same way someone can blow a kiss.)

We will make the assumption that all forms of hugging between Married People are appropriate and profoundly beneficial.

Our current purpose is more concerned with hugs between Single People.

The One-Armed Side-Hug is useful in that it maintains discretion and honors the integrity of almost any relationship. It is almost inherently platonic. I have often been good-naturedly teased about my use of this method.

The Two-Armed Embrace is much different. Discounting purely platonic interactions, there are some factors that are worth considering when it comes to two people of opposite genders taking part in a hug.

Some forms of the Two-Armed Embrace are fine. Some forms are clearly not. The intensity, the angle, and the purpose are all relevant factors. Everyone knows that a full-frontal hug can lead to complications for one or both parties. I realize that many a hugger will quickly dismiss any guidance in this matter with great disdain, but anyone with even a shred of wisdom would have to admit there are legitimate concerns.

The Full-Frontal Two-Armed embrace can easily be inappropriate. Girls are notorious for being clueless as to the effect they have on a guy, or (sad to say) very aware of the effect they have on a guy. Even though they were sometimes sabotaging the spiritual integrity of a brother-in-Christ, some of these girls thought it was funny. But these same girls would also cringe in disgust at the dude looking to steal questionable embraces under the pretense of chumminess. I remember one particular guy who orbited the devos at college latching onto one girl after another. We called him "the hug monster."

A hug can be completely innocent. A hug could be the very thing that pulls someone out of despair. A hug has the power to knock down walls of bitterness. But in the realm of Single People irresponsible hugs can cause damage.

Strangely enough it's about chemicals. Recent studies have found out much more about what's going on inside someone's brain during such things as infatuation, kissing, and even hugging. During these interactions, various chemicals come into play. One particular chemical is actually referred to as the "hug drug."

It's called oxytocin and it can link two people in a significant way. For girls in particular, when a hug becomes a prolonged embrace, oxytocin comes into play. For what it's worth, research has shown that hugging for thirty seconds can establish a false sense of connection. It actually begins to create a sense of trust in the female mind. This has proven to be unfortunate in that many of the male huggers do not deserve to be trusted.

This oxytocin factor seems like a great benefit for two people who have actually earned each other's trust. But artificial trust as a side-effect of triggered neurotransmitters—not so much.

Hugging can be a wonderful way of encouraging someone. But it can also be a powerful way of compromising someone's soul. When Single People indulge the embrace, there is more going on than meets the eye. There are chemicals. There is brain stuff going on.

Don't begrudge a hug. Don't dodge embraces of encouragement. But any true Christian woman will dispense her embraces with discretion and decorum. Any true Christian man will not take advantage of women through hugs.

It might help to consider one other way of categorizing the hug.

You can give hugs and you can take hugs.

That might be the key. When an embrace is merely theft disguised as affection, something's wrong with that. But when an embrace is given as a gift, that's where you'll find the Christian.

The Significance of Sex

Hugs can have a profound effect. So it's pretty obvious sex has an even more profound effect. Hugging is like mixing two chemicals and getting a puff of smoke. Sex is like mixing two chemicals and ending up on the evening news.

This is one of the reasons sex is intended to occur only between Married People. Just as in chemistry, there are some reactions that are so powerful, they should only take place within a very specific and exclusive arrangement. Anything else is asking for trouble. Married People are the only ones cleared for this particular reaction.

Even though the Bible is very clear about this limitation, sex is prevalent among Single People. This is nothing new. Even though we might have idealistic images of earlier times, this has always been the case. Percentages were possibly more encouraging in some instances, but all you have to do is read a thorough history book to realize your image of our ancestors might be a little optimistic. The only real difference was that back then there was more stealth.

I mention this because it's easy to think we are living in uniquely immoral times. And we are—sort of. But sexual immorality has always been an issue. You can't even get through the first book of the Bible without learning that people even from the beginning have ignored the restrictions God placed on sex.

This doesn't mean we should surrender to the times. The point here is that sex has always been an arena in which souls are in the balance. God has drawn a line, but mankind has always been quite proficient at twisting things around in order to justify crossing that line—especially when it comes to sex.

Even though the world is incredibly preoccupied with sex, it's amazing how little the world understands it. For most, sex is a thrilling but precarious encounter requiring "protection" in order to avoid such travesties as STDs and children. As long as it's between two "consenting adults," there are no restrictions. To them it's as benign as choosing a dance partner. They keep trying to shrug off the emotional damage, campaigning for the lie that sex can be consequence-free and casual. It's almost laughable. The very people who shake their head at the apparent naïve nature of Christians prove to be the most naïve of all.

When God designed sex, He restricted it to Married People for solid reasons. Hugging effects people in profound ways. Sex even more so. The cascade of chemicals in the minds of those involved is far more significant than any of us fully realize.

It is an echo of Creation. The joining of a man and woman on such an intimate level is connected to the fact that Adam and Eve were once literally "one flesh" (Genesis 2:24). This concept is what condemns prostitution. "Or do you not know that the one who joins himself to a harlot is one body with her? For He says, 'The two will become one flesh'" (I Corinthians 6:16). Any time sex takes place outside of marriage, it establishes a union not authorized by the Creator.

When God designed sex, He intended it to do more than just make Married People feel a thrill. The process transforms brains. It enables Married People to connect on more than a physical level.

In the book *Hooked* (Freda McKissic Bush and Joe S. McIlhaney Jr.), neurologists present research showing how intimacy affects the human brain. In a nutshell, they compare sex to adhesive tape. It's designed to be applied to one specific situation. Treating it casually over and over in a variety of situations makes the tape lose its bonding ability. This explains why sex outside of marriage ultimately fails. "Some individuals have been disappointed to find as they move from one sexual partner to another, that not only are they not finding ultimate pleasure but they are feeling worse about themselves and their many sexual partners" (*Hooked*, p. 26). The world's agenda for sex has a built-in descent.

People who have sex are binding themselves to each other beyond the skin. Beyond the surface of who they are. They are crossing a line that is meant to connect people in a powerful way. To make that connection just for the sake of pleasure and then ultimately break that connection to seek it with another person results in consequences. Your body and brain were designed to make that connection with one person. Beyond that, there are side-effects.

Sex is a lot like a heart transplant. After the act is over, there is a significant level of attachment. Sustaining that connection requires full attention to prevent rejection. With great care and commitment, it can turn out really well.

Sleeping around is like getting a heart transplant—over and over. You allow it to be with you for a short time. But you're not up for the commitment to this particular heart. Plus, there's this other better heart you just spotted. So you have the doctors open up your chest again. This one might work better than the last one. Or another better one might come along.

You can imagine. After a while, the wear and tear on the body makes it less and less likely to be able to fully accept yet another transplant. The graft might be successful, but the connection is more precarious now. You are more prone to rejection or just plain old heart failure.

When two Single People sleep together, it is a trial heart transplant. *Let's trade hearts for a while and see how it goes.* That's not how it works. It is meant to be a one-time, permanent decision.

So it's kind of ludicrous when couples feel they have honored sex or treated it with some kind of respect if they simply delay it for a certain amount of time. They're missing the point. It has nothing to do with the amount of time. It has to do with the amount of commitment—and time alone does not equal commitment. Even "being in love" isn't good enough. The one and only arrangement that proves commitment and thus proves itself worthy for the powerful interaction of sex is marriage.

I know, I know. The world is convinced that waiting until marriage is for oddball religious nuts and socially twisted misfits. But the truth is seen in the people around you. "Love" has become a cheap commodity that lasts about as a long as the latest sappy ballad. Unrestrained desire drives two people together and selfishness shoves them back apart. It is a collision with real damage, chipping away at souls. You can see it in the faces of those who have spent a lifetime playing by the world's rules. Some have salvaged themselves and have climbed out of the muck to find some stability. But many are faded, washed-out people who drift through the laughter, never truly connected to anyone. Even their strongest relationship trembles at the likelihood of being yet again detached or discarded.

There is no real commitment here—just chemicals and breath.

Stigma of the Virgin

And now ladies and gentlemen, I would like to present to you the ultimate outcast.
The virgin.
Believe it or not, this poor fool has somehow reached adult life without ever having had sex. Impossible, you say? Let me assure you. This pitiful creature does actually exist.

Our culture has done something pretty incredible. It has taken purity and turned it into a badge of dishonor. According to the standards of the world, if you graduate college and you're still a virgin, something must be wrong with you. Sex itself is treated like some sort of graduation. When a guy has sex, it is only then he has "become a man." When a girl has sex, it is only then she has "become a woman." Sleeping with someone has become a quest carrying all the aspirations and admiration of reaching the top of Everest.

Simply having sex with someone is not that impressive. Given suitable circumstances and a series of bad choices, sex is not only easy to achieve, it can actually be quite difficult to avoid. Add alcohol and anyone—I repeat, anyone—can find themselves no longer a virgin.

Which makes you wonder why the loss of virginity is considered such a premium. If you had to fight someone to the death or if you had to swim the English Channel or if you had to swim the English Channel while fighting someone to the death—that might deserve some admiration. But as far as effort and valor, on the grand scale of epic challenges, sleeping with someone falls just below *meh*.

Now, staying a virgin. *That* might be a little difficult. Not impossible. But it certainly takes more self-control. Losing self-control doesn't show strength. Maintaining self-control does.

The average American loses their virginity around the age of 17. That means that if you're pushing 19 without ever having had sex, you will soon be considered as odd and unlikely as Sasquatch. In some rare cases, you will be treated like a lucky charm, along the lines of a leprechaun. To others, you will be a socially inept obsolete throwback who has somehow escaped a basic-coming-of-age moment.

That's what movies usually mean when they describe the plot being about someone "coming of age." It means essentially the story deals with the protagonist making the decision to sleep with someone before marriage.

This is where the tables tilt slightly more against men than for women. Women are unfairly pressured to achieve an alien slenderness that only Photoshop can achieve. Men are pressured to "become a man" by sleeping with someone.

In the world's eyes, a female virgin is intriguing at best and laughably excluded at worst. But a male virgin is practically a sideshow freak.

Again, we reach a landmark of irony. Since God and our very design emphasize the idea of maintaining virginity until marriage, by definition those who compromise before the fact are the "freaks." Or to put it in nicer terms, the great majority of adults who cast off virginity as if it were some kind of flaw, only prove themselves to be icons of weakness. It takes stamina and determination to stay a virgin.

Legitimate

First, there are suspicions. Then there are murmurs. Eventually, it all comes to light. They were sleeping together and now she's pregnant.

In the old days, this was so scandalous that the girl was usually whisked away to visit relatives in some distant state. In some cases, she was treated almost as pariah. Tainted by her sin and thrashed by gossip, it often took decades before she was seen as anyone other than "that kind of girl."

It was difficult to know exactly how to handle the situation. One solution was the shotgun wedding. This is pretty much like a lot of weddings except when the father walks down the aisle, he's got his daughter on one arm and a double-ought Remington in the other. The idea was everything could be fixed if the couple just decided to commit to living together the rest of their lives.

I kind of understand the reasoning, but even when there isn't actually a shotgun present, urging people to get married as a kind of triage is only making one big mistake lead to another big mistake. Just because the guy can impregnate a girl doesn't mean he's suitable as a spiritual leader of the home. And that's what matters. Not what people will think, but what God will think.

Today, most of the time these kinds of situations have been handled in a much different way. In some respects, it isn't a much better approach.

When a girl becomes pregnant without being married, if she's out of high school, people barely even glance twice. As far as their concerned, that's just how the world works. If she's in high school, there is a general rush to encourage and support her. Which is great—except that it sometimes almost comes across as if she is being rewarded for a mistake. I suspect there have been more than a few overlooked young girls who considered getting pregnant as the fast-track to being the center of attention.

Being exiled or arranging a 30-caliber ceremony are not good solutions, but neither is simply patting the couple on the back and saying, "no biggie."

It's hard to strike the best tone. But I'm going to try.

First, if a Single Person is no longer a virgin—if they've already made that mistake—if they've repented, it's important to not load a bunch of grim reprimands on their shoulders. That's not our job. We don't do anyone any favors by supporting purity as anything less than a great treasure—and once that line is crossed, it can't be uncrossed. But we're also not helping if we summon storms to hover over the heads of those who have fallen. We are all sinners. It's just that some sins have different consequences. Once you're forgiven, it's as if the sin never happened. The physical consequences might remain, but the spiritual consequences have been completely removed. That person has been made spotless. To treat them as tainted in any fashion is a sin in and of itself.

It's like getting in a bad accident, in which both the driver and the car are severely damaged. The driver (your soul) can go to the hospital and be made good as new. The car (your body), however, might be permanently different. Despite time at the repair shop, it might run a little oddly or there might be a noticeable dings in the paint. But the driver is just fine.

This world makes scars. Everyone has them. It's just that some scars are more noticeable than others. The world is a sinful place and we will sometimes end up in fender-benders and sometimes we will be involved in a full-impact collision. Without God, your soul (the real you) is injured and continues to suffer from that injury. With God, it's like your soul is sent to the hospital (to the Great Physician) and you are made good as new. At that point, you can continue on just fine. Your physical self may still have some scratches, but you—you're just fine.

Even if your body is no longer a virgin, your soul is. No matter what the sin is, your soul can shine again, perfect and pure again.

When a baby is born out of wedlock, clearly there is an issue concerning the purity of the father and mother. Shrugging off the sin as a small glitch merely helps corrupt the minds of everyone involved.

But it's unfortunate when the first thought that leaps into everyone's mind is that the baby is a "problem." Discounting the sin of abortion, there are other mistakes that can be made. Suddenly everyone becomes members of a think tank focused on how to solve this baby-problem. The baby has changed the girl's life forever and if the guy is even a little more than a scumbag, he will allow the baby to change his life forever too. But the baby isn't a mistake. The baby is a soul.

During that first stretch, those involved might lie awake at night, deeply distressed because this human being now exists. Eventually everyone will probably grow to love and want the child—but the sooner that happens the better.

You've heard the term. When a baby is born out of wedlock, the baby is called "illegitimate." Wrong—at the moment of conception, that baby is legitimate. That new soul might have not been on the parents' calendar, but that new soul has always been on God's.

It all comes down to this. God is excellent at working with mistakes. Someone who is no longer a virgin—someone who has a child without being married—if everything is turned over to God immediately, the blessings will soon follow. And every single one of these blessings will be very legitimate.

Rahab Rehab

Jericho was a horrible place. When the Israelites arrived to collect the Promised Land, the area was so infected with spiritual degradation, God authorized the execution of its inhabitants. It was as if Canaan was a dying patient and the Canaanites were incurable cancer. The only feasible treatment was drastic amputation.

This is why God emphasized such a thorough annihilation. The Canaanites were a disease that killed souls. So with the strategic precision of a surgeon, Israel conducted a Jericho-ectomy.

When you imagine Jericho, don't picture a pleasant city filled with innocent people. The very existence of the city was defiance of God. The name "Jericho" was a tribute to the false moon god Yerach. The inhabitants of Jericho also worshiped a goddess named Anath. She was the very definition of sexual immorality and merciless violence. Those who worshiped her wallowed in erotic degradation. Those who worshiped her killed people because they enjoyed it. Anath was depicted by her followers as a laughing woman neck-deep in blood, while standing on a pile of human heads.

This is bad enough, but the people of Canaan were also known for doing something even more unimaginable. "They sacrificed their sons and their daughters to false gods. They shed innocent blood, the blood of their sons and daughters, whom they sacrificed to the idols of Canaan, and the land was desecrated by their blood" (Psalms 106:37-38). Jericho was such a foul place that when it was destroyed—when Joshua and his troops stood on the rubble, he sealed it with a curse (Joshua 6:26). When a man named Hiel defied this warning, it cost him two of his sons (I Kings 16:34). God was so disgusted with Jericho, He used His people to reduce it to rubble and cursed anyone who put it back together again.

The point is this. Jericho was a horrible place.

In this horrible place, there lived a woman named Rahab. In keeping with the prevalent immorality, her name meant "insolence."

If all that wasn't bad enough, she spent her days living one of the most demeaning and corrupt existences possible.

What could be worse than a pagan in Jericho? A prostitute in Jericho.

The city already reeked of perversions. But Rahab lived even below that—her life steadily sinking into spiritual rot.

And yet.

Two men of God infiltrated Jericho on a reconnaissance mission. When the king of Jericho instigated a search for the spies, Rahab hid the spies and kept them safe. She had heard about the Israelites. She knew they belonged to the real God—the One who could scorch mountains, mow down giants, and rip oceans in half (Joshua 2:9-11). That same God would soon level Jericho. So this was Rahab's chance.

When she pleaded for herself and her family, the two spies told her to hang a scarlet cord in her window. This made Rahab's home the only safe place in Jericho. Like a storm shelter, the arrangement would provide complete protection from devastation, as long as they remained inside (Joshua 2:18-19). Rahab's life in Jericho was about to come to an end.

For six days, Rahab and her family heard the Israelites' horns. Then on the seventh day, the horns sounded seven times and the world fell apart. Death came into the broken city and wiped out every single citizen of Jericho.

Almost everyone.

As the Israelites turned their backs on the remains of this horrible city, among these victors was a new family. Rahab, her father, her mother, her brothers, her sisters, and other member of her family who had all become part of the people of God.

In a sense, that scarlet cord saved Rahab's life. But it also kind of destroyed it. When all the people of Jericho were killed, one of the casualties was Rahab the Prostitute. That woman died with the rest. Rahab the Israelite walked away—a new woman.

Rahab went on to live a completely different life. Even though there were dark memories of Jericho, the blessings that came from walking away from all that must have certainly almost faded Jericho to something like a dream she once had.

Rahab went on to become a wife and mother. In fact, truth being stranger than fiction, it's very possible she actually ended up marrying one of the spies, Salmon. Turns out he was one of the princes of Judah. How's that for a happy ending?

They went on to have a son named Boaz, the great guy who ended up sweeping Ruth off her feet. You're way ahead of me. That means Rahab's great-great-grandson was King David. Which means that Rahab was one of the key links in the lineage leading to the Messiah. How's that for an even happier ending?

There are many people who have made the mistake of losing their virginity. There are many who have had children before they were married. There are many who feel they have even greater regrets than these. But all of us once lived in Jericho. Jesus knocked down the walls to get us out.

I suspect once in a while Rahab recalled Jericho. Maybe once in a while, she grew pensive. But I also suspect those moments didn't last very long. After all, it's hard to focus on the distant darkness of the past, when the present is so incredibly bright.

I have never met anyone who doesn't have regrets. But I have met lots of people who shine in the forgiveness of Jesus and have moved on.

Once, there was a prostitute in a godless city. That girl became a different girl. That girl ended up becoming the honored ancestor of the greatest lineage in history.

I wonder if she kept the scarlet cord. Not to remind her of her old self, but to remain grateful that her old self was dead and buried. This girl—the one holding her baby named Boaz. This girl lived a different life.

I heard a story once. It's one of those preacher stories, but I suspect this one is true. A young girl was given a handkerchief as a gift. It was made of silk or some other valuable material and it even had her initials embroidered on it. It was one of her most treasured possessions.

One day, she spilled ink on it. Just like that—it was ruined. It was ruined beyond repair. Needless to say, she was devastated. But tears don't remove ink stains.

A friend of the family came to visit and the handkerchief was mentioned. The friend asked if he could borrow it. The young girl shrugged and let him take it home.

The friend returned with the handkerchief and when he gave it back to the girl, she broke into tears of relief and gratitude.

You see, the friend was an incredible artist. He took the handkerchief home and using his skills, he added to the stain and transformed it into a one-of-a-kind beautiful design. The handkerchief was even more beautiful than before.

We all once lived in Jericho. We have all been stained by sin. But I know this Artist.

And He is incredibly talented at making your life beautiful again.

Foothold

One of the most challenging things about being single is to remain pure. Not just with your body, but your mind. To make the challenge even more difficult, you are surrounded by people who don't give God's standard a passing glance. Even among religious people, the standard is often ignored. So you can find yourself sometimes faltering, considering compromises.

Because of this, it's important to know the tactics of the enemy in this regard.

First of all, it's vital to remember Satan is not trying to recruit you. He is trying to destroy you. Since his agenda is so drastic, his strategies must be subtle. Any blatant attempt would probably be rejected. Sabotage is accomplished in subtle increments.

To help us understand, God has provided a warning that is brief but potent. It is an analogy that reveals a great deal about the nature of Satan and how he works. "Do not give the devil an opportunity" (Ephesians 4:27). It can also be translated as "foothold" or "place." But let's focus on the word "foothold."

The idea of a foothold implies so much. The reason you need a foothold is that you are attempting to get solid footing. In other words, you're trying to prevent your foot from slipping out of place. But the owner of the foot does not just want that secure position. A foothold is established in order to provide stability for the sake of the other foot. That other foot is waiting. Once the foothold is confirmed, that other foot will then take the next step. The first foot anchors down so that the other foot can find not only a different foothold, but a higher one.

Open your eyes. Satan is climbing.

Satan is fine with just a little bit. He's fine with you not doing big sins. Just the little sins will do for now. But each mistake is part of a process mapped out by the enemy. One sin leads to another. Little sins lead to not-so-little sins.

No one just one day starts living a life of sexual degradation. It is developed over time.

As mentioned, the word "foothold" can also be translated as "place." Don't give Satan a "place." It's like saving a seat for him. Or it's like keeping a chair at the dinner table open, or even worse, allowing him to live in the guest room.

If he openly acted like an intruder, it would be easy. If he was like someone bashing down the door or breaking through a window, we would recognize his plot right away and respond with strong opposition. We would shove him back out, chase him off. Get better locks on the doors, put bars on the windows.

But Satan doesn't typically bash down doors. He just asks for a place setting. He asks for one night in the guest room. No big deal. It's just one small thing. That's all he wants is a "place." It will do just fine for him. For now.

It's not disruptive. We might initially feel uncomfortable with him at the table. But things seem to continue on just fine. After a while, you even forget he's there.

But that's all he needs to ruin you.

The only logical solution is to never even allow him that one foothold. When he nestles his toe in, kick it back out. When he sits at your table or tries to slip into the guest room, shove him out. He is here to destroy you, one small bit at a time.

Survival will require you to fight not just the big battles, but also the tiny seemingly insignificant ones. This is how you remain pure. By not allowing the enemy to win even a little bit.

Small compromises make all the difference. This is why God emphasizes "not even a hint" (Ephesians 5:3). It's the little hints that get us.

The trick is proximity. When people see the line between right and wrong, they will often allow themselves to camp out right next to that border.

Get away from the line.

A hint of sexual immorality allows two very nice Christians to defy their God together and call it romance.

At least we're not doing what everyone else is doing. At least we're better than them.

The one who has established a foothold helps you comfort yourself with the lie that there are small sins—lesser than the "true sinners" out there.

When we are trying to guess something we often ask for a hint. That means we want the door to be slightly open. Not too much. Just enough to figure out how to open it the rest of the way.

A "hint" of sin is a slightly open door, not easy to spot. A soul guided by the Word will do better at spotting it, but even then, it's so easy to miss.

It will happen when you're having fun. It will happen when you're laughing. When you feel comfortable and accepted.

This is the way your world ends. Not with a bang, but with a foothold.

Guard Your Heart

A friend of a friend of mine had the opportunity to see the President. I'm not sure about all the details. I'm not even sure which President it was. But the friend of a friend joined a crowd of people behind a roped-off area and waited.

There were bodyguards everywhere and it was made very apparent that no one was to even think about trying to go past the ropes.

The friend of a friend was wearing a hat and a sudden gust of wind blew it off. It landed beyond the ropes. Without thinking about it, he moved toward the ropes, intending to cross over, quickly retrieve the hat and come back.

But when the friend of a friend touch the rope, there was the distinct sound of a gun being cocked. It was that famous click you hear in movies—of a bullet getting ready.

The friend of a friend changed his mind. Suddenly the hat didn't seem that important.

The reason this guy almost died for his hat was because the President is one of the most highly protected people on the planet. Security is so strict and thorough, it's almost impossible to get close enough to verify whether or not he actually is the President.

Part of it is because the President is vulnerable. Part of it is because he is so important.

Your heart is even more vulnerable and important. Your heart is like a very nice, but incompetent President. He means well, but he has a horrible track record as far as making good decisions. The only way he ever accomplishes anything good is when he is surrounded by wise advisors.

The world says, "Follow your heart." Being that your heart is a bad President, this is horrible advice. The Bible says *guard* your heart. A much better idea.

If your heart needs to be guarded, this implies it is vulnerable and important. The President's bodyguards don't just follow the President. They surround him and watch over him. Hopefully this will allow him to live long enough to get good advice and become a good President.

Your heart also needs the same strict and thorough security. However, the danger is more subtle. The enemy is not targeting your heart with a high-powered rifle. The enemy intends to simply surround it with bad advisors—to make your heart a bad President.

If you just follow your heart without guarding it, it will lead you wrong. Badgered by worldly advice, your heart will veto truth for the sake of romance. It will sign truces with infatuation. At the risk of disillusionment, it's probably safe to say most of the attacks on a Christian's heart will be disguised as "love."

Don't follow your heart. "Watch over your heart with all diligence, for from it flows the springs of life" (Proverbs 4:23). Your heart is vulnerable and your heart is important. It needs your help. Don't follow it. Guard it.

The Tree Inside Your Head

No one ever actually offered me drugs. In high school, I heard about bongs and pipes and roach clips. There was a store nearby a friend's house that kept up a pretense of selling accessories for tobacco, but everyone knew it sold paraphernalia for pot.

I heard stories of kids getting busted. A joint in someone's locker. A stash hidden at home in the sock drawer. I had a friend whose parents kicked him out of the house when they found out he was selling.

I think about all this sometimes as I drive through Denver. On some streets, there seem to be "medical" dispensaries on every other corner, each legally selling marijuana like a cross between a pharmacy and a Dunkin Donuts. One of the saddest things that has happened in my lifetime is Colorado becoming known as the land of potheads.

Of course alcohol was embraced as a legal drug long before the grass peddlers came to town. But that's a subject for another time.

It all feels kind of surreal. Whereas once you could get arrested for scoring a two-finger bag in a dark alley, now you can stop for pot on the way home with the same lack of fanfare as someone picking up a loaf of bread. The opportunity for this particular sin is everywhere.

In the Garden of Eden, sin didn't have as many convenient locations. In the beginning, there was only one location. "And the Lord commanded the man, saying 'From any tree of the garden you may eat freely; but from the tree of the knowledge of good and evil you shall not eat, for in the day that you eat from it you shall surely die'" (Genesis 2:16-17). This was the one temptation brooding in the garden.

There was only one tree. Out of all the trees in Eden, there was only one tree in particular that was doom. What it lacked for in quantity, it made up for in convenience. It was extremely convenient. It was in the middle of the garden (Genesis 3:3). To top it off, it was "good for food" and "a delight to the eyes" (Genesis 3:6). You might wonder why God didn't make it poisonous and tuck it away in a cave surrounded by giant thorns.

But it was important to God that Adam and Eve had a choice. Their choice would measure their obedience to and love for their Creator. God wanted them to face the desire of sin and turn away. That would only be possible if it was desirable and accessible.

The tree in the middle of the garden proved to be too much for them. It wasn't because there were too many trees. There was only one. The downfall of man was at least partly because the tree was just so very much, right there.

We are in the same situation, except worse. The Tree of the Knowledge of Good and Evil isn't in the middle of a garden. It's in the middle of your head. When sin flourishes in your mind, it seems good and it's pleasing to the eye. It deceives us into thinking that God is keeping us from being happy. It convinces you that you can sin and not die. All the same lies of Eden.

One particular fruit of this tree is lust. After self-preservation, the sex drive is the second most powerful instinct in a human being. It is a powerful force rooted in our minds like a prevalent and undeniable tree.

It's like a drug, but instead of having a stash hidden in a drawer or under the mattress, you carry the stash in your skull. It can be triggered by very little. A stray thought can lead to contemplation. Contemplation can lead to lust—another hit.

The result is the same as it was in Eden. We experience shame and disconnection from God.

The sex drive itself is not sin. The tree is tempting, but it is our choice that is the sin. We live in Eden with that same stupid tree and there are times when it seems we are constantly falling.

When God created us and put us in the garden, He made sure that we were not animals (Genesis 1:26). Regardless of what current documentaries say, you are not a sophisticated animal. You are a human being. God intended that you be in control of your body. God urges us to fight lust because it makes us less than human. When He condemns "those who indulge in the flesh" (II Peter 2:10), he describes these same people as "unreasoning animals born as creature of instinct" (II Peter 2:13). We, as souls, have been given freewill to determine the behavior of our body. To be less like animals and more like God. In a sense, the Tree of the Knowledge of Good and Evil was the option of turning all this down. To move the other direction.

Lust is relinquishing control and becoming a lesser creature. It is allowing the body to run things. It is one of the quickest ways to surrender your humanity. Lust makes us less than what we were created to be.

Meet the Deceiver

Jesus did a lot of damage. With incredible power, He sabotaged Satan by healing the sick, forgiving sins, and yanking demons out of people. In a way, Jesus was sort of like a heroic thief. "Or how can anyone enter the strong man's house and carry off his property, unless he first binds the strong man? And then he will plunder his house" (Matthew 12:29). In this analogy, the strong man is Satan and the property are those who are owned by Satan—his possessions. Jesus was essentially kicking down the door and liberating the lost. Those who belonged to the devil could now stop belonging to him. However, in order for this to work, it was necessary for Satan to be "tied up."

This binding of Satan was not temporary. Jesus didn't tie up the strong man only to release him again. When Jesus finished His ministry—when He walked out of the tomb and turned a defiant back on death, Satan was profoundly damaged. When Jesus left our world, He left a severely damaged enemy behind. Make no mistake, anyone who does not belong to God, belongs to Satan and is virtually possessed by Satan—but not in the sense of abduction against your will. We are promised there will always be an escape if we want it (Corinthians 10:13). This is important to know. Satan has been drastically limited.

But it is also very vital we realize our enemy continues to be dangerous. Just in different ways. He is no longer capable of making someone run around a graveyard or fall into a fire, but he is still extremely dangerous. He is extremely dangerous for at least one particular reason.

He can still lie.

This is one of Satan's best weapons. In fact, Jesus pointed out that this is a defining characteristic of our enemy. "You are of your father the devil, and you want to do the desires of your father. He was a murderer form the beginning, and does not stand in the truth, because there is no truth in him. Whenever he speaks a lie, he speaks from his own nature; for he is a liar and the father of lies" (John 8:44). There are a lot of religious people distracted by what are ultimately nonexistent dangers never perpetrated by Satan. He does not possess people. He does not brainwash us through subliminal messages. He does not whisper to us inside our head. We seem to forget that one of the most dangerous things about our enemy is the plain and simple fact that he is an exceptionally good liar.

In order for a soul to be lost, deception is key. No one would knowingly embrace condemnation. The final and ultimate downfall for the majority of humanity will be negotiated through simple trickery.

Although he certainly has numerous strategies, the basic ploy of deception remains always in play. Even modern Christians are susceptible to the old Eden scheme. We are warned of that very thing. "But I am afraid that just as Eve was deceived by the serpent's cunning, your minds may somehow be led astray from your sincere and pure devotion to Christ" (II Corinthians 11:3). Our enemy seeks to undermine our "sincere and pure devotion to Christ." And he will attempt to do it by deceiving us.

Our only hope is the Truth. It sets us apart for salvation (John 17:17). So our enemy is going to do everything he can to replace the Truth with things that are not true. If we allow it, he will interfere with our perception. "And even if our gospel is veiled, it is veiled to those who are perishing, in whose case the god of this world has blinded the minds of the unbelieving, that they might not see the light of the gospel of the glory of Christ, who is the image of God" (II Corinthians 4:3-4). Satan, the god of this world, blinds minds. It isn't necessary to literally infiltrate your brain. He simply provides lies that have the ring of truth. He fashions credible falsehoods.

He promotes WorldSpeak, that shines brightly as the "wisdom of the world" (I Corinthians 3:19). This is why our feelings alone cannot serve as a unit of measure. The world is filled with people whose feelings have led them to a sincere, genuine, heartfelt delusion. If you don't want to be the next dupe, your only hope is Scripture. The Word undeceives the deceived. A clear grasp of the Bible is the only distinction that separates those who have been made righteous from those who feel righteous.

We are surrounded by his lies. We hear them in songs, we watch them on television, we are entertained by them in movies, we are swayed by them through friends, family, online forums, sermons, blogs, texts, phone calls, and tweets. Wherever there are words, the enemy is there, ready to twist them. The result is a huge supply of excuses and loopholes, ready for the taking.

And we take them. In fact, we collect them and store them in our private arsenal, to be used at our convenience whenever we are determined to do our will instead of God's will. Certainly our enemy is to blame. But the actual responsibility is lying at our own feet. When we are tempted, the Bible is clear about who is at fault. "Let no one say when he is tempted, 'I am being tempted by God'; for God cannot be tempted by evil, and He Himself does not tempt anyone. But each one is tempted when he is carried away and enticed by his own lust. Then when lust has conceived, it gives birth to sin and when sin is accomplished, it brings forth the death" (James 1:13-15). Obviously, God is not going to have any part in tempting us. But notice that Satan isn't even mentioned here.

Satan is indeed involved as far as the deceptions of this world—developing and growing the lies. But once we pick up the temptation and carry it, at that point it isn't the devil who is running the show. It's you. Choosing from a wise selection of deceptions, you can find something to soothe your conscience long enough to sin. Unguided by the Word, you will become your own worst enemy.

In a sense, this makes Satan the second most dangerous adversary. Private Enemy Number One is you. Many have said it before. The only one who can keep you from heaven is you. Satan is adamant about undermining our salvation, but the worst culprit is you. With the help of Satan, you can become your own custom-made deceiver. God often warns us that lies are often found inside our own minds. "If anyone thinks himself to be religious, and yet does not bridle his tongue but deceives his own heart, this man's religion is worthless" (James 1:26). "If we say that we have no sin, we are deceiving ourselves, and the truth is not in us" (I John 1:8). "Let no man deceive himself. If any man among you thinks that he is wise in this age, let him become foolish that he may become wise" (I Corinthians 3:18). The Bible warns us. "Do not deceive yourselves" (I Corinthians 3:18). "Do not merely listen to the word, and so deceive yourselves. Do what it says." (James 1:22). When you sin, someone has been lying to you. And that liar is you. This is even more concerning when you consider how good we are at lying to ourselves. The whispering in your head is you.

Maybe the most frightening aspect of all this is that if you are deceived, you won't know it. Being deceived feels exactly like when you aren't being deceived. It feels just fine.

That means we cannot trust our own perception. We cannot consult our own minds alone for guidance. We are notorious liars. We lie to ourselves all the time.

Your mind has been saturated with thousands of ideas provided by the enemy. Only by being into your Bible every day will you be able to effectively identify what is false in your head. This is the only way you will ever have clarity. This the only way to remain undeceived. When it comes to anything truly significant in this life, don't be too quick to listen to you.

Captive Thoughts

My sister and my niece were detained. They were flying from Oklahoma to Colorado, when the guys in the uniforms asked them to step aside into a room for questioning. Once everyone was seated, they leveled a snake-like gaze at my sister.

"Is this your luggage?"

"Yes."

They had found something in one of the bags that incriminated her big time. Nitro glycerin. For those of you who haven't watched enough espionage movies, nitro glycerin is an explosive.

They had detected this very substance in my sister's luggage.

Fortunately, being that a young mother and her seven-year-old daughter are not your standard terrorists, the guys in the uniforms decided to consider other possible explanations.

"Does anyone in your family have heart issues?"

Bells went off in my sister's head. "Yes, my dad. My dad has heart problems."

"Does he carry nitro for his condition?"

"Why, yes he does."

For those of you who haven't watched enough medical dramas, nitro glycerin is also used as emergency medication for people suffering from heart problems. They are very small pills. About the size of an infant's fingernail. My sister had borrowed luggage from Dad.

The crazy thing is, the guys at airport didn't find an actual tablet of nitro. They found "trace elements." They explained that they had devices that could detect what was essentially a crumb of a crumb of a speck of nitro in the bag. Barely a whisper of someone who once looked at a nitro pill.

Although the delay was inconvenient, our family gained a whole new level of respect for the security system. Security has been upgraded tenfold since the old days.

In a sense, this is exactly what Jesus did. He upgraded the security system. Under the old covenant, murder was a sin. Under the new covenant, even indulging hatred is a sin (Matthew 5:21-22). Under the old covenant, adultery was a sin. Under the new covenant, even lust is a sin (Matthew 5:27-28). Jesus has put us on a much higher alert.

The danger is not just in our actions. The danger is in our thinking. We watchdog not only what we do, but also what we think. Airport security doesn't wait until you're on the plane to see if you're a threat. They make sure way before that. In the same way, Jesus expects anyone who is following Him to be on the lookout—not just for the actual sin itself, but for the "trace elements" that lead to sin.

To wait until the sin is active is like a security system at an airport that jumps into action only after the shooting starts. Not much use.

Only a strict security system will work for a Christian. All bags and passengers are detained. "We are destroying speculations and every lofty thing raised up against the knowledge of God, and we are taking every thought captive to the obedience of Christ" (II Corinthians 10:5). We do not let our thoughts wander the concourse unsupervised. The enemy has proven to be a great danger to anyone who is not wary. You can't afford to let your thoughts go about their business without some form of ID.

If any questionable thought arrives at the gates of your mind, you need to take it into a room with a bright light shining in its face. If necessary, you might even have to throw it up against the wall. *What are you doing here? What is your purpose? Where did you come from and what is your intention?* You question your thoughts. You interrogate them. Take every thought captive. Examine it closely and make sure it is willing to abide by your King.

When it comes to sinful thoughts, show no mercy. Thoughts of animosity toward another person—especially another Christian. Slam it against the wall and get it under control. Thoughts that stir up selfishness or self-pity or anger toward God. Round them up. Thoughts of impurity, anything that veer toward lust. These are particularly dangerous because they are very strong. They are notorious for ruining lives. Get them under control. Escort them from the premises. If necessary, take them out back and shoot them.

Your thoughts determine your actions. Harboring bitterness or lingering over ideas about sex and promiscuous possibilities sabotages the security system and puts your soul in great danger. It matters what you think.

There's only one way to develop an effective security system for your soul. Let your mind be shaped by the Word. "And do not be conformed to this world, but be transformed by the renewing of your mind, so that you may prove what the will of God is, that which is good and acceptable and perfect" (Romans 12:2). If you are not on the lookout, world-thinking will infiltrate your mind and get it to conform. The only hope you have to maintain a clear head is to let the Word transform your mind. Your mind is either conforming or transforming and this is determined by which thoughts you allow inside.

Appetite

Your body wants to do stuff. It wants to eat. It wants to speak. It wants to have sex. Yet, your body doesn't always get to do what it wants to do.

A great deal of being a Christian involves self-control. Left to its own devices your "self" will run rampant and the results are never good. Your self needs to be controlled.

Maybe this is one reason why Jesus said, "If anyone wishes to come after Me, let him deny himself, and take up his cross, and follow Me" (Matthew 16:24). One of the primary requirements of following Jesus is to "deny yourself." In other words, you have to say *no* to you. When your mind begins lobbying for you to do the wrong thing, you tell yourself *no*. When your body wants to defy Scripture, you say *no*. When your heart cobbles together some kind of moral loophole, you say *no*.

If you let your body end up calling the shots, you will end up very unhappy. As one writer put it, if we do not struggle to control our desires, we will fall under the "tyranny of self." Believe it or not, you make a terrible dictator. You will oppress and crush your own life. If you don't stop you, you will proceed to mercilessly run your future into the ground.

Your descent will feel like freedom, but you will actually be experiencing one of the most profound forms of slavery. It feels like you're in charge, but you're not. The truth is, you will become enslaved to appetite.

Many people are so quick to shrug off the "chains" of Scripture, only to become the ultimate slave. They think of themselves as a "free spirit," but they have merely reduced themselves to being puppets manipulated by whatever urge their body is currently experiencing. For these people, God is not their God. Their true god is "their appetite" (Philippians 3:19). They may parade a pretense of being the captain of their soul, but the truth is seen when they bow down to the Great Stomach.

Worshippers of the Great Stomach serve a mouth that never stops demanding more. This is possibly why God holds us accountable for gluttony. This is a concern mostly overlooked and yet very relevant to our spirituality.

Don't get snagged on pounds. Just because you might be heavier than some doesn't mean you are a glutton. And just because your metabolism might keep you automatically svelte, doesn't mean you're not a candidate for this sin. There's more going on here than what the scales say.

God associates people who eat too much with people who drink too much. "Do not be with heavy drinkers of wine, or with gluttonous eaters of meat" (Proverbs 23:20). Resorting to sloppy paraphrasing, we could call a glutton a "food-drunkard." This seems to have been the same sin found among the sins in Sodom. The godlessness of Sodom included "abundant food" (Ezekiel 16:49). The idea is that they were "overfed" (NIV). It seems pretty clear. If food has unlimited access to your mouth, then you serve the Great Stomach. You serve your appetite.

In another passage, the seriousness of this sin is captured by a gruesome image. "And put a knife to your throat, if you are a man of great appetite" (Proverbs 23:2). It would be silly to suggest this is merely a tip for good physical health. The idea here is that your appetite can destroy you. But notice that it doesn't even mention food. It just says appetite. This means anything your body desires can spell your demise. Whether or not you feel the blade at your jugular doesn't matter.

Our appetite for food is merely the template for all our desires. When the people of God kept criticizing how God ran things, they often brought up food. "Would that we had died by the Lord's hand in the land of Egypt, when we sat by the pots of meat, when we ate bread to the full; for you have brought us out into this wilderness to kill this whole assembly with hunger" (Exodus 16:3). "We remember the fish which we used to eat free in Egypt, the cucumbers and the melons and the leeks and the onions and the garlic, but now our appetite is gone. There is nothing at all to look at except this manna" (Numbers 11:5-6). This reveals a great deal not only about these people, but about human nature in particular. When we turn our back on God, we are then enslaved by appetite.

On the surface, it might seem like they were only complaining about the menu, but God pinpoints their hearts. "And in their heart they put God to the test by asking food according to their desire" (Psalm 78:18). Demanding that their desires be met was defiance of God.

This is why any Christian today will not just be cautious about his desire for food. He will control his desire for anger, for attention, for respect, and for sex. Whether or not he does control these things indicates the truth of his spirituality. "For the flesh sets its desire against the Spirit, and the Spirit against the flesh; for these are in opposition to one another, so that you may not do the things that you please" (Galatians 5:17). This is bad news for the worshippers of the Great Stomach. As it turns out—you don't get to "do the things that you please."

Satisfaction deferred is a symptom of someone with self-control. Food is just one of the units of measure. There's a difference between eating to survive and eating to indulge your senses. It's worth pointing out that bad food notoriously tastes better than healthy food. That's because the goal isn't sustenance, it's to trigger pleasure.

How well we do controlling our relationship with food might be a good indicator of how well we control our relationship with all are other desires. Indulging in one desire tends to allow indulgances in other areas. Maybe this is why fasting is so effective. If you can go without something you absolutely need for a while. Maybe you'll get better at going without something you merely want.

Overindulging any of our desires leads to problems. Whether it's the stomach or the eyes, or the sex drive, or the ears—your body is attuned to detect and read the world around it. But it is so easy to overdose. To become inebriated through stimuli.

Christians belong to God, not to their bodies. In fact, our bodies have been figuratively executed. "Now those who belong to Christ Jesus, have crucified the flesh with its passions and desires" (Galatians 5:24). We will indeed continue to stroll around in this contraption of flesh and bone for probably many more years. But a real Christian won't let this contraption determine the direction of his life. A real Christian will deny his appetite when necessary. He doesn't worship the Great Stomach. He already has a King and that King says, "deny yourself."

Denying yourself even in the smallest ways might lead to important victories. Hesitating before a meal. Eating only enough. Not listening to or watching everything media spews in your direction. Looking away from potential lust. It's all connected. You are inside a body designed for sensual input. It is your responsibility to limit and control that input. You are also responsible for controlling your reaction to any input that you *do* allow.

Practice saying *no* to you. It will be one of the best things you ever did for yourself.

Her Hero

I have a few things to say to us men in particular. Girls, you're welcome to listen in, but you are also welcome to skip a few pages ahead.

Anyway, men.

You're walking her home and suddenly three ninjas jump out of the shadows. You are not a military-trained lethal weapon. You have not taken classes in jujitsu or kick-boxing. But your rugged masculine instinct takes over and you somehow lay them all out, stunned and defeated—while you walk her safely back to her door.

Or you're getting popcorn and when you return, you find some guy sitting in your seat next to her, leering in her face and making crude jokes. A look of relief washes over her face when she sees you. Without hesitation, you grab this dude by the collar and toss him out one of the convenient exits, while everyone applauds.

Just about any guy would love to be *that* guy. To get the chance to flex your courage and blatantly demonstrate the lengths you are willing to go to in order to make sure your girl is safe. It's a standard daydream that seems built into all of us guys. *She gazes into your eyes. My hero.*

Chances are, no one will try to abduct your date. These scenarios rarely come along. Even if they did, they wouldn't be so tidy. Typically, even the smallest "heroic" confrontation catches the hero off guard and his reaction and handling of the situation doesn't always turn out admirable. More often than not, there will be witless cussing, awkward punching, and a whole lot of stupid.

But I have some good news. There are other ways of protecting her. Open the door for her. Help her with her coat. Do all the chivalry stuff that cause people to point and laugh. If you can take on ninjas, surely you can handle some ridicule.

How does opening a door for a girl "protect" her? It protects her from feeling inadequate. It protects her from feeling worthless. It protects her from feeling unattractive. The Bible calls her the "weaker vessel" for a reason (I Peter 3:7). Whether or not a girl can muscle the door open is beside the point. Opening it for her honors her as someone of value to be protected—even it means protecting her from doors.

Regardless of how much our culture tries to level the playing field, men and women are different. Trying to undo what the Creator did is not helping. Women being the "weaker vessel" does not mean they are less valuable or less capable. It's not a flaw. It simply means they are weaker. They're more vulnerable.

This means one of the primary jobs of the male is to protect the female. It might very well mean guarding her physically, but this also includes spiritual dangers as well. A hero isn't much good if he can't guard the girl against the greatest danger. Any man not up to watching over her soul is not a suitable suitor.

But there is yet another danger that poses a threat to your damsel.

You.

Any real man would never lift a finger against her. Any real man would not use crude language or talk down to her. But any real man would also not push her toward physical intimacy before marriage.

It's such a serious issue and yet it's treated like a game. The man sees how far he can go and it's the girl's responsibility to resist. What "kind of girl" she is ends up being determined by how long the resistance lasts. The immoral girl doesn't resist for very long. The "good" girl waits a respectable amount of time before giving in to degradation.

In this world of shadowy criminals and slouching thugs, strangely enough, the greatest threat to most woman is the very one with his arm draped protectively around her.

If any ninjas show up and you rescue her—good for you. But a man who enables the spiritual descent of a girl is not the hero. He's the other guy.

If he is any kind of hero, he will be the one saying "no," instead of constantly manipulating circumstances to compromise purity. Even if the girl is willing to cross the line, a real man demonstrates self-control. And you know why he does this?

Because he's the protector. He's the hero.

The Joseph Tactic

His brothers almost murdered him. Even though they changed their minds, they did end up tossing him into an empty well and then selling him into slavery. Later, he spent some time in a prison where it was not unheard of for a fellow prisoner to be released—and then executed.

Joseph faced more than his share of danger. However, one of the greatest threats this man ever faced would have seemed fairly mild to a passing observer. If you had been walking through Potipher's house and glanced over, you would have seen a man and a woman talking.

To understand what you're seeing, you have to know a few things. First, Joseph is a good-looking guy (Genesis 39:6). Second, Joseph works for Potipher and that woman there—that's Potipher's wife. She is currently trying to convince Joseph to sleep with her (Genesis 39:7). Seems like a recipe for what the world affectionately calls a "love affair." But watch closely. Joseph is going to do what most men wouldn't do.

He's going to say *no*.

Joseph points out to her that her husband has trusted Joseph with everything. There's no way he's going betray that trust. But more importantly, Joseph also points out the real concern. "How then could I do this great evil and sin against God?" (Genesis 39:9). Committing adultery with Potipher's wife would also be a betrayal of God. That was even more important.

I wish I could tell you that she's going to look at him with admiration and respect his moral stand. But she doesn't relent. If anything, she becomes more determined, pressing him every day to give in.

However, Joseph has strategies. He is really good at this, so pay attention. "As she spoke to Joseph day after day, he did not listen to her to lie beside her or be with her" (Genesis 39:10). Instead of wimping out and tossing aside his self-control, he demonstrates real manhood by not letting her words influence him. When necessary, he also changes location.

But she's not done. When the opportunity arrives, she actually clings to him, practically demanding that he choose sin.

This is when Joseph uses his best and most effective tactic. He ran.

"She caught him by his garment, saying, 'Lie with me!' And he left his garment in her hand and fled, and went outside" (Genesis 39:12). When his previous tactics aren't enough, Joseph resorts to drastic measures. He runs away.

It's important to pause here a moment and deduce some details.

It's probably safe to say that this woman wasn't stronger than Joseph. After all, she was not able to hang onto him. This means that Joseph would have also been strong enough to stop this straight-forward seduction.

The conclusion is simple and profound. Joseph wasn't just running from her. He was also running from himself. He was running from temptation.

When it comes to facing imminent sin, Joseph demonstrates a very effective and admirable strategy. It's like in the movies when someone rushes into a room, their eyes wide, a look of terror on their face and they say, "Run."

There's no time to stop and explain. There's no time to debate plans. There's no time.

The only wise option is to relocate as quickly as possible. This is especially true of sexual temptation. Because the threat isn't just out there. The threat is also inside. You carry it. The desire to sin lives in all of us and is eager to take the controls if you let it.

This is how God puts it. "But each one is tempted when he is carried away and enticed by his own lust" (James 1:14). When we are confronted with serious temptation, many times it's best to run. Since we can't actually escape our own tendency to sin, we must often run from the circumstances that are conducive to sin. That's why we are told to "flee youthful lusts" (James 2:22). Don't attack youthful lusts. Don't just resist youthful lusts. Get out of there. You can't leave your actual desire behind. But you can change your location.

This passage doesn't imply that a potential sinner is no longer threatened when they are no longer youthful. The idea is that youth, whether in the sinner or the subject of the lust, inherently has its own deceptive shine. It is a powerful allure that has brought many souls down to death.

But God always provides an escape. "No temptation has overtaken you but such as is common to man; and God is faithful, who will not allow you to be tempted beyond what you are able, but with the temptation will provide the way of escape also, so that you will be able to endure it" (I Corinthians 10:13). God promises we will never be put in a position where we *have* to sin. God has shown us the exits. Please take note them.

Flee and Pursue

I am really good at not cussing. I was raised in a household that considered foul language to be foul. Even though many people around me have used bad language throughout my life, I have always made it a point to never say certain words. If not cussing had been a sport, I would have been MVP.

One of my old friends knows that I don't cuss. He knows I'm a Christian. I'm pretty sure he thinks that me being a Christian basically involves not doing certain things. I live my life almost like other people, except I don't do stuff. I think that's what I pretty much thought too.

But that's actually kind of a strange way to go about it. In most cases, you don't define something by what it isn't. It would be like a doctor at a job interview, presenting his qualifications as being extremely skillful at *not* poisoning people's food and incredibly adept at *not* running down pedestrians. The interviewer might think these are commendable. *It's great you're not making things worse. But how are you at making things better?*

Don't get me wrong. There are many, many things a Christian does not do. But after you're baptized, if you want to grow—to survive, you're going to have start *doing* some things too. It's a matter of putting off, but also putting on.

Cussing can definitely be a deal breaker. "If anyone thinks himself to be religious, and yet does not bridle his tongue but deceives his own heart, this man's religion is worthless" (James 1:26). I'm still fairly astounded that so many so-called Christians have apparently not gotten this memo.

However, even though I have spent a great deal of my life feeling like I've nailed the language issue, I eventually discovered I had only accomplished half of what God expected from me in regard to my words. "Let no unwholesome word proceed from your mouth, but only such a word as is good for edification according to the need of the moment, so that it will give grace to those who hear" (Ephesians 4:29). A true Christian is not only going to stop using bad words, he's going to start using good words—specifically designed to build up other people. I can't just choose silence to break even.

So that means running away from lust and impurity is not enough. That's just the first part of the strategy. You run away—but in a specific direction. It's not a panic move, scurrying out the door with no real destination in mind.

All throughout Scripture, God indicates that belonging to Him includes the concept of "putting on" certain things. Not just putting off. "So, as those who have been chosen of God, holy and beloved, put on a heart of compassion, kindness, humility, gentleness and patience; clothe yourself with compassion, kindness" (Colossians 3:12). A Christian fights sin, but embraces righteousness. "Abhor what is evil; cling to what is good" (Romans 12:9). The way you fight sin is by putting on not-sin. If a man just empties his life of bad things, new bad things show up and "the last state of that man becomes worse than the first" (Matthew 12:45). Christianity isn't not emptiness. It's fullness.

You run away because you're chasing something. "Now flee from youthful lusts and pursue righteousness, faith, love and peace, with those who call on the Lord from a pure heart" (II Timothy 2:22). You don't just flee; you have to pursue.

When a television show starts you thinking in the wrong direction, you are being pursued. Don't just turn off the TV. Do something to fill up the space. Stumbling into passive silence can be a bad thing. The seed of temptation has been planted. You have to unplant it. You can't just stop and watch the ground.

When you hear that yet one more friend of yours is on the way to becoming happily married, don't just sit and ponder the lack of a significant other. Fill your life with lots of people, by being intent on making sure each of them is safe and happy.

Read your Bible. Pray. Fill your head with the things that matter.

You might think of it this way. Live your life more and more in such a way that there is less and less room for sin. God says to "make no provision for the flesh in regard to its lusts" (Romans 13:14). In other words, make sin inconvenient. Your schedule is so full of doing the right things, there just isn't any room left to pencil anything else in.

Playing Stupid

Just so you know, it's not always like Potipher's wife. More than likely, no one will be grabbing your coat. It will probably be more discreet.

Assuming you are the Joseph of the situation, it's important to have your eyes open. In most cases, someone will be trying to gradually manipulate the situation toward a compromise. This kind of thing can be especially dangerous since it's not always easy to spot. If you're not paying attention, it can creep up on you unnoticed, and there you are—awkward situation.

Not to say there is always conniving culprit. Situations can creep up unnoticed on both parties. But there are often times when one person is definitely shaping a "moment."

When the manipulator has less than pure intentions, there is one particular counter-move that can come in handy. Play stupid.

When someone tosses innuendos, interpret them in their most innocent form. Or simply don't notice them. When someone is obviously attempting to arrange for the two of you to be alone, invite third wheels and fourth wheels and seventeenth wheels. Become suddenly chummy with the world.

Playing stupid saves some embarrassment. It has the added bonus of keeping you from making a fool of yourself in case you've misread the other person. But it mainly helps the instigator save face. All in all, it can help avoid a lot of bad things.

Unfortunately, there is a good chance it will cost you cool points. If you're good at it, playing stupid might actually convince someone you are stupid—or at least naïve. But this is fine. Better to walk away with your integrity than to end up in a situation where the only escape might be losing your coat.

Sad to say, the more popular approach to all things iffy is to see how close you can get to the line without actually crossing it. We convince ourselves we can skim the edge without causing any damage to anyone. This is further enforced when by all appearances the encounter does seem to leave everyone spiritually unscathed. But even just toying with the hug drug is enough to hurt souls on a profound level.

If you're truly trying to approach romance on a godly level, you'll be ready to do what it takes. The first best escape might just be playing stupid. This could very well be the actual moment of truth for just about everybody. This is the spot where most people fold. Countless souls will falter in this temptation for the fear of not being cool. But this is one of the most pitiful motivations to do anything.

In this world, if you're going to walk away clean, it's going to cost you something. When you become determined to hold to God's standards, you will be seen as odd. Those who belong to the world are caught off guard when faced with someone who is actually living by the Word. This is often accompanied by animosity. "They are surprised that you do not run with them into the same excesses of dissipation, and they malign you" (I Peter 4:4). This means that sometimes you're going to have to take one for the team. You're going to have walk away with your image in shambles. I know some of you would rather lose your coat than your style, but there is an irony here that might comfort you a little.

You're only playing stupid. Without intending to sound malicious, the truth is, true stupidity is indulging yourself like everyone else. These same people will one day wish they could go back in time and play it a little smarter—possibly by playing it a little more stupid.

The Masquerade

It's a bunch of nobility waltzing around, wearing masks. Although there's some delicate romantic tension here and there, the atmosphere is classy. Lots of bowing and curtseying. Lots of chivalry and decorum.

That's the masquerade you might find in the movies. But in real life, back in the day, when masquerades were all the rage—it wasn't so classy at all.

There was a level of propriety in that these events were restricted to the upper crust, but as far as morality, many masquerades were quite decadent. That was the purpose of the mask. To give the partygoer anonymity for the sake of diving into sin. The mask kept you from being fully accountable and thus more likely to be involved in things you wouldn't normally do.

A masquerade was a group of people without faces. Or rather, without real faces. Covering their identities created an atmosphere of extreme immorality. Chances are, there were some masquerades that could have been considered respectable. But there's something about losing your identity that causes a person to become more immoral and therefore less of a person.

The masquerade lives on today. There are situations in which we can interact with other people from behind a barrier that either blurs our identity or conceals it completely. You can see it in a limited fashion when people get in their cars. Two angry people will typically get much angrier when they are in separate cars. Put the same two people face-to-face and they would be embarrassed to resort to the childish words and gestures they committed from behind the steering wheel.

The masquerade-effect is even greater online. Behind the mask of a username, when a person is upset, they will often abandon all tact and kindness. The humanity of the exchange is dulled by miles of distance and the virtual buffer of the screen.

This is not only true of anger, but also of infatuation. A car full of girls will flirt with a car full of guys. There is strength in numbers, but the separation allows them to risk a more direct approach. Most girls, even in the strength of a gaggle, won't be as brave outside the car. In some ways, a car is a mask that provides enough of a barrier for a person to become another person.

Transfer this same concept to the digital realm and suddenly there is a great lack of restraint. Secure in the distance and facelessness of texting, a guy and a girl will resort to "sexting." This doesn't mean the same two people would show any self-control in person, but the initial anonymity lends itself to smoothing the way for additional sins.

We have constructed several masks that provide anonymity. Through social networking, online dating, and whatever the next big means of communication is right at this moment, we are throwing the biggest masquerade party in history.

These systems can do a lot of good. but they provide a lot of opportunities to do bad. The realm of anonymity lures a Married Person into seeking comfort from someone online. It's a worn-out story. The lonely housewife finds a comforting voice. The discouraged husband connects with a woman who understands him. The screen is like a window. We gaze out at the world, developing our dissatisfaction and eventually someone sets out and follows through on all the words that have been exchanged. The window becomes a door.

Without the masquerade-effect, it's possible that wisdom would have prevailed or that logic would have intervened. But it's so much easier to cross lines when you're wearing a mask.

Loneliness can be painful. But one of the most foolish things you can do about loneliness nowadays is get swept up in the masquerade. Online dating is not so bad. I know several couples who are solid Married People who met through computers or phones. Maybe it's just the modern version of bumping into each other at a well in Israel.

But watch out for the masks. First take off your mask. Pretending to be someone else is never a wise move. But also watch out for the masks other people wear. This party has been going on for a long time and there is a lot of fake out there.

The Last List

Remember Mary and her list? She was the girl in 6th grade that made a list of all the boys in the order of her preferences. It was my first real awareness of there being criteria out there that I would have to aspire to. I suspect you were confronted with some equivalent. If you're a guy, I bet you were haunted by your own Mary. If you're a girl, maybe you were hoping to rate high on Marvin's List.

Later, you feel like there's an unofficial Master List that looks down on you. Inadvertently, you begin to let this List determine your self-worth. The guy scale is measured in athletes and musicians. Girls are calibrated with models and models—and on occasion, models.

Life becomes a kind of endless campaign trail; your schedule is mapped out according to anything that will help you do better in the polls. The mirror eventually just shakes its head. *Sorry, but I can only reflect the truth.*

Yet, even as you trudge under the oppression of the Master List, you discover you are a hypocrite. You too have a list that is firmly tacked up on the inside of your skull. There are certain things you are looking for in a potential romance. These bullet points welcome or dismiss potential matches that cross your path.

Again, there's nothing wrong with physical attraction. That's part of our design. The problem of course is when our list is only about attraction or if attraction ranks above more important things such as the person's spiritual condition or capability as a parent.

Every person's list is different. What you find attractive can be affected by your family ideals or by your cultural background. Your first bout with puppy love or your first actual crush has probably affected your list more than you think. You might be able to trace a lot of your criteria just back to movies. This list is what you are referring to when you describe someone as being (or not being) your "type."

Modern media has tainted your list with icons no one can achieve. Even the icons themselves can't achieve what they appear to be. They are figments. Artistic make-up, gracious lighting, and tailored clothing are photographed from a hundred different angles. Then a handful of shots are selected and even photo-shopped to create an illusion. The icons then change back into their sweats and once again, become another part of frumpy humanity just like us.

It's kind of sad really. We feel bitter when we don't qualify on someone's list and then feel justified in disqualifying someone else because of our own list.

For a lot of people, if enough time goes by, their list tends to get shorter. Sometimes this happens to us because we're fearful our standards will keep us from finding anyone. We whittle it down to the point of "settling." I saw a lot of people end up in bad marriages because of this.

Sometimes we shorten our list because we have grown more mature. We have learned that hair color and income are not as important as we thought they were.

But despite all this, there's something not quite right about the whole concept of a list.

I heard about this guy who kept his list on the refrigerator. The list included all the things he was looking for in a wife. It was a relatively admirable list. In addition to certain factors of attraction, it also included things of a more spiritual nature. As far as he was concerned, he had a good standard. It was visible and specific, like a wanted poster, except without the head shot. As far as he was concerned, it was just a matter of time before he found his dream girl.

Well, he didn't find her. Some time went by and then some more time. And still—he didn't find her.

Then one day, at the suggestion of a friend, he took down that list and replaced it with a different one. It wasn't a list of things he wanted. It was a list of things he needed to be.

The story goes that soon after putting this list up, he found the girl of his dreams. Instead of spending his time and energy every day searching the world for possible matches, he spent his time and energy becoming a better man. This apparently is what did the trick. His earlier plan was focused on what the girl could offer him. But he captured his dream girl's heart because when he met her, he had something to offer her.

There's an old story / joke about a guy who comes home to tell his roommate he has found Miss Right.

"That's great!" the roommate said.

"Not so great," the guy said. "She was looking for *Mr. Right.*"

Many Single People are severely intent on finding someone who will make them happy. They are so focused on catching someone, they forget to spend time making sure they themselves are worth being caught. They might spiffy up the exterior, but as far as honesty and depth and any kind of real spiritual maturity, all of that is left for another day.

In reality, the only "list" we should answer to is the expectations of our Creator. We're supposed to be determine to improve our "compassion, kindness, humility, gentleness, and patience" (Colossians 3:12). These things don't always rate high on everyone's list, but don't knock it. These attributes have also been known to be quite attractive. Either way, even if you don't find someone to marry, there is one small fringe benefit. You end up being a better person.

The Curse of Good Looks

Almost everyone wants to be good-looking. Guys want to be handsome and bulkier. Girls want to be gorgeous and skinnier. If there were actually genies in hidden bottles, waiting to be summoned to do our biddings, one of the three wishes would most certainly be good looks.

Everyone likes it if someone finds them attractive. Even the most aloof person who sneers at all the shallow games of desire—they too will smile to themselves if they are admired for their physical appearance.

What's really weird is that we take credit for it. If someone says you are handsome or pretty, you thank them for it.

I appreciate that. It took some time to sculpt the skull. Making the eyes were kind of a challenge and it took me several tries to get the skin just right. But hey—thanks.

You may very well have done some tidying up (arranging hair, removing hair), but just because you hosed down the exterior doesn't make you the architect. As any little kid in Bible class knows, God made you.

What you get is what you see. Discounting upgrades through exercise or even extreme measures of cosmetic surgery, you have to deal with what you got.

But what if you were to wake up one day and suddenly be attractive to everyone of the opposite sex? Let's just say it—if everyone thought you were *hot*. That would be one of the best things to ever happen to you, right?

You could hypothetically have your pick of anyone. You would only be the rejecter and never the rejectee. Surely that would make anyone happy.

During my field work among Married People and Single People, on occasion there have been sightings of the exceptionally good-looking. And although their attractive appearance has sometimes been a blessing, my observations indicate it is often more of a curse.

There are some very real drawbacks to being overly attractive.

One of the most significant drawbacks is that there is a strong likelihood you will end up emotionally connected to someone who is only truly interested in the container you inhabit. Being that this container will eventually become more functional than aesthetic (and ultimately even less than functional), this leads to a great deal of unhappiness on both sides. You—the actual you—can remain unloved. Sure, there have been times when the allure has led to some genuine form of love, but not as often as you might think.

Here's how it works most of the time. A good-looking person finds another good-looking person and if there is some kind of "chemistry," they cling and smile. Their collective bedazzlements upgrade the standard infatuation to a level that seems to resound with genuine love. The buzz of their hormones deafen rational thought. They end up being very happy, then very disillusioned, then very unhappy as all the candy coating eventually wears off. The "chemistry" becomes another common high school class title—history. Rinse, repeat.

A good-looking person often ends up becoming a Married Person sooner than others. This is not always a good thing. It's an old, old story. A beautiful girl does not last long on the market. Romance sweeps her away and that momentum is deceptive. Once she arrives in marriage, it is a rude awaking to discover that hubba-hubba doesn't hold as much currency as it used to.

As odd as it might sound, good looks can be bad.

Joseph was pursued to the point of imprisonment because he was good-looking (Genesis 39:6). Based on Michal's tendency toward shallowness, I suspect her relationship with David was also shallow, based primarily on his looks (I Samuel 17:42). Jezebel was intent on being in full-makeup at her window, just before she was thrown out of it (II Kings 9:30). From where I'm standing, it seems that for these people good looks added an element that led to many troubles.

Good looks can be spiritually risky. If you are extremely attractive, if you're not careful, your stunning eyes or husky frame can lead your soul into all kinds of spiritual disasters. They will get you into the party. They will draw you into the shadows. They will fade your soul to irrelevancy. Being attractive has been the fatal flaw for many a person.

So average is not so bad. Below average is not the worst. Many a person has made his or her looks comfortably secondary, by growing their spirituality, their sense of humor, and being a real person. These can end up not only making a person more attractive, but they also have a much greater endurance.

So a word of warning. If you do happen to be one of the beautiful people, watch out. Don't shrug this off with token modesty. In this culture, you will be easy fodder for the enemy. It's okay if you're beautiful. Just make sure your soul is, too.

Written in the Stars

We really want the stars to be in charge. Even if you don't believe in astrology, there is a prevalent fondness for the idea that those constellations are somehow calling the shots. As far as we're concerned, life would be so much better if we turned things over to those giant gobs of blazing hydrogen gas.

After all, true love between two people is "written in the stars." That bit of magical thinking is really hard to not buy. We've seen so many films about people being led by destiny that it's almost impossible to completely let go of the concept. It just seems nice.

Somewhere out there is someone for you—a soul mate who will be your perfect love. That person and that person alone is the only one who can truly make you happy. Any fulfillment in this life is dependent on you finding this person. But never fear, it is fate. Inevitably your paths will cross. Cue music and fade.

Not true—or as one of my friends liked to say—"Pig Water." It's like hogwash, but worse.

Don't get me wrong. God definitely intended that a Married Person be devoted to one and only one person as long as they are both living this life. The only possible tragedies that can bypass this are death or adultery.

But there's no destiny. Not in the sense of two souls fated to be together because the giant gobs of gas say so. I think God does indeed know who will find who. I think He knows who will get married and who will not. His knowledge and awareness are perfect and supersede time and space. But we still have the power to make choices.

It's important to be up front about this because so many are misled by the destiny idea. When a marriage becomes difficult, Married People have been known to consider "alternate universes," in which they are married to someone else. This is a dangerous waste of time. Being that there is only one universe and you can only make choices in this one universe, pondering fictional what-ifs only breeds selfish discontent.

You know how it works. An unhappy Married Person convinces themselves that the one sitting across the table is a mistake. As it turns out, that person they married isn't their destined soul-mate. So the unhappy Married Person owes it to both of them to end the marriage and go find the one who the giant gobs of gas have picked out for them.

Again, I say—Pig Water.

Truth is better than destiny. The magic is that you get to choose. You and the other person get to choose to stay together for keeps. You choose each other on your wedding day. You choose each other the following day. Then you keep choosing no matter what, for the rest of your life.

It's not scribbled in the constellations. It's not mapped with Tarot cards or even greeting cards. You have the free will to seek out someone who also has freewill and together you can decide to join together in a romance that is stronger than all the movie nonsense.

I realize there have been arranged marriages in which both the man and woman had no real choice in the matter. But that was due to the free will of others. Again, the stars had nothing to do with it. In fact, even in these cases, choice has been known to transform this obligation into actual love.

The idea of the predetermined soul mate is poetic and fun. But it is also dangerous. Because, what if after you've committed to someone, you meet someone new and that new person just seems so-right-how-can-it-be-wrong? This whole approach undermines the essence of marriage. It is meant to be a choice that endures regardless of the ups and downs. When you're in the middle of one of the downs and you spot someone who catches your fancy, the myth of destiny can enable you to abandon Choice #1 for the sake of the newly star-endorsed Choice #2.

Let's just call it what it is. Self-serving superstition.

Someone Who Can Live Without You

My great uncle died in the kitchen. He had lived a long life and when he breathed his last, he happened to be sitting at the kitchen table, not far from the stove.

A year later, his wife (my great aunt) died in the same spot.

This might sound gruesome to some, but there's part of us that likes the idea of one person not being able to abide life without the presence of another person. There have even been cases of someone dying right after their spouse died.

At the risk of waxing grim, it's kind of romantic. "I can't live without you" has given many a love song that extra punch it needed to really ring true. If you die, I die. Romeo and Juliet had it all figured out. *Happy Anniversary, pass the poison.*

When I was in my 20s, a good friend of mine was killed in an accident. From a spiritual standpoint, since he was a Christian, he got out of here just fine. But earth-side, it was a tragedy that left his wife and their small child alone.

His wife was young, so she did not die a year later at the kitchen table. She went on to live many years and lives even today. Eventually she remarried and she has found a new and wonderful life.

But not long after my friend died, while his wife was still newly single, I remember wondering whether or not she would end up marrying a Christian again. There was nothing in particular that made me doubt her wisdom, but my wandering bachelor mind pondered the possibility that even though she had married a godly man once, she might not make the same best choice the second time.

If she married a man who did not belong to God, or even if she just simply floundered spiritually on her own, that could spell spiritual disaster for not only her, but for her child as well. The soul of the child was at stake.

That's when it hit me. If I ever did get married, it had to be someone whose spirituality wasn't built on mine. The stability of my wife's soul could not depend on the stability of my soul. The souls of my children would be in her hands. That essentially meant I would need to find someone who could live without me.

She would have to be more than just someone who "went to church." In order for my hypothetical children to be truly safe, her relationship with God would have to be far beyond our cultural standard of "Christian." It would have to be the real thing.

When a Christian is "looking for someone," one of the most important considerations is the impact this search will have on those who have yet to be born. One of the greatest criteria any Christian can have while searching for someone, is to make sure that person has their own secure relationship with God. Even if you are not eventually removed from the situation through a tragedy, the criteria is still profoundly significant. If you cannot imagine the other person standing firm without you, then it might very well indicate whether or not they're the one for you. There are more than two souls at stake.

The Single Single

So here you are. The last one. All your family and friends have walked the aisle except you.

You've stood by your standards and now you stand with your standards all alone.

For a while, the possible panache of being an "eligible bachelor" gave me some comfort. As more and more of my friends got married, that status seemed to shine a little brighter. Even though we were barely into our second decade, it seemed like all my guy friends were dropping like flies. I expressed a certain amount of disdain to these early traitors. My friends might be quickly shackled by a small ring, but I was going to enjoy being footloose and fancy free.

From where I was standing, Married People seemed somewhat immobile. Because he was now a family man, the husband ended up working in a career he didn't enjoy. Women lugged the children around. Married People didn't go to movies. They stayed home, trying to patch together some kind of mundane fun with construction paper and glue-sticks.

But as for me and my house—or rather my small apartment—I could go to movies whenever I wanted. As long as I kept my credit card happy, I could pretty much get whatever I wanted without having to answer to the stern eyebrows of a wife, waiting over a cold bowl of macaroni and cheese.

Not me. I was occasionally enthralled with one girl or another, but for the most part I stayed loose. I knew that if I didn't watch my step, a little flash and dazzle of romance could be my undoing. I could end up a Married Person.

I won't lie. Sex always sounded incredibly intriguing, but I knew that marriage was a choice you couldn't un-choose. I wanted to find someone. But I was addicted to freedom.

Time went by.

My twenties were not completely solitary. I was often in the company of other people in my same situation, including girls. There was the occasional fun of flirting, but mainly just a lot of plain fun in the form of late night games and coffee. Lots of coffee.

Always lingering in the background was the faint possibility that there might be a new girl at church or at the next singles' devotional. I was patient.

I hit thirty and still, I wasn't worried about it. I was now the older one in the singles' group. Among the college students and young professionals, I was the antiquated one who still had some life in him, allowed to participate along the lines of a mascot. But I could tell. I was beginning to shift to the periphery of the game.

Then I hit forty and forty sort of hit back. I didn't have a midlife crisis. It was more of a midlife DEFCON 3. No real crisis yet, but on standby. I knew I was venturing into unusual territory. This was not standard procedure. I couldn't really hang out with most singles without being an obvious outsider.

I was ready to be single for the rest of my life. But I just wanted to know one way or the other. If I was going to end up being married, I wanted to know. If I was going to end up single, I wanted to know. It was the not-knowing that was getting to me. But I'm sure you already know. That's not how it works. The future is a perfectly blank sheet of paper. The psychics are frauds and even the weather experts are just really good guessers. As far as marriage, a person is given absolutely no information about their final status. In fact, a person is given absolutely no information about the future at all. Except for the fact that there is a limited amount of future and that at the end of it, Jesus will be arriving.

This is all for a very simple reason—faith. "Now faith is the assurance of things hoped for, the conviction of things not seen" (Hebrews 11:1). Not the assurance that you will get married. Not the conviction that you will get married. It's the assurance and conviction that your Creator exists and "causes all thing to work together for good" for those who belong to Him (Romans 8:28). Whether or not the "good" involves nuptial bliss depends on your choices. But it also depends on His perfect wisdom and knowledge of the future.

That's why I wasn't given any clue about my future. Because God wants me to have faith. Not faith in romance, but in Him.

During my thirties and forties, people would occasionally try to set me up. Most of the time, these well-meaning matchmakers seemed to be using a very limited standard. *Hey, you're single and they're single! This will work!* I always appreciated the gesture. I felt honored these matchmakers even considered me a candidate for someone, but it often led to some pretty awkward situations.

At one point during all this, I became an uncle. I loved being an uncle. My uncle-ship made my thirties and forties incredibly fun.

Then I hit fifty and I was more than just alone. I didn't know anyone like me. I became my own demographic.

Being just one person became very natural. I tried to give up on "finding someone." A romance movie might trigger a pang of loneliness, but it would fade. Going to yet another wedding and driving home alone made me feel a little down. More than a few times, when I spotted a happy couple on a Friday night, I'm sorry to report that I felt nothing less than jealousy. Just being honest. The pain was often exquisite.

I brooded over my looks, my regrets, and even wondered if there was some key piece missing in my relationship with God. *After all, if I was doing this right, shouldn't I be married by now?*

Turns out, a lot of Single People think the same thing. *Maybe I'm not married because I still haven't gotten my act together yet. God is putting everything on hold until I get a better grip on my spirituality. He doesn't think I'm ready. He doesn't think I deserve anyone.*

Say it with me. *Not true.* First of all, the blessing of marriage has been given to a whole lot of people who certainly didn't deserve it. You could even argue no one truly deserves that blessing.

Part of it is the price of a higher standard. It's actually pretty easy to get married if you throw your spirituality out the window. It just depends on the price you're willing to pay. If you're not willing to endanger your soul by uniting with someone who doesn't belong to God, then you may very well end up alone. A small price to pay when you see things clearly.

But I get it. It's one thing being single. It's a whole different game to be the only single. As we continue on toward the end of this field study, please don't think I take your loneliness lightly. That desolate wasteland is very familiar to me. However, if you'll stick with me just a little longer, I think there are some things to be said that might salvage something very good in all this.

Woe is You

Friday nights were bad. It seemed like the whole world was out on a date except for me. I went to a lot of movies by myself, which wasn't that bad. I didn't have to consider what anyone else wanted to see and I didn't have to share my popcorn.

Despite this, more than once I kind of froze up, wondering how it turned out that I was alone. I have to admit. sometimes the loneliness was almost fun. There's something about feeling sorry for yourself that is actually kind of enjoyable. If you settle into your misery, you can let the songs and the movies wash over you like a spa. You can wallow in woe and even if you feel a little tearful or destitute, there is something that resonates and makes you feel like the center of the universe. A grim universe, but still.

Naomi settled into this kind of bleak perspective. She had gotten married but then her husband died. On top of that, there was a famine. At this crossroads of despair, she recommended that her daughters-in-law ditch her for more viable company. "It is harder for me than for you, for the hand of the Lord has gone forth against me" (Ruth 1:13). As far as Naomi was concerned, God was working against her and from here on out, things would only get worse.

Her daughter-in-law Ruth messed up the plan right away by staying with her and helping her. There's nothing worse when you're trying to be depressed and a good friend starts making things better.

But Naomi was determined to be a downcast and destitute tale of sorrow. Determined to hang onto hopelessness, when she reached her hometown, she told everyone to not call her Naomi any more. She wanted to change her name. "She said to them, 'Do not call me Naomi; call me Mara, for the Almighty has dealt very bitterly with me. I went out full, but the Lord has brought me back empty. Why do you call me Naomi, since the Lord has witnessed against me and the Almighty has afflicted me?'" (Ruth 1:20-21). Naomi wasn't messing around. To prove it, she would actually go by the name Mara, which means "bitter." She was done with hope. She was confident in a grim future in which she would pine away as Mara—the woman who was once Naomi.

One of my favorite things about the book of Ruth is the number of times the name "Mara" shows up. *Once.* In fact, in the whole Bible, the only time the word "Mara" shows up is right here when Naomi called herself by that name.

Even though she adamantly insisted on this new name, there is no record of anyone calling her that. More importantly, God never even acknowledges the name. Because as He knew and we know and Naomi eventually knew—He wasn't done with blessing her just yet.

Naomi had had a hard road. She had lost her husband and both of her sons. Everything about her life indicated clear to partly dark days ahead. But where she went wrong was thinking that God was against her. Even though her surroundings convinced her otherwise, her Creator was on the job, building a shining future, custom-made for Naomi—the woman who would never be called Mara.

Her problem was that her perspective was messed up. She didn't have all the information. She was gazing at the blank white page of the future and assuming she knew everything yet to be written.

As you know, Naomi set up Ruth with Boaz. Then Ruth and Boaz got married and had a little baby boy. One day, Naomi held that little baby boy on her lap. "Then Naomi took the child and laid him in her lap, and became his nurse. The neighbor women gave him a name, saying, 'A son has been born to Naomi!' So they named him Obed. He is the father of Jesse, the father of David" (Ruth 4:16-17). As it turns out, Naomi (the woman who was Mara for about thirty seconds) became one of the greatest matchmakers in history.

On the way into Bethlehem, Naomi was thinking, "It's over." There was nothing left for her to do—expect feel sorry for herself a lot.

God, on the other hand, was thinking, *No.*

Actually, you will be playing a key role in setting up the greatest earthly king and eventually the King of Kings. But other than that, yes, you're all done.

Jacob also felt like God was against him. He "refused to be comforted" (Genesis 37:25) because as he said, "All these things are against me" (Genesis 42:36). He also didn't have all the information. The future would turn out so much better than he planned. Instead of a son that was lost, he ended up with a son who was in charge of Egypt.

There was a more obscure man named Baruch who also was down on life. He was in a bad spot too. He was sidekick to Jeremiah and things were not going well. The king in power at the time was not a fan of the Truth and it looked very grim for Baruch because he was the one writing it all down.

When Baruch spiraled down into self-pity, God called him on it. "You said, 'Ah, woe is me. For the Lord has added sorrow to my pain; I am weary with my groaning and have found no rest'" (Jeremiah 45:3). God went on to point out some priorities. "'But you, are you seeking great things for yourself? Do not seek them; for behold, I am going to bring disaster on all flesh,' declares the Lord, 'but I will give your life to you as booty in all the places where you may go'" (Jeremiah 45:5). Baruch was going to survive to see another day and his soul was also intact. That alone added up to a pretty good day. Anything else was gravy.

Then there was me. Shortly after yet another Valentine's Day, I ended up visiting my sister. As one of my best friends, I knew she genuinely empathized with my singleness and probably suffered for it more than I even did. I knew I could confide in her during the times I felt romantically destitute.

I have spent many Valentine's Days unaccompanied. Most of the time I felt little if any sadness about going stag through life for yet another year. But for some reason this year in particular felt a little more hollow, a little more bitter. I shared as much with my sister and her response was not what I expected. Instead of saying what I wanted to hear, she said what I needed to hear.

"Good thing life is short, huh?"

She didn't tell me to not lose hope. She didn't assure me that I would find someone. She didn't promise me there was someone out there for me. She didn't advise me to follow my heart or my online profile. She just told it like it was.

Life is short.

This tiny bit of wisdom implied so many things. I could spend my time whining about how lonely I was or I could get busy living the life I had been given. Pity parties don't really change anything and there's never any cake.

Regardless of circumstances, God is very good at how He shapes your life. This is easy to say, hard to live. When I doubt it, I think about Naomi entering Bethlehem, insisting that everyone call her Mara. And like everyone else, I just shake my head and smile and think, you just wait. Things are going to turn out much better than you think.

Yes, I Expect You to Be Alone

This might come as a shock, but regardless of how unbelievable this is—what I'm about to say has been confirmed. A lack of sex will not kill you.

The world pushes the idea that sex is such a vital "need" that if you don't participate in it on a fairly regular basis, then you will go into cardiac rest or you will spontaneously combust.

Don't get me wrong. The sex drive is incredibly powerful. It is definitely near the top of the list of "Wants." But when you look at the list of "Needs," many people would be surprised to discover that sex just isn't there.

I always chuckle to myself whenever there's a movie in which someone gets to "make passionate love" just before they die of some disease or get run over by a snowplow. Everyone is supposed to think, "Well, at least they got to have sex before they died."

For our purposes, it's important to know the truth. It is very possible to live without sex. You will not die. It is also not fatal to never hold hands with someone or never wear a wedding ring.

The reason I bring this up is because there is a prevalent belief that being single is a fate worse than death. You mainly hear it in the aftermath of a divorce not authorized by Scripture. Many who find themselves in this position present an appeal that is meant to trigger extreme shock. *You expect me to remain single the rest of my life?*

This plea also surfaces among those who are tired of being alone and make huge spiritual compromises such as living with someone or marrying a non-Christian. When confronted with the foolishness of both choices, they often resort to the same question. *You expect me to remain single the rest of my life?*

Apparently, they expect a response such as *No, of course not. I see your point now; go ahead and defy everything God has said concerning marriage.*

It is a question that has often been used to ward off anyone trying to interfere with someone's "needs."

You expect me to remain single the rest of my life?

Here's the short answer—Yes.

Now for the long answer.

Just because something is tough or offends your sense of fairness doesn't make it any less true.

Once again we have let the world twist up our thinking. We have been told that the worst possible thing that can happen to a person is to end up alone.

O the despair. O the agony. See the pining shadow of the person, discarded by love.

I'm not trying to mock anyone who is in the middle of experience loneliness, but I do feel qualified to poke a little fun since I experienced half a century of the stuff.

Being alone isn't always fun. Believe, me, I know. If you end up at the age of ninety-nine, living off Ramen in a secluded cabin, going stag even into death because you have no friends or family, then that would indeed be a real bummer. But good luck conjuring up that scenario. You would have to be very selfish and vicious to alienate yourself to that degree.

Any Christian knows very well that as a member of the church, you will have a difficult time ever considering yourself truly alone. Sure, if you're just playing church, keeping your brothers and sisters at a distance as Sunday morning acquaintances, then you could very well end up with your bitter loneliness intact. But that's your choice. Anyone who is truly a member of the church will not only let others be involved in their life, but they will also be busy making sure other people aren't lonely.

Any true Christian is going to have dozens of sisters and brothers. Dozens of fathers and mothers. You will never be alone. And just for the record—even that hypothetical pitiful geezer in the cabin isn't alone if he's connected with God. Being totally and utterly alone actually takes a lot of effort. If you live a selfish life and alienate everyone and also cut yourself off from God, then yes—prepare to be one and only one.

Whether or not you get a dose of Hollywood romance along the way, in the grand scheme of things, it's like a spoiled rich kid on Christmas morning complaining because he didn't also get a Ferrari.

I realize that sometimes it seems like everyone else in the world has a Ferrari. All the movies are about people getting Ferraris. All the songs on the radio are about finding a Ferrari. You have always dreamed of having a Ferrari.

You expect me to not have a Ferrari the rest of my life?
Why yes. Yes, I do.

If that's what it takes to keep your soul safe, then yes. If that's what it takes to keep you out of a relationship that daily chips away at your happiness with worry and horrible pressures. Then yes. I would wish that on anyone. For a thousand lifetimes.

A lot of people believe being single is just short of a death sentence. That's the world in your head. Married People are creatures that are actually very earthly and temporary. If you get to be one of them, congratulations. If you don't get to be one of them, congratulations. Either way, the things that matter are playing out just fine and if you trust God, He will fill your life with blessings. Not consolation prizes, but real and profound blessings.

Pricey, Wonderful You

There are no suitors knocking on your door. None of the model agencies have left any messages. You will not be on the cover of Cosmopolitan.

There are no girls who consider you a suitor. You will not be in the NFL draft pick this season. You will not be the star of your own reality show.

But you are special.

Let me shudder for you.

Shudder.

Saying "you are special" doesn't really do much nowadays. Maybe you'll spot a poster with similar sentiments. *You're one of a kind. There's no one like you. No one else can be you except you.*

All very true, but somehow they don't really break the spell. In a world that measures people in units of attraction, you just don't feel that special at all.

Your body has some market value. The chemicals you're made of would sell for just under ten bucks. However, among your assorted components, you have enough chlorine in you to disinfect five swimming pools, enough salt to fill one salt shaker, enough carbon to make 9,000 pencils, and enough iron to make one nail. All of that could give you a decent mark-up.

There's also your net worth as far as your income. If you want to find out your value in that regard, just look at your last tax return. K-ching! There's your worth!

What you think of yourself is key. Who you let determine what you think of yourself is the lock that goes with that key.

It's not a good idea to let you determine your value. You're too untrustworthy. Either you'll spiral into self-loathing or mutate into self-admiration.

The mirror does tell the truth. But the eyes looking into the mirror can lie to you.

Like most people, you might end up letting the world determine your worth. It's just a matter of finding your spot on the spectrum of beautiful people.

Or there's another option.

Let the One who made you have some input on the matter. After all, He did create you. He did design you. And make no mistake. Even though there is a wild array of possible combinations when it comes to DNA, your design was no roll of the dice. You know the way your hair does that one thing? And how your nose looks? And your eyes? God did that. He made you that way.

Wait a second. If that's true—if God didn't leave your looks to chance, then why didn't He make you a little more appealing? Instead, you've got that odd body flaw thing going on, not to mention that one particular facial feature you have often thought of as a curse.

Let's just get to the real question. Why didn't He make you hot?

Good question. So here's a good answer.

God didn't make you hot because hotness doesn't really matter. In the grand scheme of things, the hotness of your face and body mean almost nothing.

You see, God is primarily interested in getting souls to heaven. Everything He's done and everything He will do can all be traced back to that one essential goal. Getting souls to heaven.

To get too hung up on your physical appearance is kind of silly. We all do it, but it is kind of silly if you think about it. God says it's a lot like a piece of clay complaining to the potter, "Why did you make me like this?" (Romans 9:20). The potter doesn't owe the clay an explanation. It's implied the potter knows what He's doing. He can do whatever He wants.

When you mentally criticize your looks, tell yourself to be quiet. While you're at it, tell the world to close its mouth too. Your worth is determined only by God. He made you a human being with free will. You have the ability to affect lives in such a way that will resound for eternity. Whether or not your looks allow you to smooch it up with someone is really beside the point.

So in case, you aren't convinced, the reviews are in. You are incredibly valuable. There has never been anyone like you and never will be. This includes your face and your frame, your talents and interests and everything that makes you the once-in-a-lifetime you. You are the only one who can mark the world with your own specific signature.

If you're a Christian, God paid the highest price possible for you. As far as He's concerned, you're the most expensive kind of human being there is.

Quit lingering in disappointment at the mirror. Take God's word for it. You are incredibly valuable.

Opportunity Knocks, So Don't Knock Opportunity

Shortly after college, a good friend who was also single at the time (before he too betrayed me like the rest and got married) suggested the possibility that God allows some people to remain single longer than other people for a reason. It's not that they are overlooked or that they blew it. It's just that being single is their assignment.

I believe that. Most of the blessings I have experienced during my prolonged bachelorhood would have never happened if I had gotten married when everyone else had. Of course, there would have been other blessings as a Married Person, but my life has had a unique angle as a direct result of me being single.

God specifically addresses the potential benefits. "One

who is unmarried is concerned about the things of the Lord, how he may please the Lord; but one who is married is concerned about the things of the world, how he may please his wife, and his interests are divided" (I Corinthians 7:32-34). This doesn't mean that Married People can't be pleasing to God. It also certainly doesn't mean that being single meant you will always be focused on God.

But the point still stands. Being single is an opportunity. That time by yourself can allow you mobility and freedom to develop a better focus than most people. There are a lot of Married People living the dream right now—the dream you often long for—who would love to have it as bad as you.

A non-Christian friend once asked me if I had found anyone yet. When I said no—that I was still single, he asked, "Is it because of your religion?"

I said, "I hope not."

If he had meant that I was single because of my moral standards, I would have said, "Yep, I like to think so."

But I knew him and the context of the conversation well enough to realize he was wondering if I was abstaining from all things nuptial for bonus Christian points. In his mind, I was pursuing this Christian thing to the point of being some kind of quasi-monk.

I think that's what more than a few people thought about me. They had the idea I was consciously making the decision to stay single for religious purposes. In a way, I guess they were right. My Christianity did automatically interfere with me being involved in dating situations that would have led to disaster. It also prevented me from being places where I didn't need to be. So I guess in that sense I was single for religious reasons.

But I wasn't afraid women would interfere with my meditation sessions. It wasn't that at all. It was just that I was determined to not marry someone unless they belonged to God. Frankly, there aren't a lot of women out there who belong to God. There were plenty of girls who "went to church." But a great majority of these were only running demos. So I continued on, unhitched.

But the way things played out, I had so many opportunities to be involved in such things that many people would kill to do even one of. I had the pity parties, but most of the time, instead of wallowing in the blues, I did stuff. A lot of stuff that I had time to do because I was single.

If I could go back and arrange for me to get married back then, I'm not sure I would. In retrospect, it all played out really well. I was given life and I lived it.

Being single makes you very portable. There will be certain things you won't be eligible to be a part of, but there will be a whole lot of stuff that you get to do that Married People don't have time for.

Being single is an opportunity. It's an opportunity to become a better servant. It is an opportunity to develop your creativity and talents. It's an opportunity to get over yourself and scrape off any selfishness so you can be happier. God has created you as a treasure of vast possibilities. Now it's up to you whether or not you're going to see where all of it might lead.

Five Seconds in Front of the Whole World

Before I wrap this section up with one more contemplation, I want to tell you what I would say to the whole world if I had the chance.

Picture this. A microphone attached to speakers all over the planet—and I get five seconds to speak to all 7 billion human beings.

This is what I would say:
"Read the Bible every day!"
That's it.

I know it sounds pretty simple. But it's the one straightforward phrase that if taken to heart by any person would change everything for them.

All of the things I've been rambling out—all the problems and frustrations that surround Married People and the Single People who want to be Married People—would smooth out quickly if a person would daily spend time listening to the Creator speak to their soul.

So I guess this is one last effort to point in the right direction. Even if you dismiss all the things *I've* said, please don't write off what God has written. He knows you so well. He has some things to say to you.

This microphone / book might only be reaching one person, but I'm going to stick to the same plan. So let's make it official.

Testing, testing. Is thing on? Okay, here I go.

Read your Bible every day!

The Art of Being Alone

God has promised He will be faithful (II Thessalonians 3:3). God has promised if you look for Him with all your heart, you will find Him (Jeremiah 29:13). God has promised He will never allow you to be tempted beyond what you can bear (I Corinthians 10:13). God has promised He will always love you (Lamentations 3:22). He has promised that if you belong to Him He will rescue you from death and give you a permanent life in a place that far outshines this one (Romans 6:5). He has made numerous and incredible promises.

But He never promised we would all get married. The only guarantee about the future is that you will be rescued when the world burns up.

With that in mind, I have some things to say to try and sum up. Since we've been hanging out for a while now, I'm not going to insult our friendship by being too tactful. It will help us both to get straight to the point. But I do apologize for the somewhat abrasive tone.

Stop feeling sorry for yourself. It doesn't change anything. If the romance movies make you feel bad, then I've got a solution. Stop watching them. If there are songs that make you feel lonely, here's an idea. Stop listening to them. If you seeing people in love makes you jealous or bitter or whatever, make the choice. Stop being like that.

Next, get close to God. Then get closer. That always results in good things. Don't draw near on a conditional basis. Go all in and trust Him for the results. The blessings may or may not include romance, but getting closer to God is absolutely vital. Take it or leave it. If you're not married and there are no foreseeable changes in that regard in the near future, don't be fooled. Everything is going great. If you stick close to God, you'll be doing just fine.

Next, choose happiness. A better word might be "joy." It is a choice. Happiness depends on what happens (hence the word). Joy, however, can be indestructible and it's a choice. It must be, because God says to do it—always. "Rejoice always" (I Thessalonians 5:16).

Next, get busy helping other people. Look for other people who need help and then help them. Make that a daily goal. Be aware of the lost and look for opportunities to rescue them.

When you're single for a long time, if you end up focusing on your solitary despair, you can forget we are on a doomed planet covered with doomed people. To feel sorry for ourselves while we walk among the doomed is to be honest, a very heightened form of selfishness. Who cares whether or not you get to ride off into the sunset? There are lost souls all around you and time is running out.

I also recommend daily heavy doses of laughter. Once your joy is installed and running, find humor in yourself in those around you and laugh. A lot.

As we get older, we laugh less. Be the one who enjoys laughing.

Finally, have fun.

Eating alone at a table and mourning the loss of all your romantic daydreams accomplishes nothing.

Being happy alone is an art. Like any form of art it takes practice and dedication. But also like any form of art, when you get it right, it can actually be quite beautiful.

Get busy belonging to God and serving people and see what happens.

It works.

Every single time.

PART 7

The End OF THE **Comedy**

I have a confession to make. When I started writing this book, I was a bachelor with no prospects in sight.

I promise.

But during the long stretch of putting all of my thoughts down about being single, I ended up becoming *not* single.

I met someone.

If I were you, I would feel at least a little deceived. *Here's this guy going on for pages and pages, implying he has at least some kind of insight on being unmarried.* "Boo hoo, I was the only single groomsman at the wedding." "Waah, I went to so many movies all by myself." *But as it turns out, he's just like the rest.*

Traitor.

It's true. I'm married now.

I'm sorry. But I'm not sorry.

Here's what happened.

While I was putting all my bachelor thoughts on paper, I met Sarah. Actually, I met her a long, long time ago. But it was only relatively recently that I "found" her. But that's another story for another time—or another book.

When I "found" Sarah, to a certain extent, this encouraged me to finish this book while my Single Person brain was still somewhat intact, before my Married People brain forgot what it was like to be unattached. That being said, I believe I have been true to the bachelor I once was.

But now there's a real possibility that as I wrap up this book it will come across as a tidy moral-of-the-story kind of thing.

Just when the author really for sure called it quits and wrote down all his thought about how he would be permanently single, lo and behold, God gave him a wife.

That's not really true. Well, it's sort of true.

I don't believe that if you give up, you automatically find someone. I don't believe that if you write a book about being single, you will end up getting married. All I know is, God decided to bless me with Sarah.

But if this book had ended with me signing off and strolling stylishly away down the street, still a solitary figure on the

Boulevard of Eligibility, I still would have held fast to all the things I've said. At the very least, all the parts built on Scripture would definitely be the same.

Even though I now have the brain of a Married Man, I have five decades in my head of being on my own. It's still there. In fact, that bachelor-ness kind of complicated things for a little while.

Let me explain.

Even when I "found" Sarah, it took me forever to ask her to marry me. I suppose this was partly because of the timing. I think I actually *was* in the process of settling into the reality that I would be single my whole life. I noticed that I didn't listen to romantic songs as much as I used to. I stopped keeping my eyes peeled for promising introductions at gatherings and various events.

Sarah caught me off guard. She was not on my calendar at all. And I'm still amazed she would agree to be my wife. I think I'm still a little stunned.

But before my Married People brain completely takes over, at the risk of sounding ominous, let me share some things about my final days as a Single Man. They be of use to you.

When I started spending time with Sarah, I was not dating anyone. I was not pursuing anyone. In fact, it had been an exceptionally long time since I had been in that arena at all. Which makes it all the more surprising that when Sarah and I did begin to consider a future together, I hesitated.

Sarah is an incredible, beautiful Christian woman, but still I dallied. For a year and half, I dallied.

You would think that after being single for so long, that once I found someone like Sarah, that I would jump—nay, leap at the chance to get married. You would think I would sprint to the jewelry store, grab a ring, and drop to my knees as soon as possible. But I did not.

I hesitated.

Part of it was probably because I had been single for so long. I had some momentum as a Single Person. Despite all my talk about the wisdom of not being selfish, I think I was very selfish. (I will always have to fight selfishness.) Getting married would involve me having to take into consideration what another person wanted. I had my routines. I had my habits. I had my stuff. Getting married would change all that.

Part of my hesitation was also probably because I had so thoroughly trained my brain to veer away from possible bad situations that when a great situation arrived, I automatically veered. *Surely, this can't be that easy. Surely, something will surface soon about me or even her that will indicate the best choice would be to walk away. Again.*

I had gotten good at walking away. There are a few girls who deserve a book-long apology from me for my immaturity that resulted in hurting them. I am not proud of that.

For a long time, my default setting was walking away. I knew that if I ever did get married, I would never dream of walking away. I wanted to make absolutely sure I realized the reality of being fully and permanently committed. So I hesitated.

But I think there was another reason. I shared this reason with Sarah while she patiently waited for me to get my act together and propose.

It was like there was this beautiful building called Marriage. All the Married People lived inside it. Over the years, I'd witnessed countless people going inside and rumor had it that life was really great in that building.

But in reality, about half of the people who went inside, came back out devastated. Some of these even went back in and came back out a second time, devastated again.

In addition to that, from where I was standing, I caught a few glimpses of those who actually stayed inside and from what I could tell, a lot of them didn't look very happy at all. Many of them even looked back out at me with envy—or even despair on their face, wishing silently they had stayed outside.

So maybe you can understand my hesitation.

It wasn't Sarah. I wasn't me. It certainly wasn't any disillusionment about God's design for marriage. It's just that for the most part, Marriage just seemed like an unhappy place.

I finally came to my senses. It was because I realized there was another part of the building. It was a less familiar, easy-to-miss part of the building.

In this part, there were Married People who were incredibly happy. They had their share of ups and downs, but they were glad they were married and they were blessed with the confidence they were on their way to heaven together.

So Sarah and I decided to get married and live in that part.

While I was writing this book, as I got closer to reaching the end, I remembered something from my days as an English literature major.

Back in Shakespeare's time there were essentially just two kinds of stories. Which kind of story it was depended on the ending.

A story was either a tragedy or a comedy. If it was a tragedy, it ended with a bunch of people dying. If it was a comedy, it ended with a wedding. One or the other. A funeral or a wedding. Just Buried or Just Married. This is why at some theaters, you often see those two masks—one frowning, one smiling. Tragedy and comedy.

So I guess this is the end of a comedy.

It ends with a wedding, in a small town where Sarah grew up, in the foothills of the Rocky Mountains.

But the real reason this doesn't end as a tragedy is not because I got married. This story ends well because I belong to God. That's how you get a happy ending. You belong to God.

The frown or the smile. Whether you're one of the Married People or the Single People, I think you get to choose. The frown is waiting for anyone who tails into world-thinking without God. The smile is there for anyone who turns their life over to God and stays with Him to the end. That's what I did. That's what I will continue to do.

I choose the smile.

Acknowledgments

This book came about as a direct result of my friends—many of whom are Married People. Sometimes I would joke with them that I was like Diane Fossey living among the apes. Even though I technically didn't belong, they accepted me as one of their own. I want to thank these married friends for letting me be the extra wheel. I was the better for it—then and now. You know who you are.

Thank you to Mike Byron for being the first person to read through this—twice, and offering incredibly helpful suggestions.

Thank you to Robert West for your extensive notes and your insight. You have proven yet again how cool you are—in particular for knowing the correct molecular formula for chocolate.

Thank you to Cherie Byron who texted me while she read the book and made my day.

Thank you to Logan Cates and Shera Wilcox for reading some of the first few chapters and not yawning very much.

Thank you to LeNae West who took her shiny green pen and hacked her way through a tiresome rough draft and survived to tell the tale. Plus, she told me how to improve the final edits.

And thank you to Sarah—for reading this and still saying you Like-Like me.

Sources

The Fellowship of Marriage by Ron Carter
The Sacred Romance by Brent Curtis and John Eldredge
Point Man by Steve Farrar
I Kissed Dating Goodbye by Joshua Harris
Sex is Not the Problem (Lust Is) by Joshua Harris
Build Your Walls! Guard Your Gates! by Michael S. Kientz
Christian Sexuality in a Sex-Crazed World by Steve Nicholson (podcast)
Save the Males by Kathleen Parker
Hooked by Joe S. Mcilhaney Jr. M.D., and Freda McKissic Bush, M.D.
Male Spiritual Leadership by F. Lagard Smith
Federal Husband by Douglas Wilson

These sources helped to influence the writing of this book. The author benefited a great deal from their insight. This does not mean the author necessarily agrees with everything they said. For further information on which sources the author would recommend, please feel free to contact him.

Bret Carter lives with his wife and daughter in Denver, Colorado. His short stories have appeared in *Perihelion Magazine*, *Boston Literary Magazine*, *CrossTIME Science Fiction Anthology Volume V*, *Gruff Variations*, and *Mysterion*. His non-fiction includes the book *God's Words*, which deals with the integrity of the Bible and *Paper Bullets*, a book of essays on writing. Bret has written and produced over 30 plays, including 3 musicals, most of them with his father Ron Carter. Over a dozen of the plays have been produced at the Broomfield Theater in Denver. He has been a teacher for over twenty years. He currently teaches at Hyland Christian School and preaches part-time at the Miller Street church of Christ.

www.bretcarter.blogspot.com
www.nosmallcommotion.blogspot.com
@AlmostBruce

Made in the USA
Middletown, DE
05 August 2019